The Girl of the Period and other Social Essays

(Volume I)

E. Lynn Linton

Alpha Editions

This edition published in 2020

ISBN : 9789354043727

Design and Setting By
Alpha Editions
www.alphaedis.com
email - alphaedis@gmail.com

As per information held with us this book is in Public Domain.
This book is a reproduction of an important historical work. Alpha Editions uses the best technology to reproduce historical work in the same manner it was first published to preserve its original nature. Any marks or number seen are left intentionally to preserve its true form.

THE
GIRL OF THE PERIOD

AND OTHER

Social Essays

BY

E. LYNN LINTON

AUTHOR OF 'THE ATONEMENT OF LEAM DUNDAS' 'UNDER WHICH LORD?'
'THE REBEL OF THE FAMILY' 'IONE' ETC.

IN TWO VOLUMES
VOL. I.

LONDON
RICHARD BENTLEY & SON, NEW BURLINGTON STREET
Publishers in Ordinary to Her Majesty the Queen
1883

[All rights reserved]

𝔇𝔢𝔡𝔦𝔠𝔞𝔱𝔢𝔡

TO

ALL GOOD GIRLS

AND

TRUE WOMEN

PREFACE.

So MANY false reports followed the appearance of these essays, that I am grateful to the authorities of the *Saturday Review* for their present permission to republish them under my own name, even though the best of the day has a little gone by, and other forms of folly have been flying about since these were shot at. The essays hit sharply enough at the time, and caused some ill-blood. 'The Girl of the Period' was especially obnoxious to many to whom women were the Sacred Sex above criticism and beyond rebuke; and I had to pay pretty smartly in private life, by those who knew, for what they termed a libel and an untruth. With these passionate repudiators on the one hand, on the other were some who, trading on the enforced anonymity of the paper, took spurious credit to themselves for the authorship. I was twice introduced to the 'Writer of the "Girl of the Period."' The first time he was a clergyman who had boldly told my friends that he had written the paper; the second, she was a lady of rank well known in London society, and to this hour believed by her own circle to have written this and other of the articles included in the present collection. I confess that, whether for praise or blame, I am glad to be able at last to assume the full responsibility of my own work.

In re-reading these papers I am more than ever convinced that I have struck the right chord of condemnation, and advocated the best virtues and most valuable characteristics of women. I neither soften nor retract a line of what I have said. One of the modern phases of womanhood—hard, unloving, mercenary, ambitious, without domestic faculty and devoid of healthy natural instincts—is still to me a pitiable mistake and a grave national disaster. And I think now, as I thought when I wrote these papers, that a public and professional life for women is incompatible with the discharge of their highest duties or the cultivation of their noblest qualities. I think now, as I thought then, that the sphere of human action is determined by the fact of sex, and that there does exist both natural limitation and natural direction. This creed, which summarizes all that I have said *in extenso*, I repeat with emphasis, and maintain with the conviction of long years of experience.

E. LYNN LINTON.

1883.

CONTENTS

OF

THE FIRST VOLUME.

	PAGE
THE GIRL OF THE PERIOD	1
MODERN MOTHERS (I.)	10
MODERN MOTHERS (II.)	19
PAYING ONE'S SHOT	27
WHAT IS WOMAN'S WORK?	37
LITTLE WOMEN	48
IDEAL WOMEN	58
PINCHBECK	69
AFFRONTED WOMANHOOD	79
FEMININE AFFECTATIONS	88
INTERFERENCE	99
THE FASHIONABLE WOMAN	109
SLEEPING DOGS	119
BEAUTY AND BRAINS	128
NYMPHS	137
MÉSALLIANCES	147

CONTENTS OF THE FIRST VOLUME.

	PAGE
WEAK SISTERS	157
PINCHING SHOES	167
SUPERIOR BEINGS	176
FEMININE AMENITIES	184
GRIM FEMALES	193
MATURE SIRENS	203
PUMPKINS	213
WIDOWS	223
DOLLS	234
CHARMING WOMEN	244
APRON-STRINGS	254
FINE FEELINGS	264
SPHINXES	273
FLIRTING	281
SCRAMBLERS	290
FLATTERY	299
LA FEMME PASSÉE	309
SPOILT WOMEN	317
DOVECOTS	325
BORED HUSBANDS	335

ESSAYS

UPON

SOCIAL SUBJECTS.

THE GIRL OF THE PERIOD.

TIME was when the phrase, 'a fair young English girl,' meant the ideal of womanhood; to us, at least, of home birth and breeding. It meant a creature generous, capable, modest; something franker than a Frenchwoman, more to be trusted than an Italian, as brave as an American but more refined, as domestic as a German and more graceful. It meant a girl who could be trusted alone if need be, because of the innate purity and dignity of her nature, but who was neither bold in bearing nor masculine in mind ; a girl who, when she married, would be her husband's friend and companion, but never his rival ; one who would consider his interests as identical with her own, and not hold him as just so much fair game for spoil ; who would make his house his true home and place of rest, not a mere passage-place for vanity and ostentation to pass through; a tender mother, an industrious housekeeper, a judicious mistress.

We prided ourselves as a nation on our women. We thought we had the pick of creation in this fair young English girl of ours, and envied no other men their own. We admired the languid grace and subtle fire of the South; the docility and childlike affectionateness of the East seemed to us sweet and simple and restful; the vivacious sparkle of the trim and sprightly Parisienne was a pleasant little excitement when we met with it in its own domain; but our allegiance never wandered from our brown-haired girls at home, and our hearts were less vagrant than our fancies. This was in the old time, and when English girls were content to be what God and nature had made them. Of late years we have changed the pattern, and have given to the world a race of women as utterly unlike the old insular ideal as if we had created another nation altogether. The Girl of the Period, and the fair young English girl of the past, have nothing in common save ancestry and their mother-tongue; and even of this last the modern version makes almost a new language, through the copious additions it has received from the current slang of the day.

The Girl of the Period is a creature who dyes her hair and paints her face, as the first articles of her personal religion—a creature whose sole idea of life is fun; whose sole aim is unbounded luxury; and whose dress is the chief object of such thought and intellect as she possesses. Her main endeavour is to outvie her neighbours in the extravagance of fashion. No matter if, in the time of crinolines, she sacrifices decency; in the time of trains, cleanliness; in the time of tied-back skirts, modesty; no matter either, if she makes herself a nuisance and an inconvenience to every one she meets;—the Girl of the Period has done away with such moral muffishness as consideration for others, or regard for counsel and rebuke. It was all very well in old-fashioned times, when fathers and mothers had some authority and were treated with respect, to be tutored and made to obey, but she is far too fast and flourishing to be stopped in mid-career by these slow old morals; and as she lives to please herself, she does not care if she displeases every one else.

Nothing is too extraordinary and nothing too exaggerated for her vitiated taste; and things which in themselves would be useful reforms if let alone become monstrosities worse than those which they have displaced so soon as she begins to manipulate and improve. If a sensible fashion lifts the gown out of the mud, she raises hers midway to her knee. If the absurd structure of wire and buckram, once called a bonnet, is modified to something that shall protect the wearer's face without putting out the eyes of her companion, she cuts hers down to four straws and a rosebud, or a tag of lace and a bunch of glass beads. If there is a reaction against an excess of Rowland's Macassar, and hair shiny and sticky with grease is thought less nice than if left clean and healthily crisp, she dries and frizzes and sticks hers out on end like certain savages in Africa, or lets it wander down her back like Madge Wildfire's, and thinks herself all the more beautiful the nearer she approaches in look to a negress or a maniac.

With purity of taste she has lost also that far more precious purity and delicacy of perception which sometimes mean more than appears on the surface. What the *demi-monde* does in its frantic efforts to excite attention, she also does in imitation. If some fashionable *dévergondée en évidence* is reported to have come out with her dress below her shoulder-blades, and a gold strap for all the sleeve thought necessary, the Girl of the Period follows suit next day; and then she wonders that men sometimes mistake her for her prototype, or that mothers of girls not quite so far gone as herself refuse her as a companion for their daughters. She has blunted the fine edges of feeling so much that she cannot understand why she should be condemned for an imitation of form which does not include imitation of fact. She cannot be made to see that modesty of appearance and virtue in deed ought to be inseparable; and that no good girl can afford to appear bad, under pain of receiving the contempt awarded to the bad.

This imitation of the *demi-monde* in dress leads to something in manner and feeling, not quite so pronounced perhaps, but far too like to be honourable to herself or satisfactory to her friends. It leads to slang, bold talk and general fastness; to the love of pleasure and indifference to duty; to the desire of money before either love or happiness; to uselessness at home, dissatisfaction with the monotony of ordinary life, horror of all useful work; in a word, to the worst forms of luxury and selfishness—to the most fatal effects arising from want of high principle and absence of tender feeling.

The Girl of the Period envies the queens of the *demi-monde* far more than she abhors them. She sees them gorgeously attired and sumptuously appointed, and she knows them to be flattered, fêted, and courted with a certain disdainful admiration of which she catches only the admiration while she ignores the disdain. They have all that for which her soul is hungering; and she never stops to reflect at what a price they have bought their gains, and what fearful moral penalties they pay for their sensuous pleasures. She sees only the coarse gilding on the base token, and shuts her eyes to the hideous figure in the midst and the foul legend written round the edge. It is this envy of the pleasures, and indifference to the sins, of these women of the *demi-monde* which is doing such infinite mischief to the modern girl. They brush too closely by each other, if not in actual deeds, yet in aims and feelings; for the luxury which is bought by vice with the one is that thing of all in life most passionately desired by the other, though she is not yet prepared to pay quite the same price. Unfortunately, she has already paid too much—all that once gave her distinctive national character.

No one can say of the modern English girl that she is tender, loving, retiring or domestic. The old fault so often found by keen-sighted Frenchwomen, that she was so fatally *romanesque*, so prone to sacrifice appearances and social advantages for love, will never be set against the Girl of the Period. Love indeed is the last thing she thinks of, and the least of the dangers besetting her. Love in a cottage—that seductive dream which used to vex the heart and disturb the calculations of the prudent mother—is now a myth of past ages. The legal barter of herself for so much money, representing so much dash, so much luxury and pleasure—that is her idea of marriage ; the only idea worth entertaining. For all seriousness of thought respecting the duties or the consequences of marriage, she has not a trace. If children come, they find but a stepmother's cold welcome from her ; and if her husband thinks that he has married anything that is to belong to him—a *tacens et placens uxor* pledged to make him happy—the sooner he wakes from his hallucination and understands that he has simply married some one who will condescend to spend his money on herself, and who will shelter her indiscretions behind the shield of his name, the less severe will be his disappointment. She has married his house, his carriage, his balance at the banker's, his title ; and he himself is just the inevitable condition clogging the wheel of her fortune; at best an adjunct, to be tolerated with more or less patience as may chance. For it is only the old-fashioned sort, not Girls of the Period *pur sang*, who marry for love, or put the husband before the banker. But the Girl of the Period does not marry easily. Men are afraid of her; and with reason. They may amuse themselves with her for an evening, but they do not readily take her for life. Besides, after all her efforts, she is only a poor copy of the real thing; and the real thing is far more amusing than the copy, because it is real. Men can get that whenever they like; and when they go into their mothers' drawing-rooms, with their sisters and their sisters' friends, they want something of quite a different flavour. *Toujours perdrix* is bad providing all the world over; but a continual weak imitation of *toujours perdrix* is worse.

If we must have only one kind of thing, let us have it genuine, and the queens of St. John's Wood in their unblushing honesty rather than their imitators and make-believes in Bayswater and Belgravia. For, at whatever cost of shocked self-love or pained modesty it may be, it cannot be too plainly told to the modern English girl that the net result of her present manner of life is to assimilate her as nearly as possible to a class of women whom we must not call by their proper—or improper—name. And we are willing to believe that she has still some modesty of soul left hidden under all this effrontery of fashion, and that, if she could be made to see herself as she appears to the eyes of men, she would mend her ways before too late.

It is terribly significant of the present state of things when men are free to write as they do of the women of their own nation. Every word of censure flung against them is two-edged, and wounds those who condemn as much as those who are condemned; for surely it need hardly be said that men hold nothing so dear as the honour of their women, and that no one living would willingly lower the repute of his mother or his sisters. It is only when these have placed themselves beyond the pale of masculine respect that such things could be written as are written now. When women become again what they were once they will gather round them the love and homage and chivalrous devotion which were then an Englishwoman's natural inheritance.

The marvel in the present fashion of life among women is, how it holds its ground in spite of the disapprobation of men. It used to be an old-time notion that the sexes were made for each other, and that it was only natural for them to please each other, and to set themselves out for that end. But the Girl of the Period does not please men. She pleases them as little as she elevates them; and how little she does that, the class of women she has taken as her models of itself testifies. All men whose opinion is worth having prefer the simple and genuine girl of the past, with her tender little ways and pretty bashful modesties, to this loud and rampant modernization, with her false red hair and painted skin, talking slang as glibly as a man, and by preference leading the conversation to doubtful subjects. She thinks she is piquante and exciting when she thus makes herself the bad copy of a worse original; and she will not see that though men laugh with her they do not respect her, though they flirt with her they do not marry her; she will not believe that she is not the kind of thing they want, and that she is acting against nature and her own interests when she disregards their advice and offends their taste. We do not understand how she makes out her account, viewing her life from any side; but all we can do is to wait patiently until the national madness has passed, and our women have come back again to the old English ideal, once the most beautiful, the most modest, the most essentially womanly in the world.

MODERN MOTHERS.

I.

No human affection has been so passionately praised as maternal love, and none is supposed to be so holy or so strong. Even the poetic aspect of that instinct which inspires the young with their dearest dreams does not rank so high as this; and neither lover's love nor conjugal love, neither filial affection nor fraternal, comes near the sanctity or grandeur of the maternal instinct. But all women are not equally rich in this great gift; and, to judge by appearances, English women are at this moment wonderfully poor. It may seem a harsh thing to say, but it is none the less true:—society has put maternity out of fashion, and the nursery is nine times out of ten a place of punishment, not of pleasure, to the modern mother.

Two points connected with this subject are of growing importance at this present time—the one is the increasing disinclination of married women to be mothers at all; the other, the large number of those who, being mothers, will not, or cannot, nurse their own children. In the mad race after pleasure and excitement now going on through English society the tender duties of motherhood have become simply disagreeable restraints, and the old feeling of the blessing attending the quiver full is exchanged for one the very reverse. With some of the more intellectual and less instinctive sort, maternity is looked on as a kind of degradation; and women of this stamp, sensible enough in everything else, talk impatiently among themselves of the base necessities laid on them by men and nature, and how hateful to them is everything connected with their characteristic duties.

This wild revolt against nature, and specially this abhorrence of maternity, is carried to a still greater extent by American women; with grave national consequences resulting; but though we have not yet reached the Transatlantic limit, the state of feminine feeling and physical condition among ourselves will disastrously affect the future unless something can be done to bring our women back to a healthier tone of mind and body. No one can object to women declining marriage altogether in favour of a voluntary self-devotion to some project or idea; but, when married, it is a monstrous doctrine to hold that they are in any way degraded by the consequences, and that natural functions are less honourable than social excitements. The world can get on without balls and morning calls; it can get on too without amateur art and incorrect music; but not without wives and mothers; and those times in a nation's history when women have been social ornaments rather than family home-stays have ever been times of national decadence and of moral failure.

Part of this growing disinclination is due to the enormous expense incurred now by having children. As women have ceased to take any active share in their own housekeeping, whether in the kitchen or the nursery, the consequence is an additional cost for service, which is a serious item in the yearly accounts. Women who, if they lived a rational life, could and would nurse their children, now require a wet-nurse, or the services of an experienced woman who can 'bring up by hand,' as the phrase is; women who once would have had one nursemaid now have two; and women who, had they lived a generation ago, would have had none at all, must in their turn have a wretched young creature without thought or knowledge, into whose questionable care they deliver what should be the most sacred obligation and the most jealously-guarded charge they possess.

It is rare if, in any section of society where hired service can be had, mothers give more than a superficial personal superintendence to nursery or schoolroom—a superintendence about as thorough as their housekeeping, and as efficient. The one set of duties is quite as unfashionable as the other; and money is held to relieve from the service of love as entirely as it relieves from the need of labour. And yet, side by side with this personal relinquishment of natural duties, has grown up, perhaps as an instinctive compensation, an amount of expensive management specially remarkable. There never was a time when children were made of so much individual importance in the family, yet were in so little direct relation with the mother—never a time when maternity did so little and social organization so much. Juvenile parties ; the kind of moral obligation apparently felt by all parents to provide heated and unhealthy amusements for their boys and girls during the holidays ; extravagance in dress, following the same extravagance among the mothers ; the increasing cost of education ; the fuss and turmoil generally made over them—all render children real burdens in a house where money is not too plentiful, and where every child that comes is not only an additional mouth to feed and an additional body to clothe, but a subtractor by just so much from the family fund of pleasure. Even where there is no lack of money, the unavoidable restraints of the condition, for at least some months, more than counterbalance any sentimental delight to be found in maternity. For, before all other things in life, maternity demands unselfishness in women ; and this is just the one virtue of which women have least at this present time—just the one reason why motherhood is at a discount, and children are regarded as inflictions instead of blessings.

Few middle-class women are content to bring up their children with the old-fashioned simplicity of former times, and to let them share and share alike in the family, with only so much difference in their treatment as is required by their difference of state; fewer still are willing to take on themselves the labour and care which must come with children in the easiest-going household, and so to save in the expenses by their own work. The shabbiest little wife, with her two financial ends always gaping and never meeting, must have her still shabbier little drudge to wheel her perambulator, so as to give her an air of fine-ladyhood and being too good for such work; and the most indolent housekeeper, whose superintendence of domestic matters takes her just half an hour, cannot find time to go into the gardens or the square with nurse and the children, so that she may watch over them herself and see that they are properly cared for.

In France, where it is the fashion for mother and *bonne* to be together both out of doors and at home, at least the children are not neglected nor ill-treated, as is too often the case with us; and if they are improperly managed, according to our ideas, the fault is in the system, not in the want of maternal supervision. Here it is a very rare case indeed when the mother accompanies the nurse and children; and those days when she does are nursery gala-days to be talked of and remembered for weeks after. As the little ones grow older, she may occasionally take them with her when she visits her more intimate friends; but this is for her own pleasure, not their good; and going with them to see that they are properly cared for has nothing to do with the matter.

It is to be supposed that each mother has a profound belief in her own nurse, and that when she condemns the neglect and harshness shown to other children by the servants in charge, she makes a mental reservation in favour of her own, and is very sure that nothing improper nor cruel takes place in *her* nursery. Her children do not complain; and she always tells them to come to her when anything is amiss. On which negative evidence she satisfies her soul, and makes sure that all is right because she is too neglectful to see if anything is wrong. She does not remember that her children do not complain because they dare not. Dear and beautiful as all mammas are to the small fry in the nursery, they are always in a certain sense Junos sitting on the top of Mount Olympus, making occasional gracious and benign descents, but practically too far removed for useful interference; while nurse is an ever-present power, capable of sly pinches and secret raids, as well as of more open oppression—a power, therefore, to be propitiated, if only with the grim subservience of a Yezidi too much afraid of the Evil One to oppose him. Wherefore nurse is propitiated, failing the protection of the glorified creature just gone to her grand dinner in a cloud of lace and a blaze of jewels; and the first lesson taught the youthful Christian in short frocks or knickerbockers is not to carry tales down stairs, and by no means to let mamma know what nurse desires should be kept secret.

A great deal of other evil, beside these sly beginnings of deceit, is taught in the nursery; a great deal of vulgar thought, of superstitious fear, of class coarseness. As, indeed, how must it not be when we think of the early habits and education of the women taken into the nursery to give the first strong indelible impressions to the young souls under their care? Many a man with a ruined constitution, and many a woman with shattered nerves, can trace back the beginning of their sorrow to those neglected childish days when nurse had it all her own way because mamma never looked below the surface, and was satisfied with what was said instead of seeing for herself what was done. It is an odd state of society which tolerates this transfer of a mother's holiest and most important duty into the hands of a mere stranger, hired by the month, and never thoroughly known.

Where the organization of the family is of the patriarchal kind—old retainers marrying and multiplying about the central home, and carrying on a warm personal attachment from generation to generation—this transfer of maternal care has not such bad effects; but in our present way of life, without love or real relationship between masters and servants, and where service is rendered for just so much money down and for nothing more noble, it is a hideous system, and one that makes the modern mother utterly inexplicable. We wonder where her mere instincts can be, not to speak of her reason, her love, her conscience, her pride. Pleasure and self-indulgence have indeed gained tremendous power, in these later days, when they can thus break down the force of the strongest law of nature—a law stronger even than that of self-preservation.

Folly is the true capillary attraction of the moral world, and penetrates every stratum of society; and the folly of extravagant attire in the drawing-room is reproduced in the nursery. Not content with bewildering men's minds and emptying their husbands' purses for the enhancement of their own charms, women do the same by their children; and the mother who leaves the health and mind and temper and purity of her offspring in the keeping of a hired nurse takes especial care of the colour and cut of the frocks and petticoats. And there is always the same strain after show, and the same endeavour to make a little look a mickle. The children of five hundred a year must look like those of a thousand; and those of a thousand must rival the *tenue* of little lords and ladies born in the purple; while the amount of money spent on clothes in the tradesman class is a matter of real amazement to those let into the secret. Simplicity of diet, too, is going out with simplicity of dress, with simplicity of habits generally; and stimulants and concentrated food are now the rule in the nursery, where they mar as many constitutions as they make. More than one child of whom we have had personal knowledge has yielded to disease induced by too stimulating and too heating a diet ; but artificial habits demand corresponding artificiality of food, and so the candle burns at both ends instead of one.

Again, as for the increasing inability of educated women to nurse their children, even if desirous of doing so, that also is a bodily condition brought about by an unwholesome and unnatural state of life. Late hours, high living, heated blood, and constantly breathing a vitiated atmosphere are the causes of this alarming physical defect. But it would be too much to expect that women should forego their pleasurable indulgences, or do anything disagreeable to their senses, for the sake of their offspring. They are not famous for looking far ahead on any matter ; but to expect them to look beyond themselves, and their own present generation, is to expect the great miracle that never comes.

MODERN MOTHERS.

II.

THERE was once a superstition among us that mothers were of use in the world; that they had their functions and duties, without which society would not prosper nor hold together; and that much of the well-being of humanity, present and future, depended on them. Mothers in those bygone days were by no means effete personages or a worn-out institution, but living powers exercising a real and pervading influence; and they were credited with an authority which they did not scruple to use when required.

One of the functions recognized as specially belonging to them was that of guarding their young people from the consequences of their own ignorance —keeping them from dangers both physical and moral until wise enough to take care of themselves, and supplementing by their own experience the want of it in their children. Another was that of preserving the tone of society on a high level, and supplying the antiseptic element by which the rest was kept pure; as, for example, insisting that the language used and the subjects discussed before them were such as should not offend the modesty of virtuous women; that the people with whom they were required to associate should be moderately honest and well conducted; and, in short, as mothers, discountenancing everything in other men and women which they would not like to see imitated by their own sons and daughters.

This was one of the fond superstitions of an elder time. For ourselves, we boast of our freedom from superstition in these later days; of our proud renunciation of restraints and habits which were deemed beneficial by our forefathers; of our indifference to forms and hatred of humbug; and of all that tends to fetter what is called individualism. Hence we have found that we can go on without safeguards for our young; that society does not want its matrons as the preservative ingredient for keeping it pure; and that the world is all the merrier for the loosening of bonds which once it was the duty of women to draw closer. In fact, mothers have gone out, surviving only in the form of chaperons.

More or less on the search for her own pleasure—if by any possibility of artifice she can be taken for less than sixty, still ready for odd snatches of flirting as she can find occasion—or, with her faculties concentrated on the chance of winning the rubber by indifferent play—the chaperon's charge is not a very onerous one; and her daughters know as well as she does that her presence is a blind rather than a protection. They are with mamma as a form of speech; but they are left to themselves as a matter of fact. Any one who is in the confidence of young people of either sex knows a little of what goes on in the dark corners and on the steps of the stairs—a favourite anchorage for the loosely chaperoned in private houses where two hundred are invited and only a hundred can find room. But then the girls are 'with mamma,' and the young men are contented souls who take what they can get without making wry faces. Mamma, occupied in her own well-seasoned coquetries, or absorbed in the chances of her deep 'finesse' and the winning trick, lets the girls take care of themselves, and would think it an intolerable impertinence should a friend hint to her that her place of chaperon included vigilant personal guardianship, and that she would do better to keep her daughters in her own charge than leave them to themselves.

It is all very well for the advocates of youthful innocence to affect to resent the slur supposed to be cast on girlhood by the advocacy of this closer guardianship; or for those who do not know the world to make their ignorance the measure of another's knowledge, and to deny what they have not proved for themselves. Those who do know the world know what they say when they deprecate the excessive freedom which is too often granted to unmarried girls; and their warning is fully justified by experience when they call mothers back to their duty of stricter watchfulness. If indeed the young are capable of self-protection, then we grant with them that mothers are a mistake:—Let them abdicate without more ado. If license is more desirable than modesty, and liberty better than reticence, the girls may as well be left, as practically they are already, free from the mother's guardianship ; but if we have a doubt that way, we may as well give it the benefit of consideration, and think a little on the subject before going further on the present line.

From the first the mother, in the well-to-do classes, acts too much the part of the hen ostrich with her eggs. She trusts to the kindly influences of external circumstances rather than to her own care to make the hatching successful. Nurses, governesses, schools, in turn relieve her of the irksome duties of maternity. She sees her little ones at their stated hour, and for the other twenty-three leaves them to receive their first indelible impress from a class which she is never tired of disparaging.

As the children grow older the women by whom they are moulded become higher in the social and intellectual scale, but they are no more than before subordinated to the mother's personal supervision. She, for her part, cares only that her girls shall be taught the correct shibboleth of their station ; and for the rest, if she thinks at all, she cradles herself in a generous trust in the goodness of human nature, or the incorruptibility of her brood beyond that of any other woman's brood. When they come under her own immediate hand, 'finished' and ready to be introduced, she knows about as much of them as she knows of her neighbours' girls in the next square; and in nine cases out of ten the sole duties towards them which are undertaken by her are shirked when possible, as a *corvée* which she is too wise to bear unnecessarily. When she can, she shuffles them off on some kind neighbourly hands, and lets her daughters 'go about' with the first person who offers, glad to have a little breathing time on her own side, and with always that generous trust in providence and vicarious protection which has marked her maternal career throughout.

In the lower half of the middle class the liberty allowed to young girls grows yearly more and more unchecked. They walk alone, travel alone, visit alone; and the gravest evils have been known to arise from the habit which modern mothers have of sending their daughters of sixteen and upwards unaccompanied in London to colleges and classes. Mamma has grown stout and lazy, and has always some important matter on hand that keeps her at home, half asleep in the easy-chair, while the girls go to and fro, and take the exercise befitting their youthful energies. Of course no harm can befall them. They are *her* daughters, and the warnings given by the keener-eyed, who have had experience, are mere inventions of the enemy and slanders against the young. So they parade the streets, dressed in the most startling and meretricious costumes of the period; and that fatal doctrine of self-protection counts its victims by the score as the consequence.

The world is fond of throwing the blame of any misfortune that may arise, now on the girl, now on the man concerned ; but in honest fact that blame really belongs to the mothers who let their daughters run about the world without guide or guard. A work was given to them by nature and love to do which they have neglected, a duty which they have discarded. Whoever chooses may chaperon, accompany, mould their daughters, so long as they are freed from the trouble ; and their dependence on the natural virtue of humanity and the beneficence of circumstance runs exactly parallel with their own indolence and neglect.

In preserving the tone of society pure the modern mother is as far removed from the former ideal as she is in the duty of taking care of her girls. Too often she is found making herself prominent in support of the most objectionable movements ; or, when doubtful questions are discussed in mixed society, she forgets that regard for the purity of her daughters should keep her silent, even if her own self-respect were too weak to restrain her. When the conscienceless world, living without a higher aim than that of success and what is known by getting on, condones all kinds of moral obliquity for the sake of financial prosperity and social position, do we find that, as a rule, mothers and matrons protest against opening their houses to this gilded rascality ? If they did—if they made demerit and not poverty the cause of exclusion, virtue and not success the title to reception—there would be some check to the corruption which is so insolently rampant now.

Women have this power in their own hands, more especially those women who are mothers. If they would only set themselves to check the inclination for loose talk and doubtful discussions which is characteristic of the present moment, they could put an end to it without delay. So also they might stop in less than a year the torrent of slang with which Young England floods its daily speech; and by setting themselves against the paint and dye and meretricious make-up generally of the modern girl, they might bring next quarter's fashions back to modesty and simplicity.

Women are. apt to murmur at their lot as one without influence, variety, stirring purpose, space for action. But it is, on the contrary, a lot full of dignity and importance if properly regarded and fitly undertaken. If they do not lead armies, they make the characters of the men who lead and are led. If they are not State Ministers nor Parliamentary orators, they raise by their nobleness or degrade by their want of delicacy and refinement the souls and minds of the men who are. If they are not in the throng and press of active life, they can cheer others on to high aims, or basely reward the baser methods of existence. As mothers they are the artificers who give the initial touch that lasts for life; and as women they complete what the mother began. Society is moulded mainly by them, and they bring up their daughters on their own pattern.

It is surely weak and silly then to blame society for its ignoble tone, or the young for their disorders. All men want the corrective influence of social opinion, and it is chiefly women who create that opinion. Youth, too, will ever be disorderly if it gets the chance, and the race has not yet been born that carries old heads on young shoulders. It is for the mothers to supplement by their own wisdom the gaps left by the inexperience and ignorance of youth; it is for the mothers to guide aright the steps that are apt, without that guidance, to run astray, and to guard against passions, emotions, desires, which, if left to themselves, bring only evil and disaster, but which, guarded and directed, may be turned to the best ends. For ourselves, we deeply regret to see the rapid extinction of motherhood in its best sense, and decline to accept this modern loose-handed chaperon age as its worthy substitute. We repudiate the plea of the insubordination of the young so often put forward in defence of the new state of things, for it is simply nonsense. The young are what the mothers make them, just as society is what the matrons allow it to be; and if these mothers and matrons did their duty, we should hear no more of the wilfulness of the one or the shameless vagaries of the other. The remedy for each lies in their own hands only.

PAYING ONE'S SHOT.

It would save much useless striving and needless disappointment if the necessity of paying one's shot were honestly accepted as absolute—if it were understood, once for all, that society, like other manifestations of humanity, is managed on the principle of exchange and barter, and equivalents demanded for value received. The benevolence which gives out of its own impulse, with no hope of reward save in the wellbeing of the recipient, has no place in the drawing-room code of morals. We may keep a useless creature from starving at the cost of so much of our substance *per diem*, for the sole remuneration of thanks and the consciousness of an equivocal act of charity; but who among us opens his doors, or gives a seat at his table, to drawing-room paupers unable to pay their shot? who cares to cultivate the acquaintance of men or women who are unable to make him any return? It is not necessary that this return should be in kind—a dinner for a dinner, a champagne supper for a champagne supper, and balls with waxed floors for balls with stretched linen; but shot must be paid in some form, whether in kind or not, and the social pauper who cannot pay his quota is Lazarus excluded from the feast. This is a hard saying, but it is a true one. We often hear worthy people who do not understand this law complain that they are neglected—left out of wedding breakfasts—passed over in dinner invitations—and that they find it difficult to keep acquaintances when made. But the fact is, these poor creatures who know so much about the cold-shoulder of society are simply those who cannot pay their shot, according to the currency of the class to which they aspire; and so by degrees they get winnowed through the meshes, and fall to a level where their funds will suffice to meet all demands, triumphantly. For the rejected of one level are not necessarily the rejected of all, and the base metal of one currency is sound coinage in another. People who would find it impossible to enter a drawing-room in Grosvenor Square may have all Bloomsbury at their command; and what was caviare to My Lord will be ambrosia to his valet—all depending on the amount of the shot to be paid and the relative value of coinage wherewith to pay it.

The most simple form of payment is of course by the elemental process of reciprocity in kind; a dinner for a dinner and a supper for a supper:—a form as purely instinctive as an eye for an eye and a tooth for a tooth—the *lex talionis* of early jurisprudence administered among wine-cups instead of in the shambles. But there are other modes of payment as efficient if less evident, and as imperative if more subtle. For instance, women pay their shot—when they pay it individually, and not through the vicarious merits of their masculine relations—by dressing well and looking nice; some by being pretty; some by being fashionable; a few by brilliant talk; while all ought to add to their private speciality the generic virtue of pleasant manners. If they are not pretty, pleasant, well-dressed nor well-connected, and if they have no masculine pegs of power by which they can be hooked on to the higher lines, they are let to drop through the social meshes without an effort made to retain them, as little fishes swim away unopposed through the loops which hold the bigger ones. These things are their social duties—the final cause of their drawing-room existence; and if they fail in them they fail in the purpose for which they were created socially, and may die out as soon as convenient. They have other duties, of course, and doubtless of far higher moment and greater worth; but the question now is only of their drawing-room duties— of the qualities which secure their recognition in society—of the special coinage in which they must pay their shot if they would assist at the great banquet of social life. A dowdy, humdrum, well-principled woman, whose toilette looks as if it had been made with the traditionary pitchfork, and whose powers of conversation do not go beyond the strength of *Cobwebs to Catch Flies*, or *Mangnall's*

Questions, may be an admirable wife, the painstaking mother of future honest citizens, invaluable by a sickbed, beyond price in the nursery, a pattern of all household economies, a woman absolutely faultless in her sphere—and that sphere a very sweet and lovely one. But her virtues are not those by which she can pay her shot in society; and the motherly goodness, of so much account in a dressing-jacket and list-slippers, is put out of court when the fee to be paid is liveliness of manner or elegance of appearance. Certainly, worthy women who dress ill and look ungraceful, and whose conversation is about up to the mark of their children's easy-spelling-books, are plentiful in society—unfortunately for those bracketed with them for two hours' penance; but in most cases they have their shot paid for them by the wealth, the importance, the repute, or the desirableness of their relations. They may pay it themselves by their own wealth and consequent liberal tariff of reciprocity; but this is rare; the possession of personal superiority of any kind for the most part acting as a moral stimulus with women whom the superiority of their male belongings does not touch. And, by the way, it is rather hard lines that so many celebrated men have such dowdy wives. Artists, poets, self-made men of all kinds often fail in this special article; and, while they themselves have caught the tone of the circle to which they have risen, and pay their shot by manner as well as by repute, their wives lag behind among the ashes of the past, like Cinderellas before the advent of the fairy godmother. How many of them are carried through society as clogs or excrescences which a polite world is bound to tolerate with more or less equanimity, according to the amount of sensitiveness bestowed by nature and cultivated by art! Sometimes, however, self-made men and their wives are wise in their generation and understand the terms on which society receives its members; in which case the marital Reputation goes to the front alone, and the conjugal Cinderella rests tranquilly in the rear.

Notoriety of all kinds, short of murder or forgery, is one way of paying one's shot, specially into the coffers of the Leo Hunters, of whom there are many. It is shot paid to the general fund when one has seen an accident—better still, if one has been in it. Many a man has owed a rise in his scale of dinners to a railway smash; and to have been nearly burnt to death, to have escaped by a miracle from drowning, to have been set on by footpads or to have been visited by burglars, is worth a round of At Homes, because of the ready cash of a real adventure. To be connected more or less remotely with the fashionable tragedy of the hour is paying one's shot handsomely. To have been on speaking terms with the latest respectable scoundrel unmasked, or to have had dealings, sufficiently remote to have been cleanly, with the newest villainy, will be accepted as shot while the public interest in the matter lasts. A chance visit to ultra-grandees—grandees in ratio to the ordinary sphere—is shot paid with an air. A bad illness, or the attendance on one, with the apparently unconscious heroism of the details, comes in as part of the social fine; especially if the person relating his or her experience has the knack of epigram or exaggeration, while still keeping local colour and verisimilitude intact. Interesting people who have been abroad and seen things have good counters for a dinner-party; paying their shot for themselves and their hosts too, who put them forward as their contribution to the funds of the commonwealth, with certainty of acceptance. Some pay their shot by their power of procuring orders and free admissions. They know the manager of this theatre or the leading actor of that; they are acquainted with the principal members of the hanging committees, and are therefore great in private views; they are always good for a gratuitous treat to folks who can afford to pay twice the sum demanded for their day's pleasure. Such people may be stupid, ungainly, not specially polished, in grain unpleasant; but they circulate in society because they pay their shot and give back equivalents for value received. A country-house, where there is a good tennis-ground and a blushing bed of strawberries, is coinage that will carry the possessor very far ahead through London society; and by the same law you will find healthy, well-conditioned country folk tolerate undeniable little snobs of low calibre because of that sixteen-roomed house in Tyburnia, a visit to which represents so many concerts, so many theatres, a given number of exhibitions, and a certain quantity of operas and parties. Had those undeniable little snobs no funds wherewith to pay their shot, they would have had no place kept for them among the rose-trees and the strawberry-beds; but, bringing their quota as they do, they take their seat with the rest and are helped in their turn.

In fact, humiliating to our self-love as it may be, the truth is, we are all valued socially, not for ourselves integrally, not for the mere worth of the naked soul, but for the kind of shot that we pay—for the advantage or amusement to others that we can bring —for something in ourselves which renders us desirable as companions—or for something belonging to our condition which makes us remunerative as guests. If we have no special qualification, if we neither look nice nor talk well, neither bring glory nor confer pleasure, we must expect to be shunted to the side in favour of others who are up to the right mark and who give as much as they receive. If this truth were once fully established as a matter of social science, a great advance would be made; for nothing helps people so much as to clear a subject of what fog may lie about it. And as the tendency of the age is to discover the fixed laws which regulate the mutable affairs of man, it would be just as well to extend the inquiry from the jury-box to the dinner-table, and from the blue-book to the visiting-list. Why is it that some people struggle all their lives to get a footing in society, yet die as they have lived—social

Sisyphuses, never accomplishing their perpetually-recurring task? There must be a reason for it, seeing that nothing is ruled by blind chance, though much seems to lie outside the independent will of the individual. Enlighten these worthy people's minds on the unwritten laws of invitation, and show them that—thoroughly honest souls and to be trusted with untold gold or with their neighbour's pretty wife, which is perhaps a harder test, as they may be—they are by no means to be trusted with the amusement of a couple of companions at a dinner-table. Show them that, how rich soever they may be in the rough gold of domestic morality, they are bankrupts in the small-change which alone passes current in society—and, if invited where they aspire to be, they would be taken on as pauper cousins unable to pay their footing and good for neither meat nor garnish. Let them learn how to pay their shot, and their difficulties would vanish. They would leave off repeating the fable of Sisyphus, and attain completion of endeavour. No one need say this is a hard or a selfish doctrine, for we all follow it in practice. Among the people we invite to our houses are some whom we do not specially like, but whom we must ask because of shot paid in kind. There are people who may be personally disagreeable, ill-educated, uninteresting, ungainly, but whom we cannot cut because of the relations in which we stand towards them, and who take their place by right, because they pay their shot with punctuality. There are others whom we ask because of liking or desirability, and shot paid in some specific form of pleasantness, as in beauty, fashion, good manner, notoriety; but there are none absolutely barren of all gifts of pleasantness to the guests, of reflected honour to ourselves, and of social small-change according to the currency. We do not go into the byways and hedges to pick up drawing-room tatterdemalions who bring nothing with them and are simply so much dead-weight on the rest, occupying so much valuable space and consuming so much vital energy. The law of reciprocity may be hard on the strivers who are ignorant of its inexorable provisions; but it is a wholesome law, like other rules and enactments against remediable pauperism. And were we once thoroughly to understand that, if we would sit securely at the table we must put something of value into the pool—that we must possess advantageous circumstances, or personal desirabilities, as the shot to be paid for our place—the art of society would be better cultivated than it is now, and the classification of guests would be carried out with greater judgment. Surely, if the need of being gracious in manner, sprightly in talk, and of pleasant appearance generally—all cultivable qualities, and to be learned if not born in us by nature—were accepted as an absolute necessity, without which we must expect to be overlooked and excluded, drawing-rooms would be far brighter and dinner-tables far pleasanter than they are at present; to the advantage of all concerned! And, after all, society is a great thing in human life. If not equal in importance to the family, or to political virtue, it has its own special value; and whatever adds to its better organization is a gain in every sense.

WHAT IS WOMAN'S WORK?

THIS is a question which one half the world is at this moment asking the other half; with very wild answers as the result. Woman's work seems to be in these days everything that it was not in times past, and nothing that it was. Professions are undertaken and careers invaded which were formerly held sacred to men; while things are left undone which, for all the generations that the world has lasted, have been naturally and instinctively assigned to women to do. From the savage squaw gathering fuel or drawing water for the wigwam, to the lady giving up the keys to her housekeeper, housekeeping has been considered one of the primary functions of women. The man to provide—the woman to dispense; the man to do the rough initial work of bread-winning, whether as a half-naked barbarian hunting live meat or as a City clerk painfully scoring lines of rugged figures—the woman to cook the meat when got, and to lay out to the best advantage for the family the quarter's salary gained by casting up ledgers and writing advices and bills of lading. Take human society in any phase we like, we must come down to these radical conditions; and any system which ignores this division of labour, and confounds these separate functions, is of necessity imperfect and wrong. We have nothing whatever to say against the professional self-support of women who have no men to work for them, and who must therefore work for themselves in order to live. In what direction soever they can best make their way, let them take it. Brains and intellectual gifts are of no sex and no condition, and it is far more important that good work should be done than that it should be done by this or that particular set of workers. But we are speaking of the home duties of married women, and of those girls who have no need to earn their daily bread, and who are not so specially gifted as to be driven afield by the irrepressible power of genius. We are speaking of women who cannot help in the family income, but who might both save and improve in the home; women whose lives are one long day of idleness, *ennui* and vagrant imagination, because they despise the activities into which they were born, while seeking outlets for their energies impossible to them both by functional and social restrictions.

It is strange to see into what unreasonable disrepute active housekeeping—woman's first social duty—has fallen in England. Take a family with four or five hundred a year—and we know how small a sum that is for 'genteel humanity' in these days—the wife who is an active housekeeper, even with such an income, is an exception to the rule ; and the daughters who are anything more than drawing-room dolls waiting for husbands to transfer them to a home of their own, where they may be as useless as they are now, are rarer still. For things are getting worse, not better, and our young women are less useful even than were their mothers ; while these last do not, as a rule, come near the housekeeping ladies of olden times, who knew every secret of domestic economy and made a wise and pleasant 'distribution of bread' their grand point of honour. The usual method of London housekeeping, even in the second ranks of the middle-classes, is for the mistress to give her orders in the kitchen in the morning, leaving the cook to pass them on to the tradespeople when they call. If she be not very indolent, and if she have a due regard for neatness and cleanliness, she may supplement her kitchen commands by going up stairs through some of the bedrooms ; but after a kind word of advice to the housemaid if she be sweet-tempered, or a harsh note of censure if she be of the cross-grained type, her work in that department will be done, and her duties for the day are at an end. There is none of the clever marketing by which fifty per cent. is saved in the outlay, if a woman knows what she is about and how to buy ; none of that personal superintendence, so encouraging to servants when genially performed, which renders slighted work impossible ; none of that 'seeing to things' herself, or doing the finer parts of the work with her own hands, which used to form part of a woman's unquestioned duty. She gives her orders, weighs out her supplies, then leaves the maids to do the best they know or the worst they will, according to the degree in which they are supplied with faculty or conscience. Many women boast that their housekeeping takes them perhaps an hour, perhaps half an hour, in the morning, and no more; and they think themselves clever and commendable in proportion to the small amount of time given to their largest family duty. This is all very well where the income is such as to secure first-class servants— professors of certain specialities of knowledge and far in advance of the mistress; but how about the comfort of the house under this hasty generalship, when the maids are mere scrubs who ought to go through years of training if they are ever to be worth their salt? It may be very well too in large households governed by general system, and not by individual ruling; but where the service is scant and poor, it is a stupid, uncomfortable, as well as wasteful way of housekeeping. It is analogous to English cookery—a revolting poverty of result with flaring prodigality of means; all the pompous paraphernalia of tradespeople and their carts and their red-books for orders, with nothing worth the trouble of booking; and everything of less quantity and lower quality than would be if personal pains were taken—which is always the best economy.

What is there in practical housekeeping less

honourable than the ordinary work of middle-class gentlewomen? and why should women shrink from doing for utility, and for the general comfort of the family, what they would do at any time for vanity or idleness? No one need go into extremes, and wish our middle-class gentlewomen to become exaggerated Marthas occupied only with much serving, Nausicaas washing linen, or 'wise Penelopes' spending their lives in needlework alone. But, without undertaking anything unpleasant to her senses or degrading to her condition, a lady might do hundreds of things which are now left undone in a house, or are given up to the coarse handling of servants; and domestic life would gain in consequence. What degradation, for instance, is there in cookery? and how much more home happiness would there not be if wives would take in hand that great cold-mutton question? But women are both selfish and small on this point. Born for the most part with feebly-developed gustativeness, they affect to despise the stronger instinct in men, and think it low and sensual if they are expected to give special attention to the meals of the man who provides the meat. This contempt for good cooking is one cause of the ignorance there is among them of how to secure good living. Those horrible traditions of 'plain roast and boiled' cling about them as articles of culinary faith; and because they have reached no higher knowledge for themselves, they decide that no one else shall go beyond them. For one middle-class gentlewoman who understands anything about cookery, or who really cares for it as a scientific art or domestic necessity, there are ten thousand who do not; yet our mothers and grandmothers were not ashamed to be known as deft professors, and homes were happier in proportion to the respect paid to the stewpan and the stockpot. And cookery is more interesting now than it was then, because more advanced, more scientific, and with improved appliances; and, at the same time, it is of confessedly more importance.

It may seem humiliating, to those who go in for spirit pure and simple, to speak of the condition of the soul as in any way determined by beef and cabbage; but it is so, nevertheless; the connexion between food and virtue, food and thought, being a very close one. And the sooner wives recognize this connexion the better for them and for their husbands. The clumsy savagery of a plain cook, or the vile messes of a fourth-rate confectioner, are absolute sins in a house where a woman has all her senses, and can, if she will, attend personally to the cooking. Many things pass for crimes which are really not so bad as this. But how seldom do we find a house where the lady does look after the food of the family; where clean hands and educated brains are put to active service for the good of others! The trouble would be too great in our fine-lady days, even if there were the requisite ability; but there is as little ability as there is energy, and the plain cook with her savagery and the fourth-rate confectioner with his rancid pastry, have it all their own way, according as the election is for economy or ostentation. If by chance we stumble on a household where the woman does not disdain housewifely work, and specially does not disdain the practical superintendence of the kitchen, there we are sure to find cheerfulness and content.

There seems to be something in the life of a practical housekeeper that answers to the needs of a woman's best nature, and that makes her pleasant and good-humoured. Perhaps it is the consciousness that she is doing her duty—of itself a wonderful sweetener of the temper; perhaps the greater amount of bodily exercise keeps her liver in good case ; whatever the cause, sure it is that the homes of the active housekeepers are more harmonious than those of the feckless and do-nothing sort. Yet the snobbish half of the middle-classes holds housewifely work as degrading, save in the trumpery pretentiousness of 'giving orders.' A woman may sit in a dirty drawing-room which the slipshod maid has not had time to clean, but she must not take a duster in her hands and polish the legs of the chairs :—there is no disgrace in the dirt, only in the duster. She may do fancy-work of no earthly use, but she must not be caught making a gown. Indeed very few women could make one, and as few will do plain needlework. They will braid and embroider, 'cut holes, and sew them up again,' and spend any amount of time and money on beads and wools for messy draperies which no one wants. The end, being finery, sanctions the toil and refines it. But they will not do things of practical use ; or, if they are compelled by the exigencies of circumstances, they think themselves martyrs and badly used by the Fates.

The whole scheme of woman's life at this present time is untenable and unfair. She wants to have all the pleasures and none of the disagreeables. Her husband goes to the City and does monotonous and unpleasant work there; but his wife thinks herself very hardly dealt with if asked to do monotonous housework at home. Yet she does nothing more elevating nor more advantageous. Novel-reading, fancy-work, visiting and letter-writing, sum up her ordinary occupations ; and she considers these more to the point than practical housekeeping. In fact it becomes a serious question what women think themselves sent into the world for—what they hold themselves designed by God to be or to do. They grumble at having children and at the toil and anxiety which a family entails ; they think themselves degraded to the level of servants if they have to do any practical housework whatever ; they assert their equality with man, and express their envy of his life, yet show themselves incapable of learning the first lesson set to men—that of doing what they do not like to do. What, then, do they want ? What do they hold themselves made for ? Certainly some of the more benevolent sort carry their energies out of doors, and leave such prosaic matters as savoury dinners and fast shirt-buttons for committees and charities, where they get excitement and *kudos* together. Others give themselves to what they call keeping up society, which means being more at home in every person's house than their own; and some do a little weak art, and others a little feeble literature; but there are very few indeed who honestly buckle to the natural duties of their position, and who bear with the tedium of home-work as men bear with the tedium of office-work.

The little royalty of home is the last place where a woman cares to shine, and the most uninteresting of all the domains she seeks to govern. Fancy a high-souled creature, capable of æsthetics, giving her mind to soup or the right proportion of chutnee for the curry! Fancy, too, a brilliant creature foregoing an evening's conversational glory abroad for the sake of a prosaic husband's more prosaic dinner! He comes home tired from work, and desperately in need of a good dinner as a restorative; but the plain cook gives him cold meat and pickles, or an abomination which she calls hash, and the brilliant creature, full of mind, thinks the desire for anything else rank sensuality. It seems a little hard, certainly, on the unhappy fellow who works at the mill for such a return; but women believe that men are made only to work at the mill that they may receive the grist accruing, and be kept in idleness and uselessness all their lives. They have no idea of lightening the labour of that mill-round by doing their own natural work cheerfully and diligently. They will do everything but what they ought to do. They will make themselves doctors, committee-women, printers, what not; but they will not learn cooking, and they will not keep their own houses. There never was a time when women were less the helpmates of men than they are at present; when there was such a wide division between the interests and the sympathies of the sexes coincident with the endeavour, on the one side, to approximate their pursuits.

A great demand is being made now for more work for woman and wider fields for her labour. We confess we should feel a deeper interest in the question if we saw more energy and conscience put into the work lying to her hand at home; and we hold that she ought to perfectly perform the duties which we may call instinctive to her sex before claiming those hitherto held remote from her natural condition. Much of this demand springs from restlessness and dissatisfaction; little, if any, from higher aspirations or nobler energies unused. Indeed, the nobler the woman the more thoroughly she will do her own proper work, in the spirit of old George Herbert's well-worn line; and the less she will feel herself above that work. It is only the weak who cannot raise their circumstances to the level of their thoughts; only the poor in spirit who cannot enrich their deeds by their motives.

That very much of this demand for more power

of work comes from necessity and the absolute need of bread, we know ; and that the demand will grow louder as marriage becomes scarcer, and there are more women adrift in the world without the protection and help of men, we also know. But this belongs to another part of the subject. What we want to insist on now is the pitiable ignorance and shiftless indolence of most middle-class housekeepers; and what we would urge on woman is the value of a better system of life at home before laying claim to the discharge of extra-domestic duties abroad.

LITTLE WOMEN.

THE conventional idea of a brave, energetic, or a supremely criminal, woman has always been that of a tall, dark-haired, large-armed virago who might pass as the younger brother of her husband, and about whom nature seemed to have hesitated before determining whether to make her a man or a woman :— a kind of debateable land, in fact, between the two sexes, and almost as much the one as the other. Helen Macgregor, Lady Macbeth, Catharine de Medici, Mrs. Manning, and the old-fashioned murderesses in novels, were all of the muscular, black-brigand type, with more or less of regal grace superadded according to circumstances; and it would have been thought nothing but a puerile fancy to have supposed the contrary of those whose personal description was not already known. Crime, indeed, in art and fiction, was generally painted in very nice proportion to the number of cubic inches embodied and the depth of colour employed; though we are bound to add that the public favour ran towards muscular heroines almost as much as towards muscular murderesses, which to a certain extent redressed the overweighted balance. Our later novelists, however, have altered the whole setting of the palette. Instead of five foot ten of black and brown, they have gone in for four foot nothing of pink and yellow. Instead of tumbled masses of raven hair, they have shining coils of purest gold. Instead of hollow caverns whence flash unfathomable eyes eloquent of every damnable passion, they have limpid lakes of heavenly blue; and their worst sinners are in all respects fashioned as much after the outward semblance of the ideal saint as they have skill to design.

The original notion was a very good one, and the revolution did not come before it was wanted; but it has been a little overdone of late, and we are threatened with as great a surfeit of small-limbed yellow-headed criminals as we have had of the black-haired virago. One gets weary of the most perfect model in time, if too constantly repeated; as now, when we have all begun to feel that the resources of the angel's face and demon's soul have been more heavily drawn on than is quite fair, and that, given 'heavy braids of golden hair,' 'bewildering blue eyes,' 'a small lithe frame,' and special delicacy of feet and hands, we are booked for the companionship, through three volumes, of a young person to whom Messalina or Lucretia Borgia was a mere novice.

And yet there is a physiological truth in this association of energy with smallness—perhaps, also, with a certain tint of yellow hair, which, with a dash of red through it, is decidedly suggestive of nervous force. Suggestiveness, indeed, does not go very far in an argument; but the frequent connexion of energy and smallness in women is a thing which all may verify in their own circles. In daily life, who is the really formidable woman to encounter?—the black-browed, broad-shouldered giantess, with arms almost as big in the girth as a man's? or the pert, smart, trim little female, with no more biceps than a ladybird, and of just about equal strength with a sparrow? Nine times out of ten, the giantess with the heavy shoulders and broad black eyebrows is a timid, feeble-minded, good-tempered person, incapable of anything harsher than a mild remonstrance with her maid, or a gentle chastisement of her children. Nine times out of ten her husband has her in hand in the most perfect working order, so that she would swear the moon shone at midday if it were his pleasure that she should make a fool of herself by her submissiveness. One of the most obedient and indolent of earth's daughters, she gives no trouble to any one, save the trouble of rousing, exciting and setting going; while, as for the conception or execution of any naughty piece of self-assertion, she is as utterly incapable of either as if she were a child unborn, and demands nothing better than to feel the pressure of the leading-strings, and to know exactly by their strain where she is desired to go and what to do.

But the little woman is irrepressible. Too fragile

to come into the fighting section of humanity—a puny creature whom one blow from a man's huge fist could annihilate—absolutely fearless, and insolent with the insolence which only those dare show who know that retribution cannot follow—what can be done with her? She is afraid of nothing and to be controlled by no one. Sheltered behind her weakness as behind a triple shield of brass, the angriest man dare not touch her, while she provokes him to a combat in which his hands are tied. She gets her own way in everything and everywhere. At home and abroad she is equally dominant and irrepressible, equally free from obedience and from fear. Who breaks all the public order in sights and shows, and, in spite of King, Kaiser, or Policeman X, goes where it is expressly forbidden that she shall go? Not the large-boned, muscular woman, whatever her temperament; unless, indeed, of the exceptionally haughty type in distinctly inferior surroundings—and then she can queen it royally enough and set everything at most lordly defiance.

But in general the large-boned woman obeys the orders given, because, while near enough to man to be somewhat on a par with him, she is still undeniably his inferior. She is too strong to shelter herself behind her weakness, yet too weak to assert her strength and defy her master on equal grounds. She is like a flying fish—not one thing wholly; and while capable of the inconveniences of two lives is incapable of the privileges of either. It is not she, for all her well-developed frame and formidable looks, but the little woman, who breaks the whole code of laws and defies all their defenders—the pert, smart, pretty little woman, who laughs in your face and goes straight ahead if you try to turn her to the right hand or to the left, receiving your remonstrances with the most sublime indifference, as if you were talking a foreign language she could not understand. She carries everything before her, wherever she is. You may see her stepping over barriers, slipping under ropes, penetrating to the green benches with a red ticket, taking the best places on the platform over the heads of their rightful owners, settling herself among the reserved seats without an inch of pasteboard to float her. You cannot turn her out by main force. British chivalry objects to the public laying on of hands in the case of a woman, even when most recalcitrant and disobedient; more particularly if she be a small and fragile-looking woman. So that, if it be only a usurpation of places specially masculine, she is allowed to retain what she has got, amid the grave looks of the elders—not really displeased at the flutter of her ribbons among them—and the titters and nudges of the young fellows.

If the battle is between her and another woman, they are left to fight it out as they best can, with the odds laid heavily on the little one. All this time there is nothing of the tumult of contest about her. Fiery and combative as she generally is, when breaking the law in public places she is the very soul of serene daring. She shows no heat, no passion, no turbulence ; she leaves these as extra weapons of defence to women who are assailable. For herself she requires no such aids. She knows her capabilities and the line of attack that best suits her, and she knows, too, that the fewer points of contest she exposes the more likely she is to slip into victory ; the more she assumes and the less she argues, the slighter the hold she gives her opponents. She is either perfectly good-humoured or blankly innocent; she either smiles you into indulgence or wearies you into compliance by the sheer hopelessness of making any impression on her. She may, indeed, if of the very vociferous and shrill-tongued kind, burst out into such a noisy demonstration as makes you glad to escape from her, no matter what spoils you leave in her hands ; just as a mastiff will slink away from a bantam hen all heckled feathers and screeching cackle and tremendous assumption of doing something terrible if he does not look out. Any way the little woman is unconquerable ; and a tiny fragment of humanity at a public show, setting all rules and regulations at defiance, is only carrying out in the matter of benches the manner of life to which nature has dedicated her from the beginning.

As a rule, the little woman is brave. When the lymphatic giantess falls into a faint or goes off into hysterics, she storms, or bustles about, or holds on like a game terrier, according to the work on hand. She will fly at any man who annoys her, and she bears herself as equal to the biggest and strongest fellow of her acquaintance. In general she does it all by sheer pluck, and is not notorious for subtlety or craft. Had Delilah been a little woman she would never have taken the trouble to shear Samson's locks. She would have stood up against him with all his strength untouched on his head, and she would have overcome him too. Judith and Jael were both probably large women. The work they went about demanded a certain strength of muscle and toughness of sinew; but who can say that Jezebel was not a small, freckled, auburn-haired Lady Audley of her time, full of the concentrated fire, the electric force, the passionate recklessness of her type? Regan and Goneril might have been beautiful demons of the same pattern; we have the example of the Marchioness de Brinvilliers as to what amount of spiritual devilry can exist with the face and manner of an angel direct from heaven; and perhaps Cordelia was a tall dark-haired girl, with a pair of brown eyes, and a long nose sloping downwards.

Look at modern Jewesses, with their flashing Oriental orbs, their night-black tresses and the dusky shadows of their olive-coloured complexions. As catalogued properties according to the ideal, they would be placed in the list of the natural criminals and law-breakers, while in reality they are about as meek and docile a set of women as are to be found within the four seas. Pit a fiery little Welsh woman or a petulant Parisienne against the most regal and

Junonic amongst them, and let them try conclusions in courage, in energy, in audacity; the Israelitish Juno will go down before either of the small Philistines, and the fallacy of weight and colour in the generation of power will be shown without the possibility of denial.

Even in those old days of long ago, when human characteristics were embodied and deified, we do not find that the white-armed large-limbed Hera, though queen by right of marriage, lorded it over her sister goddesses by any superior energy or force of nature. On the contrary, she was rather a heavy-going person, and, unless moved to anger by her husband's numerous infidelities, took her Olympian life placidly enough, and once or twice got cheated in a way that did no great credit to her sagacity. A little Frenchwoman would have sailed round her easily; and as it was, shrewish though she was in her speech when provoked, her husband not only deceived but chastised her, and reduced her to penitence and obedience as no little woman would have suffered herself to be reduced.

There is one celebrated race of women who were probably the powerfully-built, large-limbed creatures they are assumed to have been, and as brave and energetic as they were strong and big—the Norse women of the sagas, who, for good or evil, seem to have been a very influential element in the old Northern life. Prophetesses; physicians; dreamers of dreams and accredited interpreters as well; endowed with magic powers; admitted to a share in the councils of men; brave in war; active in peace; these fair-haired Scandinavian women were the fit comrades of their men, the fit wives and mothers of the Berserkers and the Vikings. They had no tame nor easy life of it, if all we hear of them be true. To defend the farm and the homestead during their husbands' absence, and to keep these and themselves intact against all bold rovers to whom the Tenth Commandment was an unknown law; to dazzle and bewilder by magic arts when they could not conquer by open strength; to unite craft and courage, deception and daring, loyalty and independence, demanded no small amount of opposing qualities. But the Steingerdas and Gudrunas were generally equal to any emergency of fate or fortune, and slashed their way through the history of their time more after the manner of men than of women; supplementing their downright blows by side thrusts of craftier cleverness when they had to meet power with skill and were fain to overthrow brutality by fraud. The Norse women were certainly as largely framed as they were mentally energetic, and as crafty as either; but we know of no other women who unite the same characteristics and are at once cunning, strong, brave and true.

On the whole, then, the little women have the best of it. More petted than their bigger sisters, and infinitely more powerful, they have their own way in part because it really does not seem worth while to contest a point with such little creatures. There is nothing that wounds a man's self-respect in any victory they may get or claim. Where there is absolute inequality of strength, there can be no humiliation in the self-imposed defeat of the stronger; and as it is always more pleasant to have peace than war, and as big men for the most part rather like than not to put their necks under the tread of tiny feet, the little woman goes on her way triumphant to the end; breaking all the laws she does not like and throwing down all the barriers which impede her progress; irresistible and irrepressible in all circumstances and under any conditions.

IDEAL WOMEN.

It is often objected against fault-finders, writers or others, that they destroy but do not build up; that while industriously blaming errors they take good care not to praise the counteracting virtues; that in their zeal against the vermin of which they are seeking to sweep the house clean they forget the nobler creatures which do the good work of keeping things sweet and wholesome. But it is impossible to be continually introducing the saving clause, 'all are not so bad as these.' The seven thousand righteous who have not bowed the knee to Baal are understood to exist in all communities; and, vicious as any special section may be, there must always be the hidden salt and savour of the virtuous to keep the whole from falling into utter corruption.

This is specially true of modern women. Certainly some of them are as unsatisfactory as any of their kind who have ever appeared on earth before; but it would be very queer logic to infer therefore that all are bad alike, and that our modern womanhood is as ill off as the Cities of the Plain, which could not be saved for want of the ten just men to save them.

Happily, we have noble women among us yet; women who believe in something besides pleasure, and who do their work faithfully, wherever it may lie; women who can and do sacrifice themselves for love and duty, and who do not think they were sent into the world simply to run one mad life-long race for wealth, for dissipation, for distinction. But the life of such women is essentially in retirement; and though the lesson they teach is beautiful, yet its influence is necessarily confined, because of the narrow sphere of the teacher. When public occasions for devotedness occur, we in some sort measure the extent to which the self-sacrifice of women can be carried; but in general their noblest virtues come out only in the quiet sacredness of home, and the most heroic lives of patience and well-doing go on in seclusion, uncheered by sympathy and unrewarded by applause.

Still, it is impossible to write of one absolute womanly ideal—one single type that shall satisfy every man's fancy; for, naturally, what would be perfection to one is imperfection to another, according to the special bent of the individual mind. Thus one man's ideal of womanly perfection is in beauty, mere physical outside beauty; and not all the virtues under heaven could warm him into love with red hair or a snub nose. He is entirely happy if his wife be undeniably the handsomest woman of his acquaintance, and holds himself blessed when all men admire and all women envy. But he is blessed for his own sake rather than for her. Pleasant as her loveliness is to look on, it is pleasanter to know that he is the possessor of it. The 'handsomest woman in the room' comes into the same category as the finest picture or the most thoroughbred horse within his sphere; and if the degree of pride in his possession be different, the kind is the same. And so in minor proportions—from the most beautiful woman of all, to simply beauty as a *sine quâ non*, whatever else may be wanting. One other thing only is as absolute as this beauty, and that is its undivided possession.

Another man's ideal is a good housekeeper and a careful mother; and he does not care a rush whether his wife, if she is these, be pretty or ugly. Provided she is active and industrious, minds the house well, brings up the children as they ought to be brought up, has good principles, is trustworthy and even-tempered, he is not particular as to colour or form, and can even be brought to tolerate a limp or a squint. Given the broad foundations of an honourable home, and he will forego the lath and plaster of personal appearance which will not bear the wear and tear of years and their troubles. The solid virtues stand. His balance at the banker's is a fact; his good name and credit with the tradespeople are facts; so is the comfort of his home; so are the health, the morals, the education of his children. All these are the true realities of life to him; but the beauty which changes to deformity by small-pox, which fades under dyspepsia, grows stale by habit, and is worn threadbare by the end of twenty years, is only a skin-deep grace which he does not value. Perhaps he is right. Certainly, some of the happiest marriages amongst one's acquaintances are those where the wife has not one perceptible physical charm, and where the whole force of her magnetic value lies in what she is, not in how she looks.

Another man wants a tender, adoring, fair-haired seraph, who will worship him as a demigod and accept him as her best revelation of strength and wisdom. The more dependent she is, the better he will love her; the less of conscious thought, of active will, of originative power she has, the greater will be his regard and tenderness. To be the one sole teacher and protector of such a gentle little creature seems to him the most delicious joy and the best condition of married life; and he holds Milton's famous lines to be expressive of the only fitting relations between men and women. The adoring seraph is his ideal; Griselda, Desdemona, Lucy Ashton, are his highest culminations of womanly grace; and the qualities which appeal the most powerfully to his generosity are the patience which will not complain, the gentleness that cannot resent, and the love which nothing can chill.

Another man wants a cultivated intelligence in his ideal. As an author, an artist, a student, a statesman, he would like his wife to be able to help him by the contact of bright wit and ready intellect. He believes in the sex of minds, and holds no work complete which has not been created by the one and perfected by the other. He sees how women have helped on the leaders in troublous times; he knows that almost all great men have owed something of their greatness to the influence of a mother or a wife; he remembers how thoughts which had lain dumb and dormant in men's brains for more than half their lifetime have suddenly wakened up into speech and activity by the influence of a woman great enough to call them forth. The adoring seraph would be an encumbrance and nothing better than a child on his hands; and the soul which had to be awakened and directed by him would run great chance of remaining torpid and inactive all its days. He has his own life to lead and round off; and, so far from wishing to influence another's, he wants to be helped for himself.

Another man cares only for the birth and social position of the woman to whom he gives his name and affection. To another yellow gold stands higher than blue blood, and 'my wife's father' may have been a rag-picker, so long as rag-picking had been distilled in a sufficiently rich alembic leaving a residuum admitting no kind of doubt. Venus herself without a dowry would be only a pretty seaside girl with a Newtown pippin in her hand; but Miss Kilmansegg would be something worth thinking of, if but little worth looking at.

One man delights in a smart, vivacious little woman of the irrepressible kind. It makes no difference to him how petulant she is, how full of fire and fury; the most passionate bursts of temper simply amuse him, like the anger of a canary-bird, and he holds it fine fun to watch the small virago in her tantrums, and to set her going again when he thinks she has been a long enough time in subsidence. His ideal of woman is an amusing little plaything, with a great facility for being put up, and a dash of viciousness to give it piquancy. Another wants a sweet and holy saint whose patient humility springs from principle rather than from fear; another likes a blithe-tempered, healthy girl with no nonsense about her, full of fun and ready for everything, and he is not particular as to the strict order or economy of the housekeeping, provided only his wife is at all times willing to be his pleasant playmate and companion. Another delights in something very quiet, very silent, very home-staying. One must have first-rate music in his ideal woman; another, unimpeachable taste; a third, strict order; a fourth, liberal breadth of nature; and each has his own ideal, not only of nature but of person—to the exact shade of the hair, the colour of the eyes and the oval of the face. But all agree in the great fundamental requirements of truth and modesty and love and unselfishness; for though it is impossible to write of one womanly ideal as an absolute, it is very possible to detail the virtues which ought to belong to all alike.

If this diversity of ideals be true of individuals, it is especially true of nations, each of which has its own ideal woman varying according to what is called the genius of the country. To the Frenchman, if we are to believe Michelet and the novelists, it is a feverish little creature, full of nervous energy but without muscular force ; of frail health and feeble organization ; a prey to morbid fancies which she has no strength to control nor yet to resist ; now weeping away her life in the pain of finding that her husband—a man gross and material because husband—does not understand her, now sighing over her delicious sins in the arms of the lover who does ; without reasoning faculties but with divine intuitions which are as good as revelations; without cool judgment but with the light of burning passions which guide her just as well ; thinking by her heart and carrying the most refined metaphysics into her love ; subtle ; incomprehensible by the coarser brains of men and women who are only honest ; a creature born to bewilder and to be misled, to love and to be adored, to madden men and to be destroyed by them.

It does not much signify that the reality is a shrewd, calculating, unromantic woman, with a hard face and keen eyes, who for the most part makes a good practical wife to her common-sense middle-aged husband, who thinks more of her social position than of her feelings, more of her children than of her lovers, more of her purse than of her heart, and whose great object of life is a daily struggle for centimes. It pleases the French to idealize their eminently practical and worldly-wise women into this queer compound of hysterics and adultery; and if it pleases them it need not displease us. To the German his ideal is of two kinds—one, his Martha, the domestic broad-faced *Hausmutter*, who cooks good dinners at small cost, and mends the family linen as religiously as if this were the Eleventh Commandment specially appointed for feminine fingers to keep, the poetic culmination of whom is Charlotte cutting bread and butter; the other, his Mary, his Bettina, full of mind and æsthetics and heart-uplifting love, yearning after the infinite with holes in her stockings and her shoes down at heel. For what are coarse material mendings to the æsthetic soul yearning after the Infinite and worshipping at the feet of the prophet?

In Italy the ideal woman of late times was the ardent patriot, full of active energy, of physical force, of dauntless courage. In Poland it is the patriot too, but of a more refined and etherealized type, passively resenting Tartar tyranny by the subtlest feminine scorn, and living in perpetual music and mourning. In Spain it is a woman beautiful and impassioned, with the slight drawback of needing a world of looking after, of which the men are undeniably capable. In Mohammedan countries generally it is a comely smooth-skinned Dudù, patient and submissive, always in good humour with her master, economical in house-living to please the meanness, and gorgeous in occasional attire to gratify the ostentation, of the genuine Oriental; but by no means Dudù ever asleep and unoccupied. For, if not allowed to take part in active outside life, the Eastern's wife or wives have their home duties and their maternal cares like all other women, and find to their cost that, if they unduly neglect them, they will have a bad time of it with Ali Ben Hassan when the question comes of piastres and sequins, and the dogs of Jews who demand payment, and the pigs of Christians who follow suit.

The American ideal is of two kinds, like the German—the one, the clever manager, the woman with good executive faculty in the matters of buckwheat cakes and oyster gumbo, as is needed in a country so poorly provided with 'helps;' the other, the aspiring soul who puts her aspirations into deeds, and goes out into the world to do battle with the sins of society as editress, preacher, stump-orator and the like. It must be rather embarrassing to some men that this special manifestation of the ideal woman at times advocates miscegenation and free love; but perhaps we of the narrow old conventional type are not up to the right mark yet, and have to wait until our own women are thoroughly emancipated before we can rightly appreciate these questions. At all events, if this kind of thing pleases the Americans, it is no more our business to interfere with them than with the French compound; and if miscegenation and free love seem to them the right manner of life, let them follow it.

In all countries, then, the ideal woman changes, chameleon-like, to suit the taste of men; and the great doctrine that her happiness does somewhat depend on his liking is part of the very foundation of her existence. According to his will she is bond or free, educated or ignorant, lax or strict, house-keeping or roving; and though we advocate neither the bondage nor the ignorance, yet we do hold to the principle that, by the laws which regulate all human communities everywhere, she is bound to study the wishes of man and to mould her life in harmony with his liking. No society can get on in which there is total independence of sections and members, for society is built up on the mutual dependence of all its sections and all its members. Hence the defiant attitude which women have lately assumed, and their indifference to the wishes and remonstrances of men, cannot lead to any good results whatever. It is not the revolt of slaves against their tyrants which they have begun—in that we could sympathize—but it is a revolt against their duties.

And this it is which makes the present state of things so deplorable. It is the vague restlessness, the fierce extravagance, the neglect of home, the indolent fine-ladyism, the passionate love of pleasure which characterises the modern woman, that saddens men and destroys in them that respect which their very pride prompts them to feel. And it is the painful conviction that the ideal woman of truth and modesty and simple love and homely living has somehow faded away under the paint and tinsel of this modern reality which makes us speak out as we have done, in the hope—perhaps a forlorn one—that if she could be made to thoroughly understand what men think of her, she would, by the very force of natural instinct and social necessity, order herself in some accordance with the lost ideal, and become again what we once loved and what we all regret.

PINCHBECK.

NOT many years ago no really refined gentlewoman would have worn pinchbeck. False jewelry and imitation lace were touchstones with the sex, and the woman who would condescend to either was assumed, perhaps not quite without reason, to have lost something more than the mere niceness of technical taste. This feeling ran through the whole of society, and pinchbeck was considered as at once despicable and disreputable. The successful speculator, sprung from nothing, who had made his fortune during the war, might buy land, build himself a mansion and set up a magnificent establishment, but he was never looked on by the aboriginal gentry of the place as more than a lucky adventurer; and the blue blood, perhaps nourishing itself on thin beer, turned up its nose disdainfully at the claret and Madeira which had been personally earned and not lineally inherited. This exclusiveness was narrow in spirit and hard in individual working; and yet there was a wholesome sentiment underlying its pride which made it valuable in social ethics, if immoral on the score of natural equality and human charity. It was the rejection of pretentiousness, however gilded and glittering, in favour of reality, however poor and barren; it was the condemnation of make-believe—the repudiation of pinchbeck. It is not a generation since this was the normal attitude of society towards its *nouveaux riches* and Brummagem jewelry ; but time moves fast in these later days, and national sentiments change as quickly as national fashions.

We are in the humour to rehabilitate all things, and pinchbeck has now its turn with the rest. The lady of slender means who would refuse to wear imitation lace and false jewelry is as rare as the country society which would exclude the *nouveau riche* because of his newness, and not adopt him because of his riches. The whole anxiety now is, not what a thing is, but how it looks—not its quality, but its appearance. Every part of social and domestic life is dedicated to the apotheosis of pinchbeck. It meets us at the hall-door, where miserable stuccoed pillars are supposed to confer a quasi-palatial dignity on a wretched jerry-built little villa run up without regard to one essential of home comfort or of architectural truth. It goes with us into the cold, conventional drawing-room, where all is for show and nothing for use, in which no one lives, and which is just the mere pretence of a dwelling-room, set out to deceive the world into the belief that its cheap finery is the expression of the every-day life and circumstances of the family. It sits with us at the table, which a confectioner out of a back street has furnished and where everything, down to the very flowers, is hired for the occasion. It glitters in the brooches and bracelets of the women, in the studs and signet-rings of the men. It is in the hired broughams, the hired waiters, the pigmy page-boys, the faded paper flowers, the cheap champagne, and the affectation of social consideration that meet us at every turn. The whole of the lower section of the middle-classes is penetrated through and through with the worship of pinchbeck; and for one family that holds itself in the honour and simplicity of truth, ten thousand lie, to the world and to themselves, in frippery and pretence.

The greatest sinners in this are women. Men are often ostentatious, often extravagant, and not unfrequently dishonest in that broad way of dishonesty which is called living beyond their means—sometimes making up the deficit by practices which end in the dock of the Old Bailey; but, as a rule, they go in for the real thing in details, and their pinchbeck is at the core rather than on the surface. Women, on the contrary, give themselves up to a more general pretentiousness, and, provided they can make a show, care very little about the means; provided they can ring their metal on the counter, they ignore the want of the hall-stamp underneath. Locality, dress, their visiting-list and domestic appearances are the four things which they demand shall be in accord with their neighbours'; and for these four surfaces they will sacrifice the whole internal fabric. They will have a showy-looking house, encrusted with base ornamentation and false grandeur, though it lets in wind, rain and noise almost as if it were made of mud or canvas, rather than a plain and substantial dwelling-place, with comfort instead of stucco, and moderately thick walls instead of porches and pilasters. Most of their time is necessarily passed at home, but they will undergo all manner of house discomfort resulting from this preference of cheap finery over solid structure, rather than forego their 'genteel locality' and stereotyped ornamentation. A family of daughters on the one side, diligent over the 'Battle of Prague;' a nursery full of crying babies on the other; more Battles of Prague opposite, diversified by a future Lind practising her scales unweariedly; water-pipes bursting in the frost; walls streaming in the thaw; the lower offices reeking and green with damp; the upper rooms too insecure for unrestricted movement — all these, and more miseries of the same kind, a woman given over to the worship of pinchbeck willingly encounters rather than shift into a locality relatively unfashionable to her sphere, but where she could have substantiality and comfort for the same rent that she pays now for flash and show.

In dress it is the same thing. She must look like her neighbours, no matter whether they can spend pounds to her shillings, so runs up a milliner's bill beyond what she ought to afford for the whole family expenses. If others can buy gold, she can manage pinchbeck. Glass that looks like jet, like filagree work, like anything else she fancies, is every bit to her as good as the real thing; and if she cannot compass Valenciennes and Mechlin, she can go to Nottingham and buy machine-made imitations that will make quite as fine a show. How poor soever she may be, she must hang herself about with ornaments made of painted wood, of glass, of vulcanite; she must break out into spangles and beads and chains and *benoîtons*, which are cheap luxuries and, as she thinks, effective decorations. Flimsy silks make as rich a rustle to her ear as the stateliest brocade; and cotton velvet delights the soul that cannot aspire to Genoa. The love of pinchbeck is so deeply ingrained in her that even if, in a momentary fit of aberration into good taste, she condescends to a simple material about which there can be neither disguise nor pretence, she must load it with that detestable cheap finery of hers till she makes herself as vulgar in a muslin as she was in a cotton velvet. The *simplex munditiis*, which used to be held as a canon of feminine good taste, is now abandoned altogether, and the more she can bedizen herself according to the pattern of a Sandwich islander the more beautiful she thinks herself—the more certain the fascination of the men and the greater the jealousy of the women. This is the cause of all the tags and streamers, the bits of ribbon here and flying ends of laces there, the puffed-out chignons, and the trailing curls cut off some dead girl's head, wherewith the modern Englishwoman delights to make herself hideous. It is pinchbeck throughout.

But we fear woman is past praying for in the matter of fashion; and that she is too far given over to the abomination of pretence to be called back to truth for any ethical reason whatsoever, or indeed by anything short of high examples. And then, if simplicity became the fashion, we should have our pinchbeck votaries translating that into extremes as they do now with ornamentation; if my lady took to plainness, they would go to nakedness.

Another bit of pinchbeck is the visiting-list—the cards of invitation stuck against the drawing-room glass—with the grandest names and largest fortunes put forward, irrespective of dates or tenses. The chance contact with the people represented may be quite out of the ordinary circumstances of life, but their names are paraded as if an accident, which has happened once and may never occur again, were in the daily order of events. They are brought to the front to make others believe that the whole social substance is of the same quality; that generals and admirals and lords and ladies are the common elements of the special circle in which the family habitually moves; that pinchbeck is good gold, and that 'composition' means marble. Women are exceedingly tenacious of these pasteboard appearances. In a house with its couple of female servants, where formal visitors are very rare and invitations, save by friendly word of mouth, rarer still, you may see a cracked china bowl or cheap mock *patera* on the hall table, to receive the cards which are assumed to come in the thick showers usual with high people who have hall-porters and a thousand names or more on their books. The pile gets horribly dusty to be sure, and the upper layer turns by degrees from cream-colour to brown; but antiquity is not held to weaken the force of grandeur. The titled card left on a chance occasion more than a year ago still keeps the uppermost place, still represents a perpetual renewal of aristocratic visits and an unbroken succession of social triumphs. Yellowed and soiled, it is none the less the trump-card of the list; and while the outside world laughs and ridicules, the lady at home thinks that no one sees through this puerile pretence, and that the visiting-list is accepted accordding to the status of the fugleman at the head. She is very happy if she can say that the pattern of her dress, her cap, her bonnet, was taken from that of Lady So and So's; and we may be quite sure that all personal contact with grand folks so expresses itself and perpetuates the memory of the event, by such imitation—at a distance. It is too good an occasion for the airing of pinchbeck to be disregarded; consequently, for the most part it is turned to this practical account. Whether the fashion be suited to the material or to the other parts of the dress, is quite a secondary consideration; it being of the essence of pinchbeck to despise both fitness and harmony.

There is a large amount of pinchbeck in the appearance of social influence, much cultivated by women of a certain activity of mind and with more definite aims than all women have. This belongs to a grade higher than the small pretences of which we have been speaking—to women who have money, and so far have one reality, but who have not, by their own birth or their husbands', the original standing which would give them this social influence as of right. Some make themselves notorious for their drawing-room patronage of artists, which however does not include buying their pictures; others gather round them scores of obscure authors, whose books they talk of but do not read; a few, a short time since, were centres of spiritualistic circles and got a queer kind of social influence thereby, so far as Philistine desire to witness the 'manifestations' went; and one or two are names of weight in the emancipated ranks, and take chiefly to what they call 'working women.' These are they who attend Ladies' Committees, where they talk bosh and pound away at utterly uninteresting subjects as diligently as if what they said had any point in it, and what they did any ultimate issue in probability or common sense. But beyond the fact of having a large house, where their several sets may assemble at stated periods, these would-be lady patronesses are utterly impotent to help or to hinder; and their patronage is just so much pinchbeck, not worth the trouble of weighing.

In all this gaudy attempt at show, this restless dissatisfaction with what they are and ceaseless endeavour to appear something they are not, our middle-class ladies are doing themselves and society infinite mischief. They set the tone to the world below them; and the small tradespeople and the servants, when they copy the vices of their superiors, do not imitate her grace the duchess, but the doctor's wife over the way, and the lawyer's lady next door, and the young ladies everywhere, who all try to appear like women of rank and fortune, and who are ashamed of nothing so much as of industry, truth and simplicity. Hence the rage for cheap finery in the kitchen, just a trifle more ugly and debased than that worn in the drawing-room; hence the miserable pretentiousness and pinchbeck fine-ladyism filtering like poison through every pore of our society, to result God only knows in what grave moral cataclysm, unless women of mind and education will come to the front and endeavour to stay the plague already begun. Chains and brooches may seem but small material causes for important moral effects, but they are symbols; and, as symbols, they are of deep national value.

No good will be done till we get back some of our fine old horror of pinchbeck, and once more insist on Truth as the foundation of our national life. Education and refinement will be of no avail if they do not land us here; and the progress of the arts and sciences must not be brought to mean chiefly the travesty of civilized ladies into the semblance of savages, by the cheap imitation of costly substances. Women are always rushing about the world eager after everything but their home business. Here is something for them to do—the regeneration of society by means of their own energies; the bringing people back to the dignity of truth and the beauty of simplicity; the substitution of that self-respect which is content to appear what it is, for the feeble pride which revels in pinchbeck because it cannot get gold, which endeavours so hard to hide its real estate and to pass for what it is not and never can be.

AFFRONTED WOMANHOOD.

AMONGST other queer anomalies in human nature is the difference that lies between sectarian sins and personal immoralities, between the intellectual untruth of a man's creed and the spiritual evil of his own nature. Rigid Calvinism, for instance, which narrows the issues of divine grace and shuts up the avenues of salvation from all but a select few, is a sour and illiberal faith; and yet a rigid Calvinist, simply continuing to believe in predestination and election as he was taught from the beginning, may be a generous, genial, large-hearted man. An inventor scheming out the deadliest projectile that has yet been devised is not necessarily indifferent to human life on his own account; nor is every American who talks tall talk about the glorious destinies of his country and the infinite superiority of his countrymen, as conceited personally as he is vainglorious nationally. In fact, he may be a very modest fellow by his own fireside; and though in his quality of American he is of course able to whip universal creation, in his mere quality of man he is quite ready to take the lower seat at the table and to give honour where honour is due.

This kind of distinction between the faults of the sect and the person, the nature and the cause, is very noticeable in women; and especially in all things relating to themselves. Individually, many among them are meek and long-suffering enough, and would be as little capable of resenting a wrong as of revenging it. Being used from the cradle to a good deal of snubbing, they take to it kindly as part of the inevitable order of things, and kiss the chastening rod with edifying humility; but, collectively, they are the most impatient of rebuke, the most arrogant in moral attitude, and the most restive of all created things sought to be led or driven. The woman who will bear to hear of her personal faults without offering a word in self-defence, and who will even say peccavi quite humbly if hard pressed, fires up into illimitable indignation when told that her foibles are characteristic of her sex, and that she is no worse than nature meant her to be. Personally she is willing to confess that she is only a poor worm grovelling in the dust—perhaps an exceptionally poor worm, if of the kind given to spiritual asceticism—but by her class she claims to be considered next door to an angel, and arrogates to her sex virtues which she would blush to claim on her own behalf.

Men, as men, are all sorts of bad things, as every one knows. They are selfish, cruel, tyrannical, sensual, unjust, bloodthirsty—where does the list end? and human nature in the abstract is a bad thing too, given over to lies and various deadly lusts; but women, as women, are exempt from any special share in the general iniquity, and only come under the ban with universal nature—with lambs and doves and other pretty creatures—not quite perfection, because of the Fall which spoilt everything, and yet very near it. As children of the rash parents who corrupted the race they certainly suffer from the general infection of sin that followed, but, as daughters contrasted with the sons, they are so far superior to those evil-minded brethren of theirs that their comparative virtues by sex override their positive vices by race. As individuals, they are worms; as human beings, they are poor sinful souls; but by their womanhood they are above rebuke.

Women have been so long wrapped in this pleasant little delusion about the sacredness of their sex, and the perfections belonging thereto by nature, that any attempt to show them the truth and convince them that they too are guilty of the mean faults and petty ways common to a fallen humanity —whereof certain manifestations are special to themselves—is met with the profound scorn or shrill cries of affronted womanhood. A man who speaks of their faults as they appear to him, and as he suffers by them, is illiberal and unmanly, and the rage of the more hysterically indignant would not be very far below that of the Thracian Mænads, could they lay hands on the offending Orpheus of the moment; but a woman who speaks from knowledge, and touches the weak places and the sore spots known best to the initiated, is a traitress even baser than the rude man who perhaps knows no better.

The whole life and being of womanhood must be held sacred from censure, exalted as it is by a kind of sentimental apotheosis that will not bear reasoning about, to something very near divinity. Even the follies of fashion must be exempt from both ridicule and rebuke, on the ground of man's utter ignorance of the merits of the question; for how should a poor male body know anything about trains or crinolines, or the pleasure that a woman feels in making herself ridiculous or indecent in appearance and a nuisance to her neighbours? while, for anything graver than the follies of fashion, it is in a manner high treason against the supremacy of the sex to assume that they deserve either ridicule or rebuke. Besides, it is indelicate. Women are made to be worshipped, not criticized; to be reverenced as something mystically holy and incomprehensible by the grosser masculine faculties; and it is indiscreet, to say the least of it, when vile man takes it on himself to test the idol by the hard mechanical tests of truth and common-sense, and to show the world how much alloy is mingled with the gold.

This is in ethics what the Oriental's reserve about his harem is in domestic life. The sacredness of a Mohammedan's womankind must be so complete that they are even nameless to the coarser sex ; and not, 'How is your wife ? ' 'How are your daughters ? ' but, ' How is your house ? ' is the only accepted form of words by which Ali may ask Hassan about the health of his Fatimas and Zuliekas. In much the same way our women must be kept behind the close gilded gratings of affected perfectness, and, above all things, never publicly discussed—much less publicly condemned.

It is by no means a proof of wisdom, or of the power of logically reasoning out a position and its consequences, that women should thus demand to be treated as things superior to the faults and follies of humanity at large. They are clamouring loudly, and with some justice, for an equal share in the world's work and wages, and it is wonderfully stupid in them to stand on their womanly dignity and their quasi-sacredness, when told of their faults and measured according to their shortcomings, not their pretensions. If they come down into the arena to fight, they must fight subject to the conditions of the arena. They must not ask for special rules to be made in their behalf—for blunted weapons on the one side and impregnable defences on the other. If they demand either mystic reverence or chivalric homage they must be content with their own narrow but safe enclosure, where they have nothing to do but to look at the turmoil below, and accept with gratitude such portions of the good things fought for as the men to whom they belong see fit to bring them. They cannot at one and the same time have the good of both positions—the courtesy claimed by weakness and the honour paid to prowess. If they mingle in the *mêlée* they must expect as hard knocks as the rest, and must submit to be bullied when they hit foul and to be struck home when they hit wide. If they do not like these conditions, let them keep out of the fray altogether; but if they choose to mingle in it, no hysterics of affronted womanhood, however loud the shrieks, will keep them safe from hard knocks and rough treatment.

Time out of mind women have been credited with all the graces and virtues possible in a world which 'the trail of the serpent' has defiled. To be sure they have been cursed as well, as the causes of most of the miseries of society from Eve's time to Helen's, and later still. *Teterrima causa*. But the praise alone sticks, so far as their own self-belief is concerned, and men, who create the curses, may arrange them to their own liking. The poet says they are 'ministering angels;' the very name of mother is to some men almost as holy as that of God, and the most solemn oath a Frenchman can take in a private way is not by his own honour, but by the name or the head or the life of his mother.

As wives—well, save in the old nursery doggrel which sets forth that they are made of 'all that's good if well understood'—as wives certainly they get not a few ungentle rubs. But then only a husband knows where the shoe pinches, and if he blasphemes during the wearing of it, on his own head be the guilt as is already the punishment. As maidens they are confessedly the most sacred manifestation of humanity, and to be approached with the reverence rightfully due to the holiest thing we know; while in the new spiritualistic world we are told to look for the time when the moral supremacy of woman shall be the recognized law of human life and the reign of violence and tears and all iniquity shall therefore be at an end. Thus the moral loveliness of collective womanhood is a dogma which men are taught from their boyhood as an article of faith if not a matter of experience, and women naturally keep them up to the mark—theoretically, at all events. Yet for all this lip-homage, of which so much account is made, women are often ill-used and brutalized, and in spite of their superior pretensions as often fall below men in every quality but that of patience. And patience is eminently the virtue of weakness, and therefore woman's cardinal grace; speaking broadly and allowing for exceptions. But what women do not see is that all this poetic flattery comes originally from the idealizing passion of men, and that, left to themselves, with only each other for critics and analyzers, they would soon find themselves stripped of their superfluous moral finery and reduced to the bare core of uncompromising truth. And this would be the best thing for them in the end. If they could but rise superior to the weakness of flattery, they would rise beyond the power of much that now degrades them.

If they would but honestly consider the question of their own shortcomings when told where they fail, and what they cannot do, and what they will be sure to make a mess of if they attempt, they would prove their title to man's respect far more than they prove it now by the shrill cries and indignant remonstrances of affronted womanhood.

This is the day of trial for many things—among others, for the capacity of women for an enlarged sphere of action and more public exercise of power. Do women think they show their fitness for nobler duties than those already assigned them, by their impatience under censure, which is, after all, but one mode of teaching? Are they qualifying themselves to act in concert with men, by assuming an absolute moral supremacy which it is a kind of sacrilege to deny? If they think they are on the right road as at present followed, let them go on in heaven's name. When they have wandered sufficiently far perhaps they will have sense enough to turn back, and see for themselves what mistakes they have made and might have avoided, had they had the wisdom of self-knowledge in only a small degree. Certainly, so long as womanhood is held to confer, *per se*, a special and unassailable divinity, so long will women be rendered comparatively incapable of the best work through vanity, through ignorance, and through impatience of the teaching that comes by rebuke. Nothing is so damaging in the long run as exaggerated pretensions; for by-and-by, after a certain period of uncritical homage, the world is sure to believe that the silver veil which it has so long respected hides deformity, not divinity, and that what is too sacred for public use is too poor for public honour. If the faults of women are not to be discussed, nor their follies condemned, because womanhood is a sacred thing and a man naturally respects his mother and sisters, then women must be content to live in a moral harem, where they will be safe from both the gaze and the censure of the outside world; they must not come down into the battle-fields and the workshops, where they forfeit all claim to protection and have to accept the man's law of 'no favour.' It must be one thing or the other. Either their merits must be weighed and their capacity assayed in reference to the place they want to take—and in doing this their faults must be boldly and distinctly discussed—or they must be content with their present condition; and, with the mystic sanctity of their womanhood, they must accept also its moral seclusion—belonging, by their very nature, to things too sacred for criticism and too perfect for censure. It rests with themselves to decide which it is to be.

FEMININE AFFECTATIONS.

THE old form of feminine affectation used to be that of a die-away fine lady afflicted with a mysterious malady known by the name of the vapours, or one, no less obscure, called the spleen. Sometimes it was an etherealized being who had no capacity for homely things, but who passed her life in an atmosphere of poetry and music, for the most part expressing her vague ideas in halting rhymes which gave more satisfaction to herself than to her friends. She was probably an Italian scholar and could quote Petrarch and Tasso, and did quote them pretty often; she might even be a Della Cruscan by honourable election, with her own peculiar wreath of laurel and her own silver lyre; any way she was 'a sister of the Muses,' and had something to do with Apollo or Minerva, whom she was sure to call Phœbus or Pallas Athene, as being the more poetical name of the two. Probably she had dealings with Diana too—for this kind of woman does not in any age affect the 'seaborn,' save in a hazy sentimental way that bears no fruits—a neatly-turned sonnet or a clever bit of counterpoint being to her worth all the manly love or fireside home delights that the world can give. What is the touch of babies' dimpled fingers or the rosy kisses of babies' lips compared to the pleasures of being a sister of the Muses and one of the beloved of Apollo! The Della Cruscan of former days, or her modern avatar, will tell you that music and poetry are godlike and bear the soul away to heaven, but that the nursery is a prison and babies are no dearer gaolers than any other; and that household duties disgrace the aspiring soul mounting to the empyrean. This was the Ethereal Being of last generation—the Blue-stocking, as a poetess in white satin, with her eyes turned up to heaven and her hair in dishevelled cascades about her neck. She dropped her mantle as she finally departed; and we still have the Della Cruscan essence, if not in the precise form of earlier times. We still have ethereal beings who, as the practical outcome of their etherealization, rave about music and poetry and æsthetics and culture, and horribly neglect their babies and the weekly bills.

A favourite form of feminine affectation among certain opposers of the prevalent fast type is in an intense womanliness—an aggravating intensity of womanliness—that makes one long for a little roughness, just to take off the cloying excess of sweetness. This kind is generally found with large eyes, dark in the lids and hollow in the orbit, by which a certain spiritual expression is given to the face—a certain look of being consumed by the hidden fire of lofty thought, that is very effective. It does not destroy the effectiveness that the real cause of the darkened lids and cavernous orbits is most probably internal disease, when not antimony. Eyes of this sort stand for spirituality and loftiness of thought and intense womanliness of nature ; and, as all men are neither chemists nor doctors, the simulation does quite as well as truth.

The main characteristic of these women is self-consciousness. They live before a moral mirror, and pass their time in attitudinizing to what they think the best advantage. They can do nothing simply, nothing spontaneously and without the fullest consciousness as to how they do it, and how they look while they are doing it. In every action of their lives they see themselves as pictures, as characters in a novel, as impersonations of poetic images or thoughts. If they give you a glass of water, or take your cup from you, they are Youth and Beauty ministering to Strength or Age, as the case may be ; if they bring you a photographic album, they are Titian's Daughter carrying her casket, a trifle modernized ; if they hold a child in their arms, they are Madonnas, and look unutterable maternal love though they never saw the little creature before, and care for it no more than for the puppy in the mews ; if they do any small personal office, or attempt to do it—making believe to tie a shoestring, comb out a curl, fasten a button—they are Charities in graceful attitudes, and expect you to think them both charitable and graceful. Nine times out of ten they can neither tie the string nor fasten the button with ordinary deftness—for they have a trick of using only the ends of their fingers when they do anything with their hands, as being more graceful and fitting in better, than would a firmer grasp, with the delicate womanliness of the character; and the less sweet and more commonplace woman who does not attitudinize morally and never parades her womanliness, beats them out of the field for real helpfulness, and is the Charity which the other only plays at being.

This kind too affects, in theory, wonderful submissiveness to man. It upholds Griselda as the type of feminine perfection, and—still in theory—between independence and being tyrannized over, goes in for the tyranny. 'I would rather my husband beat me than let me do too much as I liked,' said one before she married, who, after she was married, managed to get entire possession of the domestic reins and took good care that her nominal lord should be her practical slave. For, notwithstanding the sweet submissiveness of her theory, the intensely womanly woman has the most astonishing knack of getting her own way and imposing her own will on others. The real tyrant among women is not the one who flounces and splutters and declares that nothing shall make her obey, but this soft-mannered, large-eyed, intensely womanly person who says that Griselda is her ideal and that the whole duty of woman lies in unquestioning obedience to man.

In contrast with this special affectation is the mannish woman—the woman who wears a double-breasted coat with big buttons, of which she flings back the lappels with an air, understanding the suggestiveness of a wide chest and the need of unchecked breathing; who wears unmistakeable shirt-fronts, linen collars, vests and plain ties, like a man; who folds her arms or sets them akimbo, like a man; who even nurses her feet and cradles her knees, in spite of her petticoats, and makes believe that the attitude is comfortable because it is manlike. If the excessively womanly woman is affected in her sickly sweetness, the mannish woman is affected in her breadth and roughness. She adores dogs and horses, which she places far above children of all ages. She boasts of how good a marksman she is— she does not call herself markswoman—and how she can hit right and left and bring down both birds flying. When she drinks wine she holds the stem of the glass between her first two fingers, hollows her underlip, and, throwing her head well back, tosses off the whole at a draught—she would disdain the lady-like sip or the closer gesture of ordinary women. She is great in cheese and bitter-beer, in claret-cup and still champagne, but she despises the puerilities of sweets or of effervescing wines. She rounds her elbows and turns her wrist outward, as men round their elbows and turn their wrists outward. She is fond of carpentry, she says, and boasts of her powers with the plane and saw. For charms to her watchchain she wears a cork-screw, a gimlet, a big knife and a small foot-rule; and in contrast with the intensely womanly woman, who uses the tips of her fingers only, the mannish woman when she does anything uses the whole hand, and if she had to thread a needle would thread it as much by her palm as by her fingers. All of which is affectation —from first to last affectation; a mere assumption of virile fashions utterly inharmonious to the whole being, physical and mental, of a woman.

Then there is the affectation of the woman who has taken propriety and orthodoxy under her special protection, and who regards it as a personal insult when her friends and acquaintances go beyond the exact limits of her mental sphere. This is the woman who assumes to be the antiseptic element in society; who makes believe that without her the world and human nature would go to the dogs and plunge headlong into the abyss of sin and destruction forthwith; and that not all the grand heroism of man, not all his thought and energy and high endeavour and patient seeking after truth would serve his turn or the world's if she did not spread her own petty preserving nets, and mark out the boundary lines within which she would confine the range of thought and speculation. She knows that this assumption of spiritual beadledom is mere affectation, and that other minds have as much right to their own boundary lines as that which she claims for herself; but it seems to her pretty to assume that woman generally is the consecrated beadle of thought and morality, and that she, of all women, is most specially consecrated. As an offshoot of this kind stands the affectation of simplicity—the woman whose mental attitude is self-depreciation, and who poses herself as a mere nobody when the world is ringing with her praises. 'Is it possible that your Grace has ever heard of *me*?' said one of this class with prettily affected *naïveté* at a time when all England was astir about her, and when colours and fashions went by her name to make them take with the public at large. No one knew better than the fair *ingénue* in question how far and wide her fame had spread; but she thought it looked modest and simple to assume ignorance of her own value, and to declare that she was but a creeping worm when all the world knew that she was a soaring butterfly.

There is a certain like kind of affectation very common among pretty women; and this is the affectation of not knowing that they are pretty, and not recognizing the effect of their beauty on men. Take a woman with bewildering eyes, say, of a maddening size and shape and fringed with long lashes which distract you to look at; the creature knows that her eyes are bewildering, as well as she knows that fire burns and that ice melts; she knows the effect of that trick she has with them—the sudden uplifting of the heavy lid and the swift, full gaze that she

gives right into a man's eyes. She has practised it
often in the glass, and knows to a mathematical
nicety the exact height to which the lid must be
raised and the exact fixity of the gaze. She knows
the whole meaning of the look and the stirring of
men's blood that it creates ; but if you speak to her
of the effect of her trick, she puts on an air of
extremest innocence, and protests her entire ignorance as to anything her eyes may say or mean ; and
if you press her hard she will look at you in the
same way for your own benefit, and deny at the
very moment of offence. Various other tricks has
she with those bewildering eyes of hers—each more
perilous than the other to men's peace ; and all un-
sparingly employed, no matter what the result. For
this is the woman who flirts to the extreme limits,
then suddenly draws up and says she meant nothing.
Step by step she has led you on, with looks and
smiles and pretty doubtful phrases always susceptible of two meanings--the one for the ear by mere
word, the other for the heart by the accompaniments
of look and manner, which are intangible ; step by
step she has drawn you deeper and deeper into the
maze where she has gone before as your decoy ;
then, when she has you safe, she raises her eyes for
the last time, complains that you have mistaken her
cruelly and that she has meant nothing more than
any one else might mean ; and what can she do to
repair her mistake ? Love you ? marry you ? No ;
she is engaged to your rival, who counts his thou-

sands to your hundreds; and what a pity that you had not seen this all along and that you should have so misunderstood her! Besides, what is there about her that you or any one should love?

Of all the many affectations of women, this affectation of their own harmlessness when beautiful, and of their innocence of design when they practise their arts for the discomfiture of men, is the most dangerous and the most disastrous. But what can one say to them? The very fact that they are dangerous disarms a man's anger and blinds his perception until too late. That men love though they suffer is the woman's triumph, guilt and condonation; and so long as the trick succeeds it will be practised.

Another affectation of the same family is the extreme friendliness and familiarity which some women adopt in their manners towards men. Young girls affect an almost maternal tone to boys of their own age, or a year or so older; and they, too, when their wiser elders remonstrate, declare they mean nothing, and how hard it is that they may not be natural! This form of affectation, once begun, continues through life; being too convenient to be lightly discarded; and youthful matrons not long out of their teens assume a tone and ways that would befit middle age counselling giddy youth, and that might by chance be dangerous even then if the 'Indian summer' were specially bright and warm.

Then there is that affectation pure and simple

which is the mere affectation of manner, such as is shown in the drawling voice, the mincing gait, the extreme gracefulness of attitude which by consciousness ceases to be grace, and the thousand little *minauderies* and coquetries of the sex known to us all. And there is the affectation which people of a higher social sphere show when they condescend to those of low estate, and talk and look as if they are not quite certain of their company, and scarcely know if they are Christian or heathen, savage or civilized. And there is the affectation of the maternal passion with women who are never by any chance seen with their children, but who speak of them as if they were never out of their sight; the affectation of wifely adoration with women who are to be met about the world with every man of their acquaintance rather than with their lawful husbands; the affectation of asceticism in women who lead a self-enjoying life from end to end; and the affectation of political fervour in those who would not give up a ball or a new dress to save Europe from universal revolution.

Go where we will, the affectation of being something she is not meets us in woman, like a ghost we cannot lay, a mist we cannot sweep away. In the holiest and the most trivial things we find it penetrating everywhere—even in church and at her prayers, when the pretty penitent, rising from her lengthy orisons, lifts her eyes and furtively looks about to see who has noticed her self-abasement and to whom her picturesque piety has commended itself.

All sorts and patterns of good girls and pleasant women are very dear and delightful; but the pearl of great price is the thoroughly natural and unaffected woman—that is, the woman who is truthful to her heart's core, and who would as little condescend to act a pretence as she would dare to tell a lie.

INTERFERENCE.

ABOUT the strongest propensity in human nature, apart from the purely personal instincts, is the propensity to interfere. We do not mean tyranny; that is another matter—tyranny being active while interference is negative—the one standing as the masculine, the other as the feminine, form of the same principle. Besides, tyranny has generally some personal gain in view when it takes it in hand to force people to do what they dislike to do; while interference seeks no good for itself at all, but simply prevents the exercise of free-will for the mere pleasure to be had out of such prevention.

Again, the idea of tyranny is political rather than domestic; but the curse of interference is seen most distinctly within the four walls of home, where also it is most felt. Very many people spend their lives in interfering with others—perpetually putting spokes into wheels with the turning of which they have nothing to do, and thrusting their fingers into pies about the baking of which they are in no way concerned; and of these people we are bound to confess that women make up the larger number and are the greater sinners. To be sure there are some men— small, fussy, finnicking fellows, with whom nature has made the irreparable blunder of sex—who are as troublesome in their endless interference as the narrowest-minded and most meddling women of their acquaintance; but the feminine characteristics of men are so exceptional that we need not take them into serious calculation. For the most part, when men do interfere in any manly sense at all, it is with such things as they think they have a right to control— say, with the wife's low dresses or the daughter's too patent flirtations. They interfere and prevent because they are jealous of the repute, perhaps of the beauty, of their womankind; and, knowing what other men say of such displays, or fearing their effect, they stand between folly and slander to the best of their ability. But this kind of interference, noble or ignoble as the cause may be, comes into another class of motives altogether and does not belong to that kind of interference of which we are speaking.

Women, then, are the great interferers at home, both with each other and with men. They do not tell us what we are to do, beyond going to church and subscribing to their favourite mission, so much as they tell us what we are not to do. They do not command so much as they forbid. And, of all women, wives and daughters are the most given to handling these check-strings and putting on these drag-chains. Sisters, while young, are obliged to be less interfering, under pain of a perpetual round of bickering; for brothers are not apt to submit to the counsel of creatures for the most part so loftily snubbed as sisters ; while mothers nine times out of ten are laid aside for all but sentimental purposes, so soon as the son has ceased to be a boy and has learned to become a man. The queenhood, therefore, of personal and domestic interference lies with wives, and they know how to use the prerogative they assume. Take an unlucky man who smokes under protest—his wife not liking to forbid the pleasure entirely, but always grudging it and interfering with its exercise. Each cigar represents a battle, deepening in intensity according to the number. The first may have been had with only a light skirmish—perhaps a mere threatening of an attack that passed away without coming to actual onslaught; the second brings up the artillery ; while the third or fourth lets all the forces loose, and sets the big guns thundering. She could understand a man smoking one cigar in the day, she says, with a gracious condescension to masculine weakness; but when it comes to more she feels that she is called on to interfere, and to do her best towards checking such a reprehensible excess. It does not weaken her position that she knows nothing of what she is talking about. She never smoked a cigar herself, therefore does not understand the uses nor the abuses of tobacco ; but she holds herself pledged to interfere so soon as she gets the chance ; and she redeems that pledge with energy.

The man too, who has the stomach of an ostrich

and an appetite to correspond, but about whom the home superstition is that he has a feeble digestion and must take care of his diet, has also to run the gauntlet of his wife's interfering forces. He never dines nor sups jollily with his friends without being plucked at and reminded that salmon always disagrees with him; that champagne is sure to give him a headache to-morrow; and, 'My dear! when you know how bad salad is for you!' or, 'How can you eat that horrid pastry? You will be so ill in the night!' 'What! more wine? another glass of whisky? how foolish you are! how wrong!' The wife has a nervous organization which cannot bear stimulants; the husband is a strong, large-framed man who can drink deep without feeling it; but to the excitable woman her feeble limit is her husband's measure, and when he has gone beyond the range of her own short tether, she trots after him remonstrating, and thinks herself justified in interfering with his further progress. For women cannot be brought to understand the capacities of a man's life; they cannot be made to understand that what is bad for themselves may not be bad for others, and that their weakness ought not to be the gauge of a man's strength.

A pale, chilly woman, afflicted with chronic bronchitis, who wears furs and velvets in May and fears the east wind as much as an East Indian fears a tiger, does her best to coddle her husband, father, sons, in about the same ratio as she coddles herself. They must not go out without an overcoat; they must take an umbrella if the day is at all cloudy; they must not walk too far nor ride too hard; and they must be sure to be at home by a given hour.

When such women as these have to do with men just on the boundary-line between the last days of vigour and the first of old age, they put forward the time of old age by many years. We see their men rapidly sink into the softness and incapacity of senility, when a more bracing life would have kept them good for half-a-dozen years longer. But women do not care for this. They like men to be their own companions and dread rather than desire the masculine comradeship which would keep them up to the mark of virile independence; for most women—but not all—would rather have their husbands manly in a womanly way than in a manly one, as being more within the compass of their own sympathies and understanding.

The same kind of interference is very common where the husband is a man of broad humour—one who calls a spade a spade, with no circumlocution about an agricultural implement. According to the odd law of compensation which regulates so much of human action, the wife of such a man is generally one of the ultra-refined kind, who thinks herself consecrated the enduring censor of her husband's speech. As this is an example most frequently to be found in middle life and where there are children belonging to the establishment, the word of warning is generally 'papa!'—said with reproach or resentment, according to circumstances — which has, of course, the effect of drawing the attention of the young people to the paternal breadth of speech, and of fixing that special breach of decorum on their memory. Sometimes the wife has sufficient self-restraint not to give the word of warning in public, but can nurse her displeasure for a more convenient season; but so soon as they are alone the miserable man has to pass under the harrow, as only husbands with wives of a chastising spirit can pass under it, and his life is made a burden to him because of that unlucky anecdote told with such verve a few hours ago, and received with such shouts of pleasant laughter. Perhaps the anecdote was just a trifle doubtful; granted; but what does the wife take by her remonstrance? Most probably a quarrel; possibly a good-natured *peccavi* for the sake of being let off the continuance of the sermon; perhaps a yawn; most certainly not reform. If the man be a man of free speech and broad humour by nature and liking, he will remain so to the end; and what the censorship of society leaves untouched, the interference of a wife will not control.

Children come in for an enormous share of interference, which is not direction nor discipline, but simple interference for its own sake. There are mothers who meddle with every expression of individuality in their young people, quite irrespective of moral tendency, or whether the occasion is trivial or important. In the fancies, the pleasures, the minor details of dress in their children, there is always that intruding maternal finger upsetting the arrangements of the poor little pie as vigorously as if thrones and altars depended on the result. Not a game of any kind can be begun, nor a blue ribbon worn instead of a pink, without maternal interference; so that the bloom is rubbed off every enjoyment, and life becomes reduced to a kind of goose-step, with mamma for the drill-sergeant prescribing the inches to be marked. Sisters, too, do a great deal of this kind of thing among each other; as all those who are intimate in houses where there are large families of unmarried girls must have seen. The nudges, the warning looks, the deprecating 'Amy's!' and 'Oh, Lucy's!' and 'Hush, Rose's!' by which some seek to act as household police over the others, are patent to all who use their senses. In some houses the younger sisters seem to have been born chiefly as training grounds for the elders, whereon they may exercise their powers of interference; and a hard time they have of it. If Emma goes to her embroidery, Ellen tells her she ought to practise her singing; if Jane is reading, Mary recommends sewing as a more profitable use of precious time; if Amy is at her easel, Ada wants to turn her round to the piano. It is quite the exception where four or five sisters leave each other free to do as each likes, and do not take to drilling and interference as part of the daily programme.

Something of the reluctance to domestic service, so painfully apparent among the better class of working women, is due to this spirit of interference with women. The lady who wrote about the caps and gowns of servant-girls, and drew out a plan of dress, down to the very material of their gloves, was an instance of this spirit. For, when we come to analyze it, what does it really signify to us how our servants dress, so long as they are clean and decent and do not let their garments damage our goods? Fashion is almost always ridiculous, and women, as a rule, care more for dress than they care for anything else; and if the kitchen apes the parlour, and Phyllis gives as much thought to her new linsey as my lady gives to her new velvet, we cannot wonder at it, nor need we hold up our hands in horror at the depravity of the smaller person. Does one flight of stairs transpose morality? If it does not, there is no real ethical reason why my lady should interfere with poor Phyllis's enjoyment in her ugly little vanities, when she herself will not be interfered with—though press and pulpit both try to turn her out of her present path into the way which all ages have thought the best for her and the one naturally appointed. It is a thing that will not bear reasoning on, being simply a form of the old 'who will guard the guardian?' Who will direct the directress? and to whose interference will the interferer submit?

There are two causes for this excessive love of interference among women. The one is the narrowness of their lives and objects, by which insignificant things gain a disproportionate value in their eyes;

the other, their belief that they are the only saviours of society, and that without them man would become hopelessly corrupt. And to a certain extent this belief is true; but surely with restrictions! Because the clearer moral sense and greater physical weakness of women restrain men's fiercer passions and force them to be gentle and considerate, women are not, therefore, the sole arbiters of masculine life into whose hands is given the paying out of just so much rope as they think fit for the occasion. They would do better to look to their own tackle before settling so exactly the run of others; and if ever their desired time of equality is to come, it must come through mutual independence, not through womanly interference, and as much liberality and breadth given as demanded:—which, so far as humanity has gone hitherto, has not been the feminine manner of squaring accounts.

Grant that women are the salt of the earth and the great antiseptic element in society, still that does not reduce everything else to the verge of corruption which they alone prevent. Yet they evidently think that it is so, and that they are each and all the keepers of keys which give them a special entrance to the temple of morality, and by which they are able to exclude or admit the grosser body of men. Hence they interfere and restrict and pay out just so much rope, and measure off just so much gambolling ground, as they think fit; then think vile man a horribly wicked invention when he takes things into his own hand

and goes beyond their boundary-lines. It is all done in good if in a very narrow faith—that we admit willingly; but we would call their attention to the difference there is between influence and interference; which is just the difference between their ideal duty and their daily practice—between being the salt of the earth and the blister of the home.

We think it only justice to put in a word for those poor henpecked fellows of husbands at a time when the whole cry is for Woman's Rights, which seems to mean chiefly her right of making man knuckle under on all occasions and of making one will serve for two lives—and that will hers. We assure her that she would get her own way in large matters much more easily if she would leave men more liberty in small ones, and not teaze them by interfering in things which do not concern her and have only reference to themselves.

THE FASHIONABLE WOMAN.

AMONG the many odd products of a mature civilization, the fashionable woman is one of the oddest. From first to last she is an amazing spectacle; and if we take human life in any earnestness at all, whether individually, as the passage to an eternal existence the condition of which depends on what we are here, or collectively, as the highest thing we know, we can only look in blank astonishment at the fashionable woman and her career. She is the one sole capable member of the human family without duties and without useful occupation; the one sole being who might be swept out of existence altogether, without deranging the nice arrangement of things, or upsetting the balance of inter-dependent forces. We know of no other organic creation of which this could be said; but the fashionable woman is not as other creatures, being, fortunately, *sui generis*, and of a type not existing elsewhere. If we take the mere ordering of her days and the employment of her time as the sign of her mental state, we may perhaps measure to a certain extent, but not fully, the depth of inanity into which she has fallen and the immensity of her folly.

Considering her as a being with the potentiality of reason, of usefulness, of thought, the actual result is surely the saddest and the strangest thing under heaven!

She goes to bed at dawn and does not attempt to rise till noon. For the most part she breakfasts in bed, and then amuses herself with a cursory glance at the morning paper, if she have sufficient energy for so great a mental exertion; if she have not, she lies for another hour or two in that half-slumberous state which is so destructive to mind and body, weakening as it does both fibre and resolution, both muscle and good principle. At last she languidly rises, to be dressed in time for luncheon and her favoured intimates—the men who have the *entrée* at sacred hours when the world in general is forbidden. Some time later she dresses again for her drive—for the first part of the day's serious business; for paying visits and leaving cards; for buying jewelry and dresses, and ordering all sorts of unnecessary things at her milliner's; for this grand lady's ordinary 'day,' and that grand lady's extraordinary At Home; for her final slow parade in the Park, where she sees her friends as in an open air drawing-room, makes private appointments, carries on flirtations, and hears and retails gossip and scandal of a full flavour. Then she goes home to dress for tea in a 'lovely gown' of suggestive piquancy; to be followed by dinner, the opera or a concert, a *soirée*, or perhaps a ball or two; whence she returns towards morning, flushed with excitement or worn out with fatigue, feverish or nervous, as she has had pleasure and success or disappointment and annoyance.

This is her outside life; and this is no fancy picture and no exaggeration. After a certain time of such an existence, can we wonder if her complexion fades and her eyes grow dim? if that inexpressible air of haggard weariness creeps over her, which ages even a young girl and makes a mature woman substantially an old one? It is then that she has recourse to those foul and fatal expedients of which we have heard more than enough in these latter days. She will not try simplicity of living, natural hours, wholesome occupation, unselfish endeavour, but rushes off for help to paints and cosmetics, to stimulants and drugs, and attempts to restore the tarnished freshness of her beauty by the very means which further corrode it. Every now and then, for very weariness when not for idleness, she feigns herself sick and has her favourite physician to attend her. In fact the funniest thing about her is the ease with which she takes to her bed on the slightest provocation, and the strange pleasure she seems to find in what is a penance to most women.

You meet her in a heated, crowded, noisy room, looking just as she always looks, whatever her normal state of health may be; and in answer to your inquiries she tells you she has only two hours ago left her bed to come here, having been confined to her room for a week, with Dr. Blank in close attendance. If you are an intimate female friend she will whisper you the name of her malady, which is sure to be something terrific, and which, if true, would have kept her a real invalid for months instead of days; but if you are only a man she will make herself out to have been very ill indeed in a more mysterious way, and leave you to wonder at the extraordinary physique of fashionable women, which enables them to live on the most friendly touch-and-go terms with death, and to overcome mortal maladies by an effort of the will and the delights of a ducal ball. The favourite physician has a hard time of it with these ladies; and the more popular he is the harder his work. It is well for his generation when he is a man of honour and integrity, and knows how to add self-respect and moral power to the qualities which have made him the general favourite. For his influence over women is almost unlimited—like nothing so much as that of the handsome Abbé of the Regency or the fascinating Monsignore of Rome; and if he chooses to abuse it and turn it to evil issues, he can. And, however great the merit in him that he does not, it does not lessen the demerit of the woman that he could.

Sometimes the fashionable woman takes up with the clergyman instead of the physician, and coquets with religious exercises rather than with drugs; but neither clergyman nor physician can change her mode of life nor give her truth nor common-sense. Sometimes there is a fluttering show of art-patronage, and the fashionable woman has a handsome painter or well-bred musician in her train, whom she pets publicly and patronizes graciously. Sometimes it is a young poet or a rising novelist, considerably honoured by the association, who dedicates his next novel to her, or writes verses in her praise, with such fervency of gratitude as sets the base Philistines on the scent of the secret—perhaps guessing not far amiss. For the fashionable woman has always some love-affair on hand, more or less platonic according to her own temperament or the boldness of the man—a love-affair in which the smallest ingredient is love; a love-affair which is vanity, idleness, a dissolute imagination and contempt of such prosaic things as morals; a love-affair not even to be excused by the tragic frenzy of earnest passion, and which may be guilty and yet not true.

The physical effects of such a life as this are as bad as the mental, and both are as bad as the worst can make them. A feverish, overstrained condition of health either prevents the fashionable woman from being a mother at all, or makes her the mother of nervous, sickly children. Many a woman of high rank is at this moment paying bitterly for the disappointment of which she herself, in her illimitable folly, has been the sole and only cause. And, whether women like to hear it or not, it is none the less a truth that part of the reason for their being born at all is that they may in their turn bear children. The unnatural feeling against maternity existing among fashionable women is one of the worst mental signs of their state, as their frequent inability to be mothers is one of the worst physical results. This is a condition of things which no false modesty nor timid reserve should keep in the background, for it is a question of national importance, and will soon become one of national disaster unless checked by a healthier current and more natural circumstances.

Dress, dissipation and flirting make up the questionable lines which enclose the life of the fashionable woman, and which enclose nothing useful, nothing good, nothing deep nor true nor holy. Her piety is a pastime; her art the poorest pretence; her pleasure consists only in hurry and excitement alternating with debasing sloth, in heartless coquetry or in lawless indulgence, as nature made her more vain or more sensual. As a wife she fulfils no wifely duty in any grand or loving sense, for the most part regarding her husband only as a banker or an adjunct, according to the terms of her marriage settlement; as a mother she is a stranger to her children, to whom nurse and governess supply her place and give such poor makeshift for maternal love as they are enabled or inclined. In no domestic relation is she of the smallest value, and of none in any social circumstance beside the adorning of a room—if she be pretty—and the help she gives to trade through her expenditure. She lives only in the gaslight, and her nature at last becomes as artificial as her habits.

As years go on, and she changes from the acknowledged belle to *la femme passée*, she goes through a period of frantic endeavour to retain her youth ; and even when time has clutched her with too firm a hand to be shaken off, and she begins to feel the infirmities which she still puts out all her strength to conceal, even then she grasps at the departing shadow and fresh daubs the crumbling ruin, in the belief that the world's eyes are dim and that stucco may pass for marble for another year or two longer. Or she becomes a Belgravian mother, with daughters to sell to the highest bidder ; and then the aim of her life is to secure the purchaser. Her daughters are never objects of real love with the fashionable woman. They are essentially her rivals, and the idea of carrying on her life in theirs, of forgetting herself in them, occurs to her only as a forecast of death. She shrinks even from her sons, as living evidences of the lapse of time which she cannot deny, and awkward *memoria technica* for fixing dates ; and there is not a home presided over by a fashionable woman where the family is more than a mere name, a mere social convention loosely held together by circumstances, not by love.

Closing such a life as this comes the unhonoured end, when the miserable made-up old creature totters down into the grave where paint and padding, and glossy plaits cut from some fresh young head, are of no more avail ; and where death, which makes all things real, reduces her life of lies to the nothingness it has been from the beginning. What does she leave behind her? A memory by which her children may order their own lives in proud assurance that so they will order them best for virtue and for honour? Or a memory which speaks to them of time misused, of duties unfulfilled, of love discarded for pleasure, and of a life-long sacrifice of all things good and pure for selfishness?

We all know examples of the worldly old woman clinging batlike to the last to the old roofs and rafters; and we all know how heartily we despise her, and how we ridicule her in our hearts, if not by our words. If the reigning queens of fashion, at present young and beautiful, would but remember that they are only that worldly old woman in embryo, and that in a very few years they will be her exact likeness, unhappily repeated for the scorn of the world once more to follow! The traditional skeleton at the feast had a wonderfully wise meaning, crude and gross as it was in form. For though its *memento mori*, too constantly before us, would either sadden or brutalize, as we were thoughtful or licentious, yet it is good to see the end of ourselves, and to study the meaning and lesson of our lives in those of our prototypes and elder likenesses.

The pleasures of the world are, as we all know, very potent and very alluring, but nothing can be more unsatisfying if taken as the main purpose of life. While we are young, the mere stirring of the blood stands instead of anything more real; but as we go on, and the pulse flags and pleasurable occasions get rare and more rare, we find that we have been like the Prodigal Son, and that our food and his have been out of much the same trough, and come in the main to much the same thing.

This is an age of extraordinary wealth and of corresponding extraordinary luxury; of unparalleled restlessness, which is not the same thing as activity or energy, but which is the kind of restlessness that disdains all quiet and repose, as unendurable stagnation. Hence the fashionable woman of the day is one of extremes in her own line also; and the idleness, the heartlessness, the self-indulgence, the want of high morality, and the insolent luxury at all times characteristic of her were never displayed with more cynical effrontery than at present, and never called for more severe condemnation.

The fashionable women of Greece and Rome, of Italy and France, have left behind them names which the world has made typical of the vices naturally engendered by idleness and luxury. But do we wish that our women should become subjects for an English Juvenal? that fashion should create a race of Laïses and Messalinas, of Lucrezia Borgias and Madame du Barrys, out of the stock which once gave us Lucy Hutchinson and Elizabeth Fry? Once the name of Englishwoman carried with it a grave and noble echo as the name of women known for their gentle bearing and their blameless honour—of women who loved their husbands, and brought up about their own knees the children they were not reluctant to bear and not ashamed to love. Now, it too often means a girl of the period, a frisky matron, a fashionable woman—a thing of paints and pads, consorting with dealers of no doubtful calling for the purchase of what she grimly calls 'beauty,' making pleasure her only good and the world her highest god. It too often means a woman who is not ashamed to supplement her husband with a lover, but who is unwilling to become the honest mother of that husband's children. It too often means a hybrid creature, perverted out of the natural way altogether, affecting the license but ignorant of the strength of a man; as girl or woman alike valueless so far as her highest natural duties are concerned; and talking largely of liberty while showing at every turn how much she fails in that co-essential of liberty —knowledge how to use it.

SLEEPING DOGS.

THERE is a capital old proverb, often quoted but not so often acted on, called 'Let sleeping dogs lie;' a proverb which, if we were to abide by its injunction, would keep us out of many a mess that we get into now, because we cannot let well alone. Certainly we fall into trouble sometimes, or rather we drift into it —we allow it to gather round us—for want of a frank explanation to clear off small misunderstandings. At least novelists say so, and then make a great point of the anguish endured by Henry and Angelina for three mortal volumes, because they were too stupid to ask the reason why the one looked cold the other evening at the duchess's ball, and the other looked shy the next morning in the park. But then novelists, poor souls, are driven to such extravagant expedients for motives and matter, that we can scarcely take them as rational exponents of real life in any way; though the very meaning and final cause of their profession is to depict human nature as it is, and to show the reflex action of character and circumstances somewhat according to the pattern set out in the actual world. But, leaving novelists alone, on the whole we find in real life that if speech is silvern, silence is essentially golden, and that more harm is done by saying too much than by saying too little ; above all, that infinite mischief arises by not letting sleeping dogs lie.

People are so wonderfully anxious to stir up the dregs of everything, they can never let things rest. Take a man or woman who has done something queer that gets noised abroad, and who is coldly looked on in consequence by those who believe the worst reports which arise as interpretations. Now the wisest thing undoubtedly is to bear this coldness as the righteous punishment of that folly, and to trust for rehabilitation to the mysterious process called 'living it down.' If there has been absolutely no sinfulness to speak of, nothing but a little imprudence and a big glossary of scandalous explanation, a little precipitancy and a great deal of ill-nature, by all means wake up the sleeping dog and set him howling through the streets. He may do good, seeing that truth would be your friend. But if there be a core of ugly fact, even if it be not quite so ugly as the envelope which rumour has wrapped round it, then fall back on the dignity of 'living it down,' and let the dog lie sleeping and muzzled.

There is another, but an unsavoury saying, which advises against the stirring up of evil odours ; but this is just what imprudent, high-spirited people will not understand. They will take their own way in spite of society and all its laws ; they will kick over the traces when it suits them; they will do this and that of which the world says authoritatively, 'No, you shall not do it;' and then, when the day of wrath arrives, and down comes the whip on the offending back, they shriek piteously and wake up all the dogs in the town in the 'investigation of their case.' And a queer kennel enough they turn out sometimes! They would have done better to put up with their social thrashing than to have set the bloodhounds of 'investigation' on their heels.

Actions for libel often do this kind of thing, as every one may read for himself. Many a man who gets his farthing damages had better have borne the surly growl of the only half-roused dog, than have retaliated, and so waked him up. The farthing damages, representing say a cuff on the head or a kick in the ribs, or a milder 'Lie down, sir!' may be very pleasant to the feelings of the yelped-at, as so much revenge exacted—Shylock's pound of flesh, without the blood. But what about the consequences? what about the disclosure of your secret follies and the uncovering of the foundations on which the libel rested? The foundations remain immoveable to the end of time if the superstructure be disroofed, and the sleeping dog is awakened, never to be set at rest again while he has a tooth in his head that can bite.

One of the arts of peaceful living at home is contained in the power of letting sleeping dogs lie. Papa is surly—it is a way papas have—or mamma is snappish, as even the best of mammas are at times when the girls are tiresome and will flirt with ineligible younger brothers, or when the boys, who must marry money, are paying attention to dowerless beauty instead. Well, the family horizon is overcast, and the black dog keeps the gate of the family mansion. Better let it lie there asleep, if it will but remain so. It is not pleasant to have it there certainly, but it would be worse to rouse it into activity and to have a general yelping through the house.

Sometimes, indeed, in a family given to tears and caresses and easily excited feelings, a frank challenge as to reasons why is answered by a temporary storm, followed by a scene of effusion and *attendrissement*, and the black dog is not awakened, but banished, by the rousing he has got. This is a method that can be tried when you have perfect knowledge and command of your material; else it is a dangerous, and nine times out of ten would be an unsuccessful, experiment. It is nearly always unsuccessful with husbands and wives, who often sulk, but rarely for causes needing explanation. Angelina knows quite well that she danced too often the other night with that fascinating young Lovelace for whom her Henry has a special, and not quite groundless, aversion. She may put on as many airs of injured innocence as she likes, and affect to consider herself an ill-used wife suffering grievous things because of her husband's displeasure and the black dog of sulks accompanying ; but she knows as well as her Henry himself where her sin lies, and to kick at the black dog would only be to set him loose upon her, and be well barked at if not worried for her pains. The wiser course would be to muzzle him by ignoring his presence ; and so in almost all cases of domestic dog, however black.

A sleeping dog of another kind, which it would be well if women would always leave at rest, is the potential passion of a man who is a cherished friend but an impossible lover. Certain slow-going men are able to maintain for life a strong but strictly platonic attachment for certain women. If any warmer impulse or more powerful feeling give threatening notice of arising, it is kept in due subjection and a wholesome state of coolness, perhaps by its very hopelessness even if returned, perhaps by the fear or the knowledge that it would be ill-received, and that the only passport to the pleasant friendship so delighted in is in this calm and sober platonism. This is all very well so long as the woman minds what she is about ; for the passionless attachment of a man depends mainly on her desire to keep things in their present place, and on her power of holding to the line to be observed. If she oversteps this line, if she wakens up that sleeping dog of passion, it is all over with her and platonism. What was once a pleasant truth would now be a burning satire ; for friendship routed by love can never take service under its old banners again.

And yet this is what women are continually doing. They are always complaining that men are not their friends, and that they are only selfish and self-seeking in their relations with them; yet no sooner do they possess a man friend who is nothing else than they try their utmost to convert him into a lover, and are not too well pleased if they do not succeed—which might by chance sometimes happen like any other rare occurrence, but not often. And yet success ruins everything. It takes away the friend and does not give an available lover; it destroys the existing good and substitutes nothing better. If the woman be of the fishpond type, whose heart Thackeray wanted to 'drag,' she simply turns round upon the unhappy victim with one of the 'looks that kill;' if she be more weak than vain and less designing than impulsive, she regrets the momentary infatuation which has lost her her friend; but in any case she has lost him—by her own folly, not by inevitable misfortune.

Just as easy is it to rouse the sleeping dogs of hatred, of jealousy, of envy. You have a tepid well-controlled dislike to some one; and you know that he knows it. For feelings are eloquent, even when dumb, and express themselves in a thousand ways independent of words. You do not care much about your dislike—you do not nurse it nor feed it in any way, and are rather content than not to let it lie dormant, and so far harmless. But your unloved friend cannot let well alone. He will be always treading on your corns and touching you on the raw. That unlucky speculation you made ; your play that was damned ; the election you lost ; the decision that was given against you, with costs—whenever you see him he is sure to introduce some topic that rubs you the wrong way, till at last the sleeping dog gets fairly roused, and what was merely a well-ordered dislike bursts out into a frantic and ungovernable hatred. It has been his own doing. Just as in the case of the platonic friend transformed into the passionate lover by the woman's wiles, so the dislike that gave you no trouble—become now the hatred which is a real curse to your existence—results from your friend's incessant rousing up of sleeping passions.

Young people are much given to this kind of thing. There is an impish tendency in most girls, and in all boys, that makes teazing a matter of exquisite delight to them. If they know of any sleeping dog which an elder carries about under his cloak, they are never so happy as when they are rousing it to activity, though their own backs may get bitten in the fray. Let a youngster into the secret of a weakness, a sore, and if he can resist the temptation of torturing you as the result of his knowledge he may lay claim to a virtue almost unknown in boyish morals. But he sometimes pays dearly for his fun. More than one life-long dislike, culminating in a disastrous codicil or total omission from the body of the will, has been the return-blow for a course of boyish teazings which a testy old uncle or huffish maiden aunt has had to undergo. The punishment may be severe and unjust; but the provocation was great; and revenge is a human, if indefensible, instinct common to all classes.

Fathers and mothers themselves are not always sacred ground, nor are their special dogs suffered to lie sleeping undisturbed; and perhaps the favouritism and comparative coldness patent in almost every family may be traced back to the propensity for soothing or for rousing those parentâl beasts. For even fathers and mothers have personal feelings in excess of their instincts, and they, no more than any one else, like to be put through their paces by the impish vivacity of youth, and made to dance according to the piping of an irreverent lad or saucy girl. If they have dogs, they do not want their children to pry into their kennels and whistle them out at their pleasure; and those who do so most will naturally get worst off in the great division of family love. 'Let sleeping dogs lie,' certainly, as a rule for private life.

Historically, the saying does not hold good. For if the great leaders of thought and reform had not roused up the sleeping dogs of their day, and made them give tongue for all after ages to hear, we should be but poorly off at this present time. Many of our liberties have been got only by diligently prodding up that very sleepy dog, the public, till he has been forced to show his teeth; and history is full of instances of how much has been done, all the world over and in every age, by the like means. Sometimes the prodded dog flies at the wrong throat on the other side, as we have had a few notable instances of late; and then it would have been wiser to leave him quietly sleeping in the shade, whether at Mentana or elsewhere; to rouse for rending being a poor amusement at the best, and an eminently unprofitable use of leather.

BEAUTY AND BRAINS.

THAT lovely woman fulfils only half her mission when she is unpersonable instead of beautiful, all young men, and all pretty girls secure in the consciousness of their own perfections, will agree. Indeed, it is cruel to hear the way in which ingenuous youths despise ugly girls, however clever, whose charm lies in their cleverness only, with a counteraction in their plainness. To hear them, one would think that hardness of feature was, like poverty, a crime voluntarily perpetrated, and that contempt was a righteous retribution for the offence. Yet their preference, though so cruelly expressed, is to a certain extent the right thing. When we are young, the beauty of women has a supreme attraction beyond all other possessions or qualities; and there are self-evident reasons why it should be so. It is only as we grow older that we know the value of brains, and, while still admiring beauty—as indeed who does not?—admire it as one passing by on the other side—as a grace to look at, but not to hold, unless accompanied by something more lasting.

This is in the middle term of a man's life. Old

age, perhaps with the unconscious yearning of regret, goes back to the love of youth and beauty for their own sake; extremes meeting here as in almost all other circumstances. The danger is when a young man, obeying the natural impulse of his age and state, marries beauty only, with nothing more durable beneath. The mind sees what it brings, and we love the ideal we create rather than the reality that exists. A pretty face, the unworn nerves of youth, the freshness of hope that has not yet been soured by disappointment nor chilled by experience, a neat stroke at croquet and a merry laugh easily excited, make a girl a goddess to a boy who is what he himself calls in love and his friends 'spoony.' She may be narrow, selfish, spoilt, unfit to bear the burdens of life and unable to meet her trials patiently; she may be utterly unpractical and silly —one of those who never mature but only grow old —without judgment, forethought, common-sense or courage; but he sees nothing of all this. To him she is perfect; the 'jolliest girl in the world,' if he be slangy, or the 'dearest,' if he be affectionate; and he neither sees nor heeds her potential faults.

It is only when she has stepped down from her pedestal to the level of the home-threshold that he finds out she is but a woman after all, and perhaps an exceptionally weak and peevish one. Then he knows that he would have done better for himself had he married that plain brave-hearted girl who would have had him to a dead certainty if he had asked her, but whom he so unmercifully laughed at when he was making love to his fascinating charmer. As years go on and reduce the Hebe and Hecate of eighteen to much the same kind of woman at forty—with perhaps the advantage on Hecate's side if of the sort that ripens well and improves by keeping—the man feels that he has been a fool after the manner of Bunyan's Passion; that he has eaten up his present in the past, and had all his good things at once. If he had but looked at the future and been able to wait! But in those days he wanted beauty that does not last, and cared nothing for brains which do; and so, having made his election he must abide by it, and eat bitter bread from the yeast of his own brewing.

Many a man has cursed, his whole life long, the youthful infatuation that made him marry a pretty fool. Take the case of a rising politician whose fair-faced wife is either too stupid to care about his position, or who imperils it by her folly. If amiable and affectionate, and in her own silly little way ambitious, she does him incalculable mischief by exaggeration, and by saying and doing exactly the things which are most damaging to him; if stupid, she is just so much deadweight that he has to carry with him while swimming up the stream. She is very lovely certainly, and people crowd her drawing-room to look at her; but a plain-featured, sensible, shrewd woman, with no beauty to speak of but with tact and cleverness, would have helped him in his career far better than does his brainless Venus. He finds this out when it is too late to change M. for N. in the marriage service.

The successful men of small beginnings are greatly liable to this curse of wifely hindrance. A barrister once briefless and now in silk—an artist once obscure and now famous—who in the days of impecuniosity and Bohemianism married the landlady's pretty daughter and towards the meridian of life find themselves in the front ranks of *la haute volée* with a wife who drops her h's and multiplies her s's, know the full bitterness of the bread baked from that hasty brewing. Each woman may have been beautiful in her youth, and each man may have loved his own very passionately; but if she have nothing to supplement her beauty—if she have no brains to fall back on, by which she can be educated up to her husband's present social position as the wife of his successful maturity—she is a mistake. Dickens was quite right to kill off pretty childish Dora in 'David Copperfield.' If she had lived she would have been like Flora in 'Bleak House,' who indeed was Dora grown old but not matured; with all the grace and beauty of her youth gone, and nothing else to take their place.

Men do not care for brains in excess in women. They like a sympathetic intellect which can follow and seize their thoughts as quickly as they are uttered; but they do not much care for any clear or specific knowledge of facts. Even the most philosophic among them would rather not be set right in a classical quotation, an astronomical calculation, or the exact bearing of a political question by a lovely being in tarlatane whom he was graciously unbending to instruct. Neither do they want anything very strong-minded. To most men, indeed, the feminine strong-mindedness that can discuss immoral problems without blushing is a quality as unwomanly as a well-developed biceps or a 'shoulder-of-mutton' fist. It is sympathy, not antagonism—it is companionship, not rivalry, still less supremacy, that they like in women; and some women with brains as well as learning—for the two are not the same thing—understand this, and keep their blue stockings well covered by their petticoats. Others, enthusiasts for freedom of thought and intellectual rights, show theirs defiantly; and meet with their reward. Men shrink from them. Even clever men, able to meet them on their own ground, do not feel drawn to them; while all but high-class minds are humiliated by their learning and dwarfed by their moral courage. And no man likes to feel humiliated or dwarfed in the presence of a woman, and because of her superiority.

But the brains most useful to women, and most befitting their work in life, are those which show themselves in common-sense, in good judgment, and that kind of patient courage which enables them to bear small crosses and great trials alike with dignity and good temper. Mere intellectual culture, however valuable it may be in itself, does not equal the worth of this kind of moral power; for as the true domain of woman is the home, and her way of ordering her domestic life the best test of her faculties, mere intellectual culture does not help in this; and, in fact, is often a hindrance rather than a help. What good is there in one's wife being an accomplished mathematician, a sound scholar, a first-rate musician, a deeply-read theologian, if she cannot keep the accounts square, knows nothing of the management of children, lets herself be cheated by the servants and the tradespeople, has not her eyes opened to dirt and disorder, and gives way to a fretful temper on the smallest provocation?

The pretty fool who spends half her time in trying on new dresses and studying the effect of colours, and who knows nothing beyond the last new novel and the latest plate of fashions, is not a more disastrous wife than the woman of profound learning whose education has taught her nothing practical. They stand at the opposite ends of the same scale, and neither end gives the true position of women. Indeed, if one must have a fool in one's house, the pretty one would be the best, as, at the least, pleasant to look at; which is something gained.

The intellectual fool, with her head always in books and 'questions,' and her children dropping off like sheep for the want of womanly care, is something more than flesh and blood can tolerate. The pretty fool cannot help herself. If nature proved herself but a stepmother to her, and left out the best part of her wits while taking such especial care of her face, it is no fault of hers; but the intellectual fool is a case of maladministration of powers, for which she alone is responsible ; and in this particular alternative between beauty and brains, without a shadow of doubt we would go in for beauty.

Ball-rooms and dinner-tables are the two places where certain women most shine. In the ball-room Hebe is the queen, and has it all her own way without fear of rivals. A very few men who care for dancing for its own sake will certainly dance with Hecate if she is light on hand, keeps accurate time, and manages her feet with scientific precision ; but to the ruck of youths, Hebe, who jerks herself into step every second round, but whose lovely face and perfect figure make up for everything, is the partner they all besiege. Only to those exceptional few who regard dancing as a serious art would she be a bore with her three jumps and a hop ; while Hecate, waltzing like an angel, would be divine, in spite of her high cheek-bones and light green eyes à fleur de tête. But at a dinner-table, where a man likes to talk between the dishes, a sympathetic listener with pleasant manners, to whom he can air his stalest stories and recount his personal experiences, is preferable to the prettiest girl if a simpleton, only able to show her small white teeth in a silly smile, and say 'yes' and 'indeed' in the wrong places. The ball-room may be taken to represent youth; the dinner-table maturity. The one is the apotheosis of mere beauty, in clouds of millinery glory and a heaven of flirting ; the other is solid enjoyment, with brains to talk to by the side and beauty to look at opposite, in just the disposition that makes life perfect. A well-ordered dinner-table is a social microcosm; and, being so, this is the blue riband of the arrangement.

Every woman is bound to make the best of herself. The strong-minded women who hold themselves superior to the obligations of dress and manner and all the pleasant little artificial graces belonging to an artificial civilization, and who think any sacrifice made to appearance just so much waste of power, are awful creatures, ignorant of the real meaning of their sex—social Graiæ wanting in every charm of womanhood, and to be diligently shunned by the wary.

This making the best of themselves is a very different thing from making dress and personal vanity the first considerations in life. Where women in general fail is in the exaggerations into which they fall on this and on almost every other question. They are apt to be either demireps or devotees; frights or flirts; fashionable to an extent that lands them in illimitable folly and drags their husbands' names through the mire, or they are so dowdy that they disgrace a well-ordered drawing-room, and among nicely-dressed women stand out as living sermons on slovenliness. If they are clever, they are too commonly blue-stockings, and let the whole household go by the board for the sake of their fruitless studies; and if they are domestic and good managers they sink into mere servants, never opening a book save their daily ledger, and having no thought beyond the cheesemonger's bill and the butcher's prices. They want that fine balance, that accurate self-measurement and knowledge of results, which goes by the name of common-sense and is the best manifestation of brains they can give, and the thing which men most prize. It is the most valuable working form of intellectual power, and has most endurance and vitality; and it is the form which helps a man on in life, when he has found it in his wife, quite as much as money or a good connexion.

So that, on the whole, brains are before beauty in the solid things of life. For admiration and personal love and youthful enjoyment, beauty of course is supreme; but as we cannot be always young nor always apt for pleasure, it is as well to provide for the days when the daughters of music shall be brought low and the years draw nigh which have no pleasure in them.

NYMPHS.

BETWEEN the time of the raw school-girl and that of the finished young lady is the short season of the nymph, when the physical enjoyment of life is perhaps at its keenest, and a girl is not afraid to use her limbs as nature meant her to use them, nor ashamed to take pleasure in her youth and strength. This is the time when a sharp run down a steep hill, with the chance of a tumble midway, is an exercise by no means objected to; when clambering over gates, stiles, and even crabbed stone-walls is not refused because of the undignified display of ankle which the adventure involves; when leaping a ditch comes in as one of the ordinary accidents of a marshland walk; and when the fun of riding is infinitely enhanced if the horse be only half broken or barebacked.

The nymph—an out-of-door, breezy, healthy girl, more after the pattern of the Greek Oread than the Amazon—is found only in the country; and for the most part only in the remoter districts of the country. In the town she degenerates into fastness, according to the law which makes evil merely the misdirection of force, as dirt is only matter in the wrong place. But among the mountains, in the secluded midland villages, or out on the thinly-populated moorland tracts, the nymph may be found in the full perfection of her nature. And a very beautiful kind of nature it is ; though it is to be feared that certain ladies of the stricter sort would call her 'tomboy,' and that those of a still narrower way of thought, unable to distinguish between unconventionality and vulgarity, would hold her to be decidedly vulgar—which she is not—and would wonder at her mother for 'letting her go on so.'

You fall upon the nymph at all hours and in all seasons. Indeed, she boasts that no weather ever keeps her indoors, and prefers a little roughness of the elements to anything too luscious or sentimental. A fresh wind, a sharp frost, a blinding fall of snow, or a pelting shower of rain are all high jinks to the nymph, to whom it is rare fun to come in like a water-dog, dripping from every hair, or shaking the snow in masses from her hat and cloak. She prefers this kind of thing to the suggestive beauty of the moonlight or the fervid heats of summer; and thinks a long walk in the crisp sharp frost, with the leaves crackling under her feet, worth all the nightingales in the wood. And yet she loves the spring and summer too, for the sake of the flowers and the birds and the beasts and the insects they bring forth ; for the nymph is almost always a naturalist of the perceptive and self-taught kind, and has a marvellous faculty for finding out nests and rare habitats, and for tracking unusual trails to the hidden home.

There is no prettier sight among girls than the nymph when thoroughly at her ease, and enjoying herself in her own peculiar way. That wonderful grace of unconsciousness which belongs to savages and animals belongs to her also, and she moves with a supple freedom which affectation or shyness would equally destroy. To see her running down a green field, with the sunlight falling on her; her light dress blown into coloured clouds by the wind; her step a little too long for the correct town-walk—but so firmly planted and yet so light, so swift, so even!—her cheeks freshly flushed by exercise; her eyes bright and fearless; her white teeth shown below her upper lip as she comes forward with a ringing laugh, carrying a young bird which she has just caught, or a sheaf of wild flowers for which she has been perilling her neck, is to see a beautiful and gracious picture which you remember with pleasure all your life after. Or you meet her quite alone on a wide bleak moor, with her hat in her hand and her hair blowing across her face, looking for plovers' eggs, or ferns and orchids down in the damp hollows. She is by no means dressed according to the canons of *Le Follet*, and yet she always manages to have something picturesque about her—something that would delight an artist's taste, and that is in perfect harmony with herself and her surroundings—which she wears with profound ignorance as to how well it suits her—or at most with only an instinctive knowledge that it is the right thing for her. She may be shy as she meets you; if she is passing out of the nymph state into that of conscious womanhood, she will be shy; but if still a nymph with no disturbing influences at work, she will probably look at you with a fixed, perplexing, half-provoking look of frank curiosity which you can neither notice nor take advantage of; the trammels of conventional life fettering one side heavily, if not the other.

Shocking as it is to say, the nymph may sometimes be met on the top of a haycart, and certainly in the hayfield, where she is engaged in scattering the 'cocks,' if not in raising them; and where even the haymakers themselves—and they are not a notably romantic race—do not grumble at the extra trouble she gives them, because of her evident delight in her misdeeds. Besides, she has a bright word for them as she passes; for the nymph has democratic tendencies, and is frank and 'affable' to all classes alike. She needs to be a little looked after in this direction, not for mischief but for manners; for, if not judiciously checked, she may become in time coarse. There are seamy sides to everything, and the nymph does not escape the general law.

If the nymph condescends to any game at all, it is croquet, at which she is inexorably severe. She knows nothing of the little weakness which makes her elder sisters overlook the patent spooning of the favourite curate, even though he is opposed to them

—nothing of the tender favouritism which pushes on an awkward partner by deeds of helping outside the law. The nymph, who has no weakness nor tenderness of that kind, knows only the game; and the game has not elastic boundaries. Therefore she is inflexible in her justice to one side and the other. Is it not the game? she says when reproached with being disagreeable and unamiable.

But even croquet is slow to the nymph, who has been known to handle a bat not discreditably, and who is an adept at firing at a mark with real powder and ball. If she lives near a lake, a river, or the sea, she is first-rate at boating, can feather her oar and back water with the skill of a veteran oarsman, and can reef a sail or steer close without the slightest hesitation or nervousness. She is also a famous swimmer, and takes the water like a duck; and at an ordinary summer seaside resort, if by chance she ever profanes herself by showing off there, she attracts a crowd of beach-loungers to watch her feats far outside the safe barrier of the bathing-machines. She is a great walker, wherever she lives. If a mountaineer, she is a clever cragswoman, making it a point of honour to go to the top of the most difficult and dangerous mountains in her neighbourhood, and coaxing her brothers to let her join them and their friends in expeditions which require both nerve and strength.

Her greatest sphere of social glory is a picnic, where she always heads the exploring party, clambering up the rocks of the waterfall, or diving down into the close-smelling caves, or scaling the crumbling walls of the ruin before any one else can come up to her. She is specially happy at old ruins, where she flits in and out among the broken columns and under the mouldering arches, like a spirit of the place unduly disturbed. Sometimes she climbs up by unseen means, till she reaches a point where it makes one dizzy to see her; and sometimes she startles her company by the sudden bleating of a sheep, or the wild hoot of an owl. For she can imitate the sounds of animals for the most part with wonderful accuracy; though she can also sing simple ballads without music, with sweetness and correctness. She is fond of all animals and fears none. She will pass through a field thronged with wild-looking cattle without the least hesitation; and makes friends even with the yelping farm-dogs which come snapping and snarling at her heels. In winter she feeds the wood-birds by flocks, and always takes care that the horses have a handful of corn or a carrot when she goes to see them, and that the cows are the better for her visit by a bunch of lucerne or a fat fresh cabbage-leaf. The home-beasts show their pleasure when they hear her fleet footstep on the paved yard; and her favourite pony whinnies to her in a peculiar voice as she passes his stable door. These are her friends, and their love for her is her reward.

In her early days the nymph was notorious for

her dilapidated attire, perplexing mother and nurse to mend, or to understand why or how it had come about. But as her favourite hiding-place was in a forked branch midway up an old tree in the shrubbery, or a natural arbour which she had cut out for herself in the very heart of the underwood, it was scarcely to be wondered at if cloth and cotton testified to the severity of her retreats. She has still mysterious rents in her skirts, got no one knows how; and her mother still laments over her aptitude for rags, and wishes she could be brought to see the beauty of unstained apparel. She is given to early rising— to fits indeed of rising at some wild hour in the morning, for walks before breakfast and the like innocent insanities. Sometimes she takes it in hand to educate herself in certain stoicisms, and goes without butter at breakfast or without breakfast altogether, if she thinks that thereby she will grow stronger or less inclined to self-indulgence. For drink she will never touch wine nor beer; but she likes new milk, and is great in her capacity for water.

The nymph is almost always of the middle-classes. It is next to impossible indeed that she should be found in the higher ranks, where girls are not left to themselves, and where no one lives in far-away country places out of the reach of public opinion and beyond the range of public overlooking. Some years ago, before the railroads and monster hotels had made the mountain districts like Hampstead or Richmond on a Sunday afternoon, the nymph was to be found in great abundance down in Cumberland and Westmoreland. By the more remote lakes, like Buttermere and Hawes Water, and in the secluded valleys running up from the larger lakes, you would come upon square stuccoed houses, generally abominably ugly, where the nymph was mistress of the situation. She might be met riding about alone in a flapping straw hat, long before hats were fashionable headgear for women, and in a blue baize skirt for all the riding-habit thought necessary ; or she might be encountered on the wild fell sides, or on the mountain heights, or in her boat sculling among the lonely lake islets, or gathering water-lilies in the bays. In the desolate stretch of moorland country to the north of Skiddaw the whole female population a few years ago was of the nymph kind ; but railroads and the penny-post, cheap trains, fashion and fine-ladyism have penetrated even into the heart of the wild mountains, and now the nymph there is only a transitional development—not, as formerly, a fixed type.

The nymph is the very reverse of a flirt. She has no inclination that way, and looks shy and awkward at the men who pay her compliments or attempt anything like sentimentality. But she is not superior to boys, who are her chosen companions and favourites. A bold, brave boy, who just overtops her in skill and daring, is her delight ; but anything over twenty is ' awfully old,' while forty and sixty are so remote that the lines blur and blend together and have no distinction. By-and-by the nymph becomes a staid young woman, and marries. If she goes into a close town and has children, very often her vigorous health gives way, and we see her in a few years nervous, emaciated, consumptive, and with a pitiful yearning for 'home' more pathetic than all the rest. But if she remains where she is, in the fresh pure air of her native place, she retains her youth and strength long after the age when ordinary women lose theirs, and her children are celebrated as magnificent specimens of the future generation.

We often see in country places matrons of over forty who are still like young women, both in looks and bearing, both in mental innocence and physical power. They have the shy and innocent look of girls; they blush like girls; they know less evil than almost any town-bred girl of eighteen, mothers of stalwart youths though they may be; they can walk and laugh and take pleasure in their lives like girls; and their daughters find them as much sisters as mothers. It is not quite the same thing if they do not marry; for among the saddest sights of social life is that terrible fading and withering away of comely, healthy, vigorous young country girls, who slowly pass from nymphs, full of grace and beauty, of happiness and power, to antiquated virgins, soured, useless, debilitated and out of nature. Of these, too, there are plenty in country places; but perhaps some scheme will be some day set afoot which shall redress the overweighted balance and bring to the service of the future some of the healthiest and best of our women. Meanwhile the fresh, innocent, breezy nymph is a charming study ; and may the time be far distant which shall see her tamed and civilized out of existence altogether!

MÉSALLIANCES.

THE French system of parents arranging the marriage of their children without the consent of the girl being even asked, but assumed as granted, is not so wholly monstrous as many people in England believe. It seems to be founded on the idea that, given a young girl who has been kept shut up from all possibility of forming the most shadowy attachment for any man whatsoever, and present to her as her husband a sufficiently well-endowed and nice-looking man, with whom come liberty, pretty dresses, balls, admiration and social standing, and the chances are she will love him and live with him in tolerable harmony to the end of the chapter. And this idea is by no means wholly beside the truth, as we find it in practice. The parents, who are better judges of character and circumstance than the daughter can possibly be, are supposed to take care that their future son-in-law is up to their standard, whatever that may be, and that the connexion is not of a kind to bring discredit on their house; and on this and the joint income, as the solid bases, they build the not very unreasonable hypothesis that one man is as good as another for the satisfaction of a quite untouched and virginal fancy, and that suitable external conditions go further and last longer than passion. They trust to the force of instinct to make all square with the affections, while they themselves arrange for the smooth running of the social circumstances; and they are not far out in their calculations.

The young people of the two lonely lighthouse islands, who made love to each other through telescopes, are good examples of the way in which instinct simulates the impulse which calls itself love when there are two or three instead of one to look at. For we may be quite sure that had the lighthouse island youth been John instead of James, fair instead of dark, garrulous instead of reticent, short and fat instead of tall and slender, the lighthouse island girl would have loved him all the same, and would have quite believed that this man was the only man she ever could have loved, and that her instinctive gravitation was her free choice.

The French system of marriage, then, based on this accommodating instinct, works well for women who are not strongly individual, not inconstant by temperament, and not given to sentimentality. But, seeing that all women are not merely negative, and that passions and affections do sometimes assert themselves inconveniently, the system has had the effect of making society lenient to the little follies of married women, unless too strongly pronounced— partly because the human heart insists on a certain amount of free-will, which fact must be recognized—but partly, we must remember, because of the want of the young-lady element in society. In England, where our girls are let loose early, we have free-trade in flirting; consequently, we think that all that sort of thing ought to be done before marriage, and that, when once a woman has made her choice and put her neck under the yoke, she ought to stick to her bargain and loyally fulfil her self-imposed engagement.

One consequence of this free-trade in flirting and this large amount of personal liberty is that love-marriages are more frequent with us than with the French, with whom indeed, in the higher classes, they are next to impossible; and, unfortunately, the corollary to this is that love-marriages are too often *mésalliances*. There is of course no question, ethically, between virtuous vulgarity and refined vice. A groom who smells of the stable and speaks broad Somersetshire or racier Cumberland, but who is brave, faithful, honest, incapable of a lie or of meanness in any form, is a better man than the best-bred gentleman whose life is as vicious as his bearing is unexceptionable. The most undeniable taste in dress, and the most correct pronunciation, would scarcely reconcile us to cruelty, falsehood, or cowardice; and yet we do not know a father who would prefer to give his girl to the groom, rather than the gentleman, and who would think horny-handed virtue, dressed in fustian and smelling of the stable, the fitter husband of the two.

If we take the same case out of our own time and circumstances, we have no doubt as to the choice to be made. It seems to us a very little matter that honest Charicles should tell his love to Aglaë in the broad Doric tongue instead of in the polished Athenian accents to which she was accustomed; that he should wear his chiton a hand's breadth too long or a span too short; that his chlamys should be flung across his brawny chest in a way which the young bloods of the time thought ungraceful; or that, as he assisted at a symposium, he should not hold the rhyton at quite the proper angle, but in a fashion at which the refined Cleon laughed as he nudged his neighbour. Yet all these conventional solecisms, of no account whatever now, would have weighed heavily against poor Charicles when he went to demand Aglaë's hand; and the balance would probably have gone down in favour of that scampish Cleon, who was an Athenian of the Athenians, perfect in all the graces of the age, but not to be compared to his rival in anything that makes a man noble or respectable. We, who read only from a distance, think that Aglaë's father made a mistake, and that the honester man would have been the better choice of the two.

It is only when we bring the same circumstances home to ourselves that we realize the immense importance of the social element; and how, in this complex life of ours, we are unable to move in a single line independent of all it touches. Imagine a fine old county family with a son-in-law who ate peas with his knife, said 'you was' and 'they is,' and came down to dinner in a shooting-jacket and a blue bird's-eye tied in a wisp about his throat! He might be the possessor of all imaginable virtues, and, if occasion required, a very hero and a *preux chevalier*, however rough; but occasions in which a man can be a hero or a *preux chevalier* are rare, whereas dinner comes every day, and the senses are never shut. The core within a conventionally ungainly envelope may be as sound as is possible to a corrupt humanity, but social life requires manners as well as principles; and though eating peas with a knife is not so bad as telling falsehoods, still we should all agree in saying, Give us truth that does not eat peas with its knife; let us have honesty in a dress coat and pureheartedness in a clean shirt, seeing that there is no absolute necessity why these several things should be disunited.

Love-marriages, made against the will of the parents before the character is formed and while the obligations of society are still unrealized, are generally *mésalliances* founded on passion and fancy only. A man and woman of mature age who know what they want may make a *mésalliance*, but it is made with a full understanding and deliberate choice; and, if the thing turns out badly, they can blame themselves less for precipitancy than for wrong calculation. The man of fifty who marries his cook knows what he most values in women. It is not manners and it is not accomplishments; perhaps it is usefulness, perhaps good-temper; at all events it is something that the cook has and that the ladies of his acquaintance have not, and he is content to take the disadvantages of his choice with its advantages. But the boy who runs away with his mother's maid neither calculates nor sees any disadvantages. He marries a pretty girl because her beauty has touched his senses; or he is got hold of by an artful woman who has bamboozled and seduced him. It is only when his passion has worn off that he wakes to the full consequences of his mistake, and understands then how right his parents were when they cashiered his pretty Jane so soon as they became aware of what was going on, and sent that artful Sarah to the right about—just a week too late.

It is the same with girls; but in a far greater extent. If a youth's *mésalliance* is a millstone round his neck for life, a girl's is simply destruction. The natural instinct with all women is to marry above themselves; and we know on what physiological basis this instinct stands, and what useful racial ends it serves. And the natural instinct is as true in its social as in its physiological expression. A woman's honour is in her husband; her status, her social life, are determined by his; and even the few women who, having made a bad marriage, have nerve and character enough to set themselves free from the personal association, are never able to thoroughly regain their maiden place. There is always something about them which clogs and fetters them; always a kind of doubtful and depressing aura that surrounds and influences them. If they have not strength to free themselves, they never cease to feel the mistake they have made, until the old sad process of degeneration is accomplished, and the 'grossness of his nature' has had strength to drag her down. After a time, if her ladyhood has been of a superficial kind only, a woman who has married beneath herself may ease down into her groove and be like the man she has married; if, however, she has sufficient force to resist outside influences she will not sink, and she will never cease to suffer. She has sinned against herself, her class and her natural instincts; and has done substantially a worse thing than has the boy who married his mother's maid. Society understands this, and not unjustly if harshly punishes the one while it lets the other go scot-free; so that the woman who makes a *mésalliance* suffers on every side, and destroys her life almost as much as the woman who goes wrong.

All this is as evident to parents and elders as that the sun shines. They understand the imperative needs of social life, and they know how fleeting are the passions of youth and how they fade by time and use and inharmonious conditions; and they feel that their first duty to their children is to prevent a *mésalliance* which has nothing, and can have nothing, but passion for its basis. But novelists and poets are against the hard dull dictates of worldly wisdom, and join in the apotheosis of love at any cost—all for love and the world well lost; love in a cottage, with nightingales and honeysuckles as the chief means of paying the rent; Libussa and her ploughman; the princess and the swineherd, &c. And the fathers who stand out against the ruin of their girls by means of estimable men of inferior condition and with not enough to live on, are stony-hearted and cruel, while the daughters who take to cold poison in the back-garden, if they cannot compass a secret honeymoon or an open flight, have all the world's sympathy and none of its censure. The cruel parent is the favourite whipping-boy of poetry and fiction; and yet which is likely to be the better guide— reason or passion? experience or ignorance? calculation or impulse? maturity which can judge or youth which can only feel? There would be no hesitation in any other case than that of love; but the love-instinct is generally considered to be superior to every other consideration, and has to be obeyed as a divine voice, no matter at what cost or consequence.

The ideal of life, according to some, is founded on early marriages. But men are slower in the final setting of their character than women, and one never knows how a young fellow of twenty or so will turn out. If he is devout now, he may be an infidel at forty; if, under home influences, he is temperate and pure, when these are withdrawn he may become a rake of the fastest kind. His temper, morals, business power, ability to resist temptation, all are as yet inchoate and undefined; nothing is sure; and the girl's fancy that makes him perfect in proportion to his good looks, is a mere instinct determined by chance association.

A girl, too, has more character than she shows in her girlhood. Though she sets sooner than men, she does not set unalterably, and marriage and maternity bring out the depths of her nature as nothing else can. It is only common-sense, then, to marry her to a man whose character is already somewhat formed, rather than to one who is still fluid and floating.

It is all very well to talk of fighting the battle of life together, and welding together by time. Many a man has been ruined by these metaphors. The theory, partly true and partly pretty, is good enough in its degree; and, indeed, so far as the welding goes, we weld together in almost all things by time. We wear our shoe till we wear it into shape and it ceases to pinch us; but, in the process, we go through a vast deal of pain, and are liable to make corns which last long after the shoe itself fits easily. We do not advocate the French system of marrying off our girls according to our own ideas of suitableness, and without consulting them; but we not the less think that, of all fatal social mistakes, *mésalliances* are the most fatal, and, in the case of women, to be avoided and prevented at any cost short of a broken heart or a premature death. And even death would sometimes be better than the life-long misery, the enduring shame and humiliation, of certain *mésalliances*.

WEAK SISTERS.

THE line at which a virtue becomes a vice through excess can never be exactly defined, being one of those uncertain conditions which each mind must determine for itself. But there is a line, wheresoever we may choose to set it; and it is just this fine dividing mark which women are so apt to overrun. For women, as a rule, are nothing if not extreme. Whether as saints or sinners, they carry a principle to its outside limits; and of all partizans they are the most thoroughgoing, whether it be to serve God or the devil, liberty or bigotry, Bible Communism or Calvinistic Election. Sometimes they are just as extreme in their absolute negation of force, and in the narrowness of the limits within which they would confine all human expression either by word or deed —and especially all expression of feminine life. These are the women who carry womanly gentleness into the exaggeration of self-abasement, and make themselves mere footstools for the stronger creature to kick about at his pleasure; the weak sisters who think all self-reliance unfeminine, and any originality of thought or character an offence against the ordained inferiority of their sex. They are the parasitic plants of the human family, living by and on the strength of others; growths unable to stand alone, and, when deprived of their adventitious support, falling to the ground in a ruin perhaps worse than death.

It is sad to see one of these weak sisters when given up to herself after she has lived on the strength of another. As a wife, she was probably a docile, gentle kind of Medora—at least on the outside; for we must not confound weakness with amiability—suffering many things because of imperfect servants and unprofitable tradesmen, maybe because of unruly children and encroaching friends, over none of whom she had so much moral power as enabled her to hold them in check; but on the whole drifting through her days peacefully enough, and, though always in difficulties, never quite aground. She had a tower of strength in her husband, on whom she leaned for assistance in all she undertook, whether it were to give a dose of Dalby to the child, or a scolding to the maid, or to pronounce upon the soundness of two rival sects each touting for her soul. While he lived she obeyed his counsel—not always without a futile echo of discontent in her own heart—and copied his opinions with what amount of accuracy nature had bestowed on her; though it must be confessed more often making a travesty than a facsimile, according to the trick of inferior translators, and not necessarily better pleased with his opinions than with his counsels. For your weak sister is frequently peevish, and though unable to originate is not always ready to obey cheerfully; cheerfulness indeed being for the most part an attribute of power.

Still, there stood her tower of strength, and while it stood, she, the parasite growing round it, did well enough, and flourished with a pleasant semblance of individual life into the hollowness of which it was no one's business to inquire. But when the tower fell, where was the ivy ? The husband taken away, what became of the wife?—he who had been the life and she only the parasite. Abandoned to the poor resources of her own judgment she is like one suddenly thrown into deep water, not knowing how to swim. She has no judgment. She has been so long accustomed to rely on the mind of another, that her will is paralyzed for want of use. She is any one's tool, any one's echo, and worse than that, if left to herself she is any one's victim. All she wants is to be spared the hardship of self-reliance and to be directed free of individual exertion. She is utterly helpless—helpless to act, to direct, to decide ; and it depends on the mere chance of proprietorship whether her slavery shall be degradation or protection, ruin or safety. For she will be a slave, whosoever may be her proprietor ; being the pabulum of which slaves and victims are naturally formed. The old age of Medora is Mrs. Borradaile, who, if her husband had lived, would have probably ended her life in an honourable captivity and a well-directed subserviency.

We often see this kind of helpless weakness in the daughter of a man of overbearing will, or of a termagant mother fond of managing and impatient of opposition. During the plastic time of her life, when education might perhaps have developed a sufficient amount of mental muscle, and a course of judicious moulding might have fairly set her up, she is snubbed and suppressed till all power is crushed out of her. She is taught the virtue of self-abnegation till she has no self to abnegate; and the backbone of her individuality is so incessantly broken that at last there is no backbone left in her to break. She has become a mere human mollusc which, when it loses its native shell, drifts helplessly at the mercy of chance currents into the maw of any stronger creature that may fancy it for his prey. One often sees these poor things left orphans and friendless at forty or fifty years of age. They have lived all their lives in leading-strings, and now are utterly unable to walk alone. They are infants in all knowledge of the world, of business, of human life; their youth is gone, and with it such beauty and attractiveness as they might have had, so that men who liked them when fresh and gentle at twenty do not care to accept their wrinkled helplessness at forty. They have been kept in and kept down, and so have made no friends of their own; and then, when the strong-willed father dies and the termagant mother goes to the place where the wicked cease from troubling, the mollusc these have hitherto protected is left defenceless and alone.

If she has money, her chances of escape from the social sharks always on the look-out for fat morsels are very small indeed. It is well if she falls into no worse hands than those of legitimate priests of either section, whether enthusiastic for chasubles or crazy for missions; and if her money is put to no baser use than supplying church embroidery for some Brother Ignatius at home, or blankets for converted Africans in the tropics. It might go into Agapemones, into spiritual Athenæums, into Bond Street back-parlours, where it certainly would do no good, take it any way one would; for, as it must go into some side-channel dug by stronger hands than hers, the question is, into which of the innumerable conduits offered for the conveyance of superfluous means shall it be directed?

This is the woman who is sure to go in for religious excess of one kind or another, and for whom therefore, a convent with a sympathetic director is a godsend past words to describe. She is unfit for the life of the world outside. She has neither strength to protect herself, nor beauty to win the loving protection of men; she cannot be taken as a precious charge, but she will be made a pitiable victim; and, though matins and vespers come frightfully often, surely the narrow safety of a convent-cell is a better fate for her than the publicity of the witness-box at the Old Bailey! As she must have a master, her condition depends on what master she has ; and the whole line of her future is ruled according to the fact whether she is directed or 'exploited,' and used to serve noble ends or base ones.

As a mother, the weak sister is even more unsatisfactory than as a spinster left to herself with funds which she can manipulate at pleasure. She is affectionate and devoted ; but of what use are affection and devotion without guiding sense or judgment ? Even in the nursery, and while the little ones need only physical care, she is more obstructive than helpful, never having so much self-reliance nor readiness of wit as to dare a remedy for one of those sudden maladies, incidental to children, which are dangerous just in proportion to the length of time they are allowed to run unchecked. And if she should by chance remember anything of therapeutic value, she has no power to make her children take what they don't like to take, nor do what they don't like to do. In the horror of an accident she is lost. If her child were to cut an artery, she would take it up into her lap tenderly enough, but she would never dream of stopping the flow ; if it swallowed poison, she would send for the doctor who lives ten miles away ; and if it set itself on fire, she would probably rush with it into the street, for the chance of assistance from a friendly passer-by. She never has her senses under serviceable command ; and her action in a moment of danger generally consists in unavailing pity or in obstructive terror, but never in useful service nor in valuable suggestion.

But if useless in her nursery while her children are young, she is even more helpless as they get older; and the family of a weak woman grows up, unassisted by counsel or direction, just as the old Adam wills and the natural bent inclines. Her girls may be loud and fast, her sons idle and dissipated, but she is powerless to correct or to influence. If her husband does not take the reins into his own hands, or if she be a widow, the young people manage matters for themselves under the perilous guidance of youthful passions and inexperience. And nine times out of ten they give her but a rough corner for her own share. They have no respect for her, and, unless more generously compassionate than young people usually are, scarcely care to conceal the contempt they cannot help feeling. What can she expect? If she was not strong enough to root out the tares while still green and tender, can she wonder at their luxuriant growth about her feet now? She, like every one else, must learn the sad meaning of retribution, and how the weakness which allowed evil to flourish unsubdued has to share in its consequences and to suffer for its sin.

Unsatisfactory in her home, the weak sister does not do much better in society. She is there the embodiment of restriction. She can bear nothing that has any flavour or colour in it. Topics of broad human interest are forbidden in her presence because they are vulgar, improper, unfeminine. She takes her stand on her womanhood, and makes that womanhood to be something apart from humanity in the gross. There must be no cakes and ale for others if she be virtuous ; and spades are not to be called spades when she is by to hear. She is the limit beyond which no one must go, under pain of such displeasure as the weak sister can show. And, weak as she is in many things, she can compass a certain strength of displeasure ; she can condemn, persistently if not passionately.

Nothing is more curious than the way in which the weak sister exercises this power of condemnation, and nothing much more wide than its scope. If incapable of yielding to certain temptations, because incapable of feeling them, she has no pity for those who have not been able to resist ; yet, on the other hand, she cannot comprehend the vigour of those who withstand such influences as conquer her. If she be under the shadow of family protection, safe in the power of those who know how to hold her in all honour and prosperity, she cannot forgive the poor weak waif—no weaker than herself !—who has been caught up in the outside desert of desolation, and made to subserve evil ends. Yet, on the other hand, for the woman who is able to think and act for herself she has a kind of superstitious horror ; and she shrinks from one who has made herself notorious, no matter what the mode or method, as from something tainted, something unnatural and unwomanly. She has even grave doubts respecting the lawfulness of doing good if the manner of it gets into the papers and names are mentioned as well as things ; and though the fashion of the day favours feminine notoriety in all directions, she holds by the instinct of her temperament, and languidly maintains that woman is the cipher to which man alone gives distinctive value. Griselda and Medora are the types to her of womanly perfection ; and the only strength she tolerates in her own sex is the strength of endurance and the power of patience. She has no doubt in her own mind that the ordained purpose of woman is to be convenient for the highhandedness and brutality of man ; and any woman who objects to this theory, and demands a better place for herself, is flying in the face of Providence and forfeiting one of the distinctive privileges of her sex. For the weak sister thinks, like some others, that it is better to be destroyed by orthodox means than to be saved by heterodox ones ; and that if good Christians uphold moral suttee, they are only pagans and barbarians who would put out the flames and save the victim from the burning. So far she is respectable, in that she has a distinct theory about something ; but it is wonderfully eloquent of her state that it should only be the theory of Griseldadom as womanly perfection, and the beauty to be found in the moral of Cinderella sitting supinely among the ashes, and forbidden to own even the glass-pper that belonged to her. Fortunately for the world, the weak sister and her theories do not rule. Indeed we are in danger of going too much the other way in these times, and the revolt of our women against undue slavery goes very near to a revolt against wise submission. Still, women who are to be the mothers of men ought to have some kind of power, if the men are to be worth their place in the world; and if we want creatures with backbones we must not give our strength to rearing a race of molluscs.

PINCHING SHOES.

THERE are two ways of dealing with pinching shoes. The one is to wear them till you get accustomed to the pressure, and so to wear them easy ; the other is to kick them off and have done with them altogether. The one is founded on the accommodating principle of human nature by which it is enabled to fit itself to circumstances, the other is the high-handed masterfulness whereby the earth is subdued and obstacles are removed ; the one is emblematic of Christian patience, the other of Pagan power. Both are good in certain states and neither is absolutely the best for all conditions. There are some shoes indeed, which, do what we will, we can never wear easy. We may keep them well fixed on our feet all our life, loyally accepting the pressure which fate and misfortune have imposed on us ; but we go lame and hobbled in consequence, and never know what it is to make a free step, nor to walk on our way without discomfort. Examples abound ; for among all the pilgrims toiling more or less painfully through life to death, there is not one whose shoes do not pinch him somewhere, how easy soever they may look and how soft soever the material of which they may be made.

Even those proverbial possessors of roomy shoes, the traditional King and Princess, have their own little private bedroom slippers which pinch them, undetected by the gaping multitude who measure happiness by lengths of velvet and weight of gold embroidery; and the envied owners of the treasure which all seek and none find might better stand as instances of sorrow than of happiness—examples of how badly shod poor royalty is, and how, far more than meaner folk, it suffers from the pinching of its regal shoes.

The uncongeniality of a profession into which a man may have been forced by the injudicious overruling of his friends, or by the exigencies of family position and inherited rights, is one form of the pinching shoe by no means rare to find. And here, again, poor royalty comes in for a share of the grip on tender places, and the consequent hobbling of its feet. For many an hereditary king was meant by nature to be nothing but a plain country gentleman at the best—perhaps even less; many, like poor 'Louis Capet,' would have gone to the end quite happily and respectably if only they might have kicked off the embroidered shoes of sovereignty and betaken themselves to the highlows of the herd—if only they might have exchanged the sceptre for the turning-lathe, the pen or the fowling-piece. 'Je déteste mon métier de roi,' Victor Emmanuel is reported to have siad to a republican friend who sympathized with the monarch's well-known tastes in other things beside his hatred of the kingly profession; and history repeats this frank avowal in every page. But the purple is as hard to be got rid of as Deianeira's robe; for the most part carrying the skin along with it and trailed through a pool of blood in the act of transfer—which is scarcely what royalty, oppressed with its own greatness, and willing to rid itself of sceptre and shoes that it may enjoy itself in list-slippers after a more bourgeoise fashion, would find in accordance with its wishes.

Lower down in the social scale we find the same kind of misfit between nature and position as a very frequent occurrence—pinching shoes, productive of innumerable corns and tender places, being many where the feet represent the temperament and the shoes are the profession. How often we see a natural 'heavy' securely swathed in cassock and bands, and set up in the pulpit of the family church, simply because the tithes were large and the advowson was part of the family inheritance. But that stiff rectorial shoe of his will never wear easy. The man's secret soul goes out to the parade-ground and the mess-table. The glitter and jingle and theatrical display of a soldier's life seem to him the finest things in the whole round of professions, and the quiet uneventful life of a village pastor is of all the most abhorrent. He wants to act, not to teach. Yet there he is, penned in beyond all power of breaking loose on this side the grave; bound to drone out muddled sermons half an hour long and eminently good for sleeping draughts, instead of shouting terse and stirring words of command which set the blood on fire to hear; bound to rout the shadowy enemy of souls with weapons he can neither feel nor use, instead of prancing off at the head of his men, waving his drawn sword above his head in a whirlwind of excitement and martial glory, to rout the tangible enemies of his country's flag. He loves his wife and takes a mild parsonic pleasure in his roses; he energizes his schools and beats up recruits for his parish penny readings; he lends his pulpit to missionary delegates and takes the chair at the meeting for the conversion of Jews; he does his duty, poor man, so far as he knows how and so far as nature gave him the power; but his feet are in pinching shoes all his life long, and no amount of walking on the clerical highway can ever make them pleasant wearing. Or he may have a passionate love for the sea, and be mewed up in a lawyer's musty office where his large limbs have not half enough space for their natural activity; where he is perched for twelve hours out of the twenty-four on a high stool against a desk instead of climbing cat-like up the ropes; and where he is set to engross a longwinded deed of conveyance, or to make a fair copy of a bill of costs, instead of bearing a hand in a gale and saving his ship by pluck and quickness. He could save a ship better than he can engross a deed; while, as for law, he cannot get as much of that into his heavy brain as would enable him to advise a client on the simplest case of assault; but he knows all the differences of rig, and the whole code of signals, and can tell you to a nicety about the flags of all nations, and the name and position of every spar and stay and sheet, and when to reef and when to set sail, with any other nautical information to be had from books and a chance cruise as far as the Nore. That pen behind his ear never ceases to gall and fret; his shoe never ceases to pinch; and to the last day of his life the high stool in the lawyer's office will be a place of penance and the sailor's quarter-deck the lost heaven of his ambition.

No doubt, by the time the soldier wrongly labelled as a parson or the sailor painfully working the legal treadmill, comes to the end of his career, the old shoe which has pinched him so long will be worn comparatively easy. The gradual decay of manly vigour, and the slow but sure destruction of strong desires, reduce one's feet at last to masses of accommodating pulp; but what suffering we go through before this result can be attained!—what years of fruitless yearning, of fierce despair, of pathetic self-suppression, of jarring discord between work and fitness, pound all the life out of us before our bones become like wax and pinching shoes are transformed to easy-fitting slippers! For itself alone, not counting the beyond to which the hope clings, it would scarcely seem that such a life were worth the living.

Another pinching shoe is to be found in climate and locality. A man hungering for the busy life of the city has to vegetate in the rural districts, where the days drop one after the other like leaden bullets, and time is only marked by an accession of dulness. Another, thirsting for the repose of the country, has to jostle daily through Cheapside. To one who thinks Canadian salmon-fishing the supreme of earthly happiness, fate gives the chance of chasing butterflies in Brazil; to another who holds 'the common objects of the seashore' of more account than silver and gold, an adverse fortune assigns a station in the middle of a plain as arid as if the world had been made without water; and a third, who cares for nothing but the free breathing of the open moors or the rugged beauty of the barren fells, is dropped down into the heart of a narrow valley where he cannot see the sun for the trees. At first this matter of locality seems to be but a very small grip on the foot, not worth a second thought; but it is one of a certain cumulative power impossible to describe, though keen enough to him who suffers; and the pinching shoe of uncongenial place is quite as hard to bear as that of uncongenial work.

Again, a man to whom intellectual companionship means more than it does to many is thrown into a neighbourhood where he cannot hope to meet with comprehension, still less with sympathy. He is a Freethinker, and the neighbourhood goes in for the strictest Methodism or the highest ultra-Ritualism; he is a Radical, and he is in the very focus of county Toryism, where the doctrine of equality and the rights of man is just so much seditious blasphemy, while the British Constitution is held as a direct emanation from divine wisdom second only to the Bible; or he is a Tory to the backbone—and his backbone is a pretty stiff one—and he is in the midst of that blatant kind of Radicalism which thinks gentlehood a remnant of the dark ages, and confounds good breeding with servility, and loyalty to the Crown with oppression of the people. Surrounded by his kind, he is as much alone as if in the middle of a desert. An Englishman among Englishmen, he has no more mental companionship than if he were in a foreign country where he and his neighbour spoke different tongues, and each had a set of signs with not two agreeing. And this kind of solitude makes a pinching shoe to many minds; though to some of the more self-centred or defying kind it is bearable enough—perhaps even giving a sense of roominess which closer communion would destroy.

Of course one of the worst of our pinching shoes is matrimony, when marriage means bondage and not union. The mismated wife or husband never leaves off, willingly or unwillingly, squeezing the tender places; and the more the pressure is objected to the worse the pain becomes. And nothing can relieve it. A country gentleman, hating the dust and noise of London, with all his interest in his county position and all his pleasure in his place, and a wife whose love lies in Queen's balls and opera-boxes, and to whom the country is simply a slice out of Siberia wherever it may be ; a hearty hospitable man, liking to see his table well filled, and a wife with a weak digestion, irritable nerves and a morbid horror of society ; a pushing and ambitious man, with a loud voice and an imposing presence, and a shrinking fireside woman, who asks only to glide unnoticed through the crowd and to creep noiselessly from her home to her grave—are not all these shod with pinching shoes, which, do what they will, go on pinching to the end, and which nothing short of death or the Sir James Hannen of the time can remove ? The pinching shoe of matrimony pinches both sides equally—excepting indeed, one of the two is specially phlegmatic or pachydermatous, and then the grip is harmless ; but, as a rule, the ring-fence of marriage doubles all conditions, and when A. walks hobbled, B. falls lame, and both suffer from the same misfit. However, the only thing to do is to bear and wear till the upper-leather yields or till the foot takes the required shape ; but there is an eternity of pain to be gone through before either of these desirable ends comes about ; and the instinct which dreads pain, and questions its necessity, is by no means a false one. For all that, we must wear our pinching shoes of matrimony till death or the Divorce Court pulls them from our feet ; which points to the need of being more careful than we usually are about the fit beforehand.

Poverty has a whole rack full of pinching shoes very hard to get accustomed to, and as bad to dance in lightly as were the fiery slippers of the naughty little girl in the German fairy-tale. Given a large heart, generous instincts and an empty purse, and we have the conditions of a real tragedy, both individual and social. For poverty does not mean only that elemental want of food and clothing which we generally associate with its name. Poverty may have two thousand a year as well as only a mouldy crust and three shillings a week from the parish ; and poverty cursing its sore feet in a brougham is quite as common as poverty, full of corns and callosities, blaspheming behind a costermonger's barrow. The shoe may pinch horribly, though there is no question of hunger or the 'twopenny rope ;' for it is all a matter of relative degree, and the means wherewith to meet wants. But as poverty is not one of those fixed conditions of human life which no human power can remove, we have not perhaps quite so much sympathy with its grips and pinches as in other things less remediable. For while there is work still undone in the world, there is gain still to be had. The man whose energies stagnate now in a dry channel can, if he will, turn them into one more fertile ; and if he is making but a poor business out of meal, it is his own fault if he does not try to make a better out of malt. Where the shoe pinches hardest is in places which we cannot protect and with a grip which we cannot prevent ; but we cannot say this of poverty as a necessary and inalienable condition, and sympathy is so much waste when circumstances can be changed by energy or will.

SUPERIOR BEINGS.

EVERY now and then one comes across the path of a Superior Being—a being who seems to imagine itself made out of a different kind of clay from that which forms the coarser ruck of humanity, and whose presence crushes us with a sense of our own inferiority, exasperating or humiliating, according to the amount of natural pride bestowed upon us. The superior being is of either sex and of all denominations; and its superiority comes from many causes—being sometimes due to a wider grasp of intellect, sometimes to a loftier standard of morals, sometimes to better birth or a longer purse, and very often to the simple conceit of itself which simulates superiority and believes in its own apery. The chief characteristic of the superior being is that exalted pity for inferiority which springs from the consciousness of excellence. In fact, one of the main elements of superiority consists in this sublime consciousness of private exaltation, and the immense interval that separates it from the grosser condition it surveys. Rivalry is essentially angry and contentious, but confessed superiority can afford to be serene and compassionate. The little people who live in that meagre sphere of theirs, mental and social, with which not one point of its own extended circle comes in contact, are deserving of all pity and are below anything like active displeasure. That they should be content with such a meagre sphere seems inconceivable to the superior being, as it contemplates its own enlarged horizon with the complacency proper to a dweller in vastness. Or it may be that its own world is narrow; and its superiority will then be that it is high, safe, exclusive, while its pity will flow down for those poor wayfarers who wander afield in broad latitudes, and know nothing of the pleasure found in reserved places. In any case the region in which a superior being dwells is better than the region in which any other person dwells.

Take a superior being who has made up a private account with truth, and who has, in his own mind at least, unlocked the gate of the great mysteries of life, and got to the back of that eternal Why? for ever confronting us. It does not in the least degree signify how the key is labelled. It may be High Church or Low Church, Swedenborgianism or Positivism. The name has nothing to do with the thing. It is the contented certainty of having unlocked that great gate at which others are hammering in vain which confers the superiority, and how the thing has been done does not affect the result. Neither does it disturb the equanimity of the superior being when he meets with opposing superior beings who have also made up their private accounts with truth, but in quite another handwriting and with a different sum-total at the bottom of the page; who have also unlocked the gate of the great mysteries, but with a key of contradictory wards, while the gate itself is of another order of architecture altogether. But then nothing ever does disturb the equanimity of the superior being; for, as he is above all rivalry, so is he beyond all teaching. The meeting of two superior beings of hostile creed is like the meeting of the two blind kings in the story, each claiming the crown for his own and both ignorant of the very existence of a rival. It may be that the superior being has soared away into the cold region of spiritual negation, whence he regards the praying and praising multitudes who go to church and believe in Providence as grown people regard children who still believe in ghosts and fairies. Or it may be that he has plunged into the phosphorescent atmosphere of mysticism and an all-pervading superstition; and then all who hold by scientific law, and who think the test of common sense not absolutely valueless, are Sadducees who know nothing of the glorious liberty of the light, but who prefer to live in darkness and to make themselves the agents of the great Lord of Lies.

Sometimes the superior being goes in for the doctrine of love and impulse, as against reason or experience, holding the physiologist and political economist as creatures absolutely devoid of feeling; and sometimes his superiority is shown in the application of the hardest material laws to the most subtle and delicate manifestations of the mind. But on which side soever he ranks himself—as a spiritualist to whom reason and matter are stumbling-blocks and accursed, or as a materialist denying the existence of spiritual influences at all—he is equally secure of his own superiority and serene in his own conceit. That there should be two sides to any question never seems to strike him; and that a man of another creed should have as much right as himself to a hearing and consideration is the one hard saying impossible for him to receive. With a light and airy manner of playful contempt—sometimes with a heavy and Johnsonian scorn that keeps no terms with an opponent—the superior being meets all your arguments or batters down all your objections; sometimes, indeed, he will not condescend even so far as this, but when you express your adverse opinion just lifts up his eyebrows with a good-humoured kind of surprise at your mental state, but lets you see that he thinks you too hopeless, and himself too superior, to waste powder and shot upon you. It is of the nature of things that there should be moles and that there should be eagles; so much the worse for the moles, who must be content to remain blind, not seeing things patent to the nobler vision.

The superior being is sometimes a person who is above all the passions and weaknesses of ordinary men; a philosopher, or an etherealized woman dwelling on serene Olympian heights which no clouds obscure and where no earth-fogs rise. The passions which shake the human soul, as tempests shake the forest trees, and warp men's lives according to the run of their own lines, are unknown to these Olympian personages who cannot understand their power. They look on these tempestuous souls with a curious analytical gaze, speculating on the geography of their Gethsemane, and wondering why they cannot keep as calm and quiet as they themselves are. They sit in scornful judgment on the mysterious impulses regulating human nature—regulating and disturbing—and think how perfect all things would be if only passions and instincts were cut out of the great plan, and men and women were left to the dominion of pure reason. But they do not take into account the law of constitutional necessity, and they are utterly unable to strike a balance between the good and evil wrought both by the tempests of souls and by those of nature. They only know that storms are inconvenient, and that for themselves they have no need of such convulsions to clear off stagnant humours; nor are they made of elements which kindle and explode at the contact of such or such materials. And if they know nothing of all this, why then should others? If they can sit on Olympian heights serene above all passion, why should not the whole world sit with them, and fogs and fires, earthquakes and deluges, be conditions unknown?

When this kind of superior being is a woman, there is something pretty in the sublime assumption of her supremacy and the sweeping range of her condemnation. Sheltered from temptation and secure from danger, she looks out on life from the serene heights of her safe place, and wonders how men can fail and women fall before the power of trials of which she knows only the name. Her circulation is languid and her temperament phlegmatic; and the burning desire of life which sends the strong into danger, perhaps into sin, is as much unknown to her as is the fever of the tropics to a Laplander crouching in his snow-hut. But she judges none the less positively because of her ignorance; and, as she looks into your quivering face with her untroubled eyes, lets you see plainly enough how she despises all the human frailties under which you may have tripped and stumbled. Sometimes she rebukes you loftily. Your soul is sore with the consciousness of your sin, your heart is weak with the pain of life; but the superior being tells you that repentance cannot undo the evil that has been done, and that to feel pain is weak.

The superiority which some women assume over men is very odd. It is like the grave rebuke of a child, not knowing what it is that it rebukes. When women take up their parable and censure men for the wild or evil things they do, not understanding how or why it has come about that they have done them, and knowing as little of the inner causes as of the outer, they are in the position of superior beings talking unmitigated rubbish. To be sure, it is very sweet and innocent rubbish, and has a lofty air about it that redeems what else would be mere presumption ; but there is no more practical worth in what they say than there is in the child's rebuke when its doll will not stand upright on sawdust legs, nor eat a crumb of cake with waxen lips. This is one reason why women of the order of superior beings have so little influence over men ; they judge without knowledge and condemn without insight. If they could thoroughly fathom man's nature, so as to understand his difficulties, they would then have moral power if their aims were higher than his, their principles more lofty, their practice more pure. As it is, they have next to none ; and the very men who seem to yield most go only so far as to conceal what the superior being disapproves of ; they do not change because of her greater weight of doctrine.

Men show themselves as superior beings to women on another count—intellectually, rather than morally. While women rebuke men for their sins, men snub women for their follies ; the one wields the spiritual, the other the intellectual, weapon of castigation, and both hold themselves superior, beyond all possibility of rivalry, according to the chance of sex. The masculine view of a subject always imposes itself on women as something unattainable by the feminine mind. Nine times out of ten it brings them to a due sense of their own inferiority, save in the case of the superior being, to whom of course the masculine view counts for nothing against her own. But even when women do not accept a man's opinions, they instinctively recognize his greater value, his greater breadth and strength. Perhaps they cry out against his hardness, if he is a political economist and they are emotional; or against his lower morality if he goes in for universal charity and philosophical latitudinarianism, and they are enthusiasts with a clearly-defined faith and a belief in its infallibility. These are wide tracts of difference between the two minds, not to be settled by the *ipse dixit* of even a superior being; but in general the superiority of the man makes itself more felt than the superiority of the woman. While one preaches, the other ridicules; and snubbing does more than condemnation.

FEMININE AMENITIES.

A MAN's foes are those of his own household, and the keenest enemies of women are women themselves. No one can inflict such humiliation on a woman as can a woman when she chooses; for if the art of high-handed snubbing belongs to men, that of subtle wounding is peculiarly feminine, and is practised by the best-bred of the sex. Women are always more or less antagonistic to each other. They are gregarious in fashions and emulative in follies, but they cannot combine; they never support their weak sisters; they shrink from those who are stronger than the average; and if they would speak the truth boldly, they would confess to a radical contempt for each other's intellect—which perhaps is the real reason why the sect of the 'emancipated' commands so small a following.

Half a dozen ordinary men advocating 'emancipation' doctrines would do more towards leavening the whole bulk of womankind than any number of first-class women. Where these do stand by each other it is from instinctive or personal affection rather than from class solidarity. And this is one of the most striking distinctions of sex, and one cause, among others, why men have the upper hand, and why they are able to keep it. Certainly there are reasons, sufficiently good, why women do not more readily coalesce; and one is the immense difference between the two extremes—the silly being too silly to appreciate the wise, and the weak too weak to bear the armour of the strong. There is more difference between outsiders among women than there is among men; the feminine characteristic of exaggeration making a gap which the medium or average man fills. The ways of women with each other more than all else show the great difference between their *morale* and that of men. They flatter and coax as men could not do, but they are also more rude to each other than any man would be to his fellow. It is amazing to see the things they can do and will bear—things which no man would dream of standing and which no man would dare to attempt. This is because they are not taught to respect each other, and because they have no fear of consequences. If one woman is insulted by another, she cannot demand satisfaction nor knock the offender down; and it is unladylike to swear and call names. She must bear what she can repay only in kind; but, to do her justice, she repays in a manner undeniably effective and to the point.

There is nothing very pronounced about the feminine modes of aggression and retaliation; and yet each is eloquent and sufficient for its purpose. It may be only a stare, a shrug, a toss of the head; but women can throw an intensity of disdain into the simplest gesture which answers the end perfectly. The unabashed serenity and unflinching constancy with which one woman can stare down another is in itself an art that requires a certain amount of natural genius, as well as careful cultivation. She puts up her eyeglass—not being shortsighted—and surveys the enemy standing two feet from her, with a sublime contempt for her whole condition, or with a still more sublime ignoring of her sentient existence, that no words could give. If the enemy be sensitive and unused to the kind of thing, she is absolutely crushed, destroyed for the time, and reduced to the most pitiable state of self-abasement. If she be of a tougher fibre, and has had some experience of feminine warfare, she returns the stare with a corresponding amount of contempt or of obliviousness; and from that moment a contest is begun which never ceases and which continually gains in bitterness. The stare is the weapon of offence most in use among women, and is specially favoured by the experienced against the younger and less seasoned. It is one of the instinctive arms native to the sex; and we have only to watch the introduction of two girls to each other to see this, and to learn how even in youth is begun the exercise which time and use raise to such deadly perfection.

In the conversations of women with each other we again meet with examples of their peculiar amenities to their own sex. They never refrain from showing how much they are bored; they contradict flatly, without the flimsiest veil of apology to hide their rudeness; and they interrupt ruthlessly, whatever the subject in hand may be. One lady was giving another a minute account of how the bride looked yesterday when she was married to Mr. A., of somewhat formidable boudoir repute, with whom her listener had had sundry tender passages which made the mention of his marriage a notoriously sore subject. 'Ah! I see *you* have taken that old silk which Madame Josephine wanted to palm off on me last year,' said the tortured listener brusquely breaking into the narrative without a lead of any kind. And the speaker was silenced. In this case it was the interchange of doubtful courtesies, wherein neither deserved pity; but to make a disparaging remark about a gown, in revenge for turning the knife in a wound, was a thoroughly feminine manner of retaliation, and one that would not have touched a man. Such shafts fall blunted against the rugged skin of the coarser creature; and the date or pattern of a bit of cloth would not have told much against the loss of a lover. But as most women passionately care for dress, their toilet is one of their most vulnerable parts. Ashamed to be unfashionable, they tolerate anything in each other rather than shabbiness or eccentricity, even when picturesque; hence a sarcastic allusion to the age of a few yards of silk as a set-off against a grossly cruel stab was a return wound of considerable depth cleverly given.

The introduction of the womankind belonging to a favourite male acquaintance of somewhat lower social condition affords a splendid opportunity for the display of feminine amenity. The presentation cannot be refused, yet it is resented as an intrusion. 'Another daughter, Mr. C.! You must have a dozen daughters surely,' a peeress said disdainfully to a commoner whom personally she liked, but whose family she did not want to know. The poor man had but two; and this was the introduction of the second.

Very painful to a high-spirited gentlewoman must be the way in which a superior creature of this kind receives her, if not of the same set as herself. The husband of the inferior creature may be adored, as men are adored by fashionable women who love only themselves, and care only for their own pleasures. Artist, man of letters, *beau sabreur*, he is the passing idol, the temporary toy, of a certain circle; and his wife has to be tolerated for his sake, and because she is a lady and fit to be presented, though an outsider. So they patronize her till the poor woman's blood is on fire; or they snub her till she has no moral consistency left in her, and is reduced to a mere mass of pulp. They keep her in another room while they talk to her husband with their other intimates; or they admit her into their circle, where she is made to feel like a Gentile among the faithful, for either they leave her unnoticed altogether or else speak to her on subjects quite apart from the general conversation, as if she were incapable of understanding them on their own ground. They ask her to dinner without her husband, and take care that there is no one to meet her whom she would like to see; but they ask him when they are at their grandest, and express their deep regret that his wife (uninvited) cannot accompany him. They know every turn and twist that can humiliate her if she has pretensions which they choose to demolish. They praise her toilet for its good taste in simplicity, when she thinks she is one of the finest on an occasion on which no one can be too fine. They tell her that pattern of hers is perfect, and made just like the dear duchess's famous dress last season, when she believes that she has Madame Josephine's last, freshly imported from Paris. They celebrate her dinner as the very perfection of a refined family dinner without parade or cost, though it has all been had from the crack confectioner's, and though the bill for the entertainment will cause many a day of family pinching. These are the things which women say to one another when they wish to pain and humiliate; things which pain and humiliate some more than would a positive disgrace. For some women are distressingly sensitive about these little matters. Their lives are made up of trifles, and a failure in a trifle is a failure in their object of life.

Women can do each other no end of despite in a small way in society, not to speak of mischief of a graver kind. A hostess who has a grudge against one of her more famous lady-guests can always ensure her a disappointing evening under cover of doing her supreme honour and paying her extra attention. If she sees the enemy engaged in a pleasant conversation with one of the male stars, down she swoops, and in the sweetest manner possible carries her off to another part of the room, to introduce her to some school-girl who can only say yes or no in the wrong places—'who is dying for the honour of talking to you, my dear;' or to some unfledged stripling who blushes and grows hot and cannot stammer out two consecutive sentences, but who is presented as a rising genius and to be treated with the consideration due to his future. As her persecution is done under the guise of extra friendliness, the poor victim cannot cry out, nor yet resist; but she knows that whenever she goes to Mrs. So and So's she will be seated next the stupidest man at table, and prevented from talking to any one she likes in the evening; and that every visit to that lady is made in some occult manner unpleasant to her. And yet what has she to complain of? She cannot complain in that her hostess trusts to her for help in the success of her entertainment, and moves her about the room as a perambulating attraction which she has to dispense fairly among her guests, lest some should be jealous of the others. She may know that the meaning is to annoy; but who can act on meaning as against manner? How crooked soever the first may be, if the last is straight the case falls to the ground, and there is no room for remonstrance.

Often women flirt as much to annoy other women

as to attract men or amuse themselves. If a wife has crossed swords with a friend, and the husband is in any way endurable, let her look out for retaliation. The woman she has offended will take her revenge by flirting more or less openly with the husband, all the while loading the enemy with flattery if she be afraid of her, or snubbing her without much disguise if she feel herself the stronger. The wife cannot help herself, unless things go too far for public patience. A jealous woman without proof is the butt of her society, and brings the whole world of women like a nest of wasps about her ears. If wise, she will ignore what she cannot laugh at ; if sensitive, she will fret ; if vindictive, she will repay. Nine times out of ten she does the last, and, may be, with interest ; and so goes on the duel, though all the time the fighters appear to be intimate friends and on the best possible terms together.

But the range of these feminine amenities is not confined to women ; it includes men as well ; and women continually take advantage of their position to insult the stronger sex by saying to them things which can be neither answered nor resented. A woman can with the quietest face and the gentlest voice imaginable insinuate that you have just cheated at cards ; she can give you the lie direct as coolly as if she were correcting a misprint ; and you cannot defend yourself. To brawl with her would be unpardonable ; to contradict her is useless ; and the sense of society does not allow you to show her any active displeasure. In this instance the weaker creature is the stronger, and the more defenceless is the safer. You have only the rather questionable consolation of knowing that you are not singular in your discomfiture, and that when she has made an end of you she will probably have a turn with your betters, and make them too, dance to her piping, whether they like the tune or not. At all events, if she humiliates you she humiliates her sisters still more ; and with the knowledge that, hardly handled as you have been, others are yet more severely dealt with, you must learn to be content, and to practise as much of that grim kind of patience, which suffers keenly and bears silently, as your nature will permit.

GRIM FEMALES.

ALMOST all histories and mythologies embody the idea of a race of grim females. Whether as fabulous and complex monsters, like the Sphinx and the Harpies, or in the more human forms of the Fates and the Furies, unsexed women have been universally recognized as forming part of the system of nature and to be accepted among the stranger manifestations of human life. Yet it is hard to understand why they should exist at all. As moral 'sports,' they are so far interesting to the psychologists; but, as women with definite duties and fixed functions, nothing can be less admirable. They are even worse than effeminate men—which is saying everything.

The grim female must be carefully distinguished from the masculine woman; for they are by no means essentially the same, though the types may run into each other, and sometimes do. But the masculine woman, if not grim but only Amazonian, has often much that is fine and beautiful in her, as we see in her great prototype Pallas Athene; but the grim female *pur sang* is never noble, never beautiful ; and the only meaning of her existence—the only mission she seems sent into the world to fulfil—is that of serving as a warning to the young what to avoid.

The grim female is not necessarily an old maid, as would appear likely at first sight. We find her of all conditions indifferently—as maid, wife, widow, as mother and childless alike—and we do not find that her condition in any way affects her character. If born grim, she remains grim to the end ; and neither marriage nor motherhood modifies her. The grim female of novelists is generally an old maid ; but she is a caricature, painted in the broadest lines and copied from the outsides of things. She is emphatically an odd woman ; odd in her dress, her mode, her state. She wears a flapping cap, skimpy skirts and rusty brown mittens on her bony hands. She has a passionate aversion against men and matrimony ; and she lives queerly behind a barricaded house-door, with a small slavey, or an elderly female afflicted with deafness, to do her work and bear the brunt of her temper. But she is always odd, unmarried, unfashionable and unlike everybody else, and could never be mistaken for an ordinary woman from the first phrase which stamps her personality on the page to the last paragraph of her fictitious existence.

Now the grim female of real life may be one of the most conventional of her sex, and in fact, she generally is one of the most conventional of her sex. She is one who rules her household with a rod of

GRIM FEMALES.

iron carefully wrought after the pattern of her neighbours' rods, and to whom a dish set awry, or the second-best china instead of the best, counts for as great a moral delinquency in her servants as a breach of all the Ten Commandments together. She is a woman who regards being out of the fashion, or being foremost in the fashion, as equally reprehensible, and to whom dress is among the most important matters of life. Wherefore she is notorious for a certain grim grandeur of style, as one who respects herself by her clothes, and is known among other women as possessing handsome lace and costly velvet in profusion. Are not lace and velvet *de rigueur* for women of condition? and what is the grim female but the embodiment of the 'rigour of the game' in all matters? Therefore she clothes herself sumptuously, without elegance or taste; and would as soon be seen abroad in her dressing-gown and slippers as without her characteristic heavy velvet or rustling silk. But the artist's little wife, in her fresh muslin and nice admixture of colours, sails round her for grace and beauty at about one-twentieth part of what the grim female's stately ugliness has cost.

One characteristic of the grim female is her want of womanly passion for children. She may have so much maternal instinct, perverted, as to be on friendly terms with a dog or two, a cat, or may be a cockatoo; but she has no real affection for children, no comprehension of child-nature, and the 'sublime nonsense' of the nursery is a thing unknown to her from first to last. If she have children of her own, she treats them in a hard wooden way that has nothing of the ideal mother about it. She generally sees that they are properly cared for, because she is a disciplinarian; but, though she is inexorable on the score of cold baths and 'no trash,' she never condescends to the weakness of love. If her little ones are sick, they are set aside and dosed until they are well; if they are naughty, they are punished; but they never know those moments of tender indulgence which help them over a period of indisposition not severe enough for actual doctoring, yet throwing them out of gear and inducing a spell of what ignorance calls naughtiness. Rhadamanthus was a weakling compared to the grim female in the nursery; and what she is in her nursery she continues to be in the schoolroom, and the drawing-room to follow. Her children are always causes of annoyance to the grim female, and the first stirrings of individuality, the first half-unconscious trials of their young strength, are offences she cannot away with. Children and inferiors are they in her eyes, even when grown up and married; and she exacts from them the humility and deference of their lower condition. Hence she is one to whom the present generation is undeniably worse than the past; one who groans over the follies and shortcomings of the times and who thinks that good conduct died out with her own youth, and that it is not likely, by the look of things, to be restored. In fact, youth itself is the root and basis of offence; and if she coerces children, she tyrannizes over girls and snubs young men, with inexorable impartiality.

The grim female is not necessarily a strong-minded woman, nor a learned woman, like those who wear spectacles, go to scientific meetings and are great in the classics and the 'ologies. She may be of the emancipated class; it all depends on chance; and a grim female, when of the emancipated, is a very formidable person indeed. But she is not necessarily one of these. On the contrary, part of her very grimness comes from her intense conservatism and uncompromising conventionality. Nothing is so abhorrent to her as innovation or novelty in any shape. She does not hold with any one out of the narrowest groove of respectable belief, in what direction soever the diverging line may go. A Romanist or a Baptist, a Jew or an infidel, it is all one to her; each is equally dreadful to her, and each is eternally foredoomed. She is of the orthodox Church without fal-lals; as far removed from Ritualism as she is from ranting, and demanding for herself that infallibity of judgment and absolute possession of the truth which she denies to the Pope and all his Cardinals. Beware how you broach new doctrines in her presence. She has been known before now to abjure her nearest relations for no greater moral lapse than a weak belief in globules; while, as for anything like graver aberrations, say on the ape theory or on the plurality of races, on development in religions or on a republican form of government, she has no toleration whatever. If the Smithfield fires existed at the present day, the grim female would be the first to light the faggots. It is all the same if she belongs to any Dissenting persuasion; part of her grimness coming from her intolerance, and her own beliefs being simply the springboard on which she stands.

Many causes produce the grim female. It may be that she is grim from social pride as well as from natural hardness. If she has been used to live with people whom, rightly or wrongly, she considers her inferiors, she will probably queen it over them in a very unmistakeable manner. The prelatic blood is renowned for this sort of thing; and a bishop's daughter, or an archbishop's grand-daughter, or Mrs. Proudie, prelatic by marriage only, if of the grim class, is one of the grimmest of her class. The halo of sanctity round the mitre and the crozier will be greater in her eyes than even the glitter of the strawberry leaves; and she holds herself consecrated by her birth or marriage to the understanding of every moral question, and specially to the final settlement of every tough theological position. Or she may be grim because of her isolation and meagre intercourse with the world at large; such as she is found in the remoter districts. This kind comes into the exceptional or novelist's class, and is often more masculine than grim. These are the women who hunt and fish and shoot like men, and who may be found in all weathers wandering alone about the mountains in short petticoats and spatterdashes—women who affect to be essentially mannish in person, habits and attire, and who may be quite jolly easy-going fellows in their own way, or else grim and trenchant, as nature or the fit takes them. This is a kind not at all uncommon in country places among the higher class of resident ladies—ladies who are so highly placed locally that they can afford to disregard public opinion, and who are so independent by disposition that they naturally go off to the manly side, and make themselves bad imitations, as the best they can do.

The grim female tries her strength with all newcomers. She is like one of the giants or black knights of old romance, who lived in castles or caves, whence they pounced on all passers-by, and either wrung their necks if they conquered or retreated howling if discomfited. This is what the grim female does in her degree. She dashes on all who are presented to her, and has a passage of arms as the first act of the new drama. If her opponents yield out of timidity or good-breeding, or perhaps from not understanding the warlike nature of the encounter, she puts her foot on them forthwith, and ignominiously crushes them; if they defy her, and give her back blow for blow, ten to one she cuts them and becomes their enemy for ever after. For she has not breadth enough to be magnanimous, and the one thing she never forgives is successful opposition. Very grim is she in the presence of human weakness, moral and physical. Woe to that unhappy maid of hers who has slipped on the narrow path of prudence! She will be turned out to perish with no more compunction than if she were a black-beetle to be swept out of the way.

As a nurse the grim female is precise, punctual, obedient to orders, but inexorable. She would give the patient a fit of nervous hysterics which would throw him back for a week, rather than allow him five minutes' grace in the matter of a painful operation or a nauseous draught. Without variableness or weakness herself, she cannot endure it in others, and whosoever comes under her hand must be content to remain in shape, and to keep himself well braced up to the utmost rigidity of duty. If she had to lose an arm or a leg, she would go to her trouble like a Trojan; and why not others? She would merely tighten her lips and hold her breath, and then would sit down to let herself be hacked and mangled without a groan or a word. To judge by the notice given of her in her sister's life, Emily Brontë was of the grim class, and about the grimmest for her age and state that could well be found. Had she lived, and lived unsoftened, she would have been one unbroken mass of iron and granite, without a soft spot anywhere. Her very love was fiercer than other women's hate; her strength was more terrible than a man's anger; her passions were as fiery as furnace flames. Of all the examples we could cite, she seems about the fittest for our model.

GRIM FEMALES.

A grim female has no mercy. She may be just, but if so, it is in a hard uncompromizing way that makes her justice worse than others' partiality. For justice can be sympathetic, even if unwavering ; and the grim female is never sympathetic, how painful soever the work on hand and the sentence to be executed. Neither is she gay ; for she is not plastic enough to be either one or the other. She is run into an iron mould, where her nature is compressed as in a vice ; and she allows of no expansion, no lipping over, no bursting of bonds anyhow.

What would become of us if all our women were like her ? Without any of the feminine little weaknesses at which we have our laugh yet which we do not wholly dislike—without any of the pretty coaxing ways which we know warp our better judgment and take us out of the strict course ; and yet how pleasant that warping process is !—without any even of the transient petulances which give so much light and shade to a woman's character, the grim female stands like an old-world Gorgon, turning living flesh and blood to stone. When we look at her we are inclined to forgive all the smallness and silliness which sometimes vex us in the ordinary woman, and to think that there are worse things than the love of dress for which we so often reproach our wives and daughters ; that flirting, which is reprehensible no doubt, might be exchanged for something even more reprehensible ; and that vanity, of the giggling, coquettish kind, though to be steadily discouraged and sternly reproved, is not quite the worst feminine thing after all. Surely not ! A grim female who cannot flirt nor giggle nor cry, nor yet kiss and make up again when scolded, is far away a worse kind of thing than a feather-headed little puss who is always doing wrong by reason of her foolish brain, but who manages somehow to pull herself right because of her loving heart. Weak women, vain women, affected women, and the whole class of silly women, whatever the speciality of silliness exhibited, are tiresome enough, heaven knows ; but, unsatisfactory as they are, they are better than the grim female—that woman of no sex, born without softness or sympathy and living without pity and without love.

MATURE SIRENS.

NOTHING is more incomprehensible to girls than the love and admiration sometimes given to middle-aged women. They cannot understand it ; and nothing but experience will ever make them understand it. In their eyes, a woman is out of the pale of personal affection altogether when she has once lost that shining gloss of youth, that exquisite freshness of skin and suppleness of limb, which to them, in the insolent plenitude of their unfaded beauty, constitute the chief claims to admiration of the one sex from the other. And yet they cannot conceal from themselves that the pretty maid of eighteen is often deserted for the handsome woman of forty, and that the patent witchery of their own youth and brilliant colouring goes for nothing against the mysterious charms of a mature siren. What can they say to such an anomaly ? There is no good in going about the world disdainfully wondering how on earth a man could ever have taken up with such an antiquated creature !—suggestively asking their male friends what could he see in a woman of her age, old enough to be his mother ? There the fact stands ; and facts are stubborn things. The eligible suitor who has been coveted by more than one golden-haired girl has married a woman twenty years her senior, and the middle-aged siren has quietly carried off the prize which nymphs in their teens have frantically desired to win. What is the secret ? How is it done ? The world, even of silly girls, has got past any belief in spells and talismans, such as Charlemagne's mistress wore, and yet the man's fascination seems to them quite as miraculous and almost as unholy as if it had been brought about by the black art. But if they had any analytical power they would understand the *diablerie* of the mature siren clearly enough ; for it is not so difficult to understand when one puts one's mind to it.

In the first place, a woman of ripe age has a knowledge of the world, and a certain suavity of manner and moral flexibility, wholly wanting to the young. Young girls are for the most part all angles —harsh in their judgments, stiff in their prejudices, narrow in their sympathies. They are full of combativeness and self-assertion if they belong to one type of young people, or they are stupid and shy if they belong to another type. They are talkative with nothing to say, and positive with nothing known ; or they are monosyllabic dummies who stammer out Yes or No at random, and whose brains become hopelessly confused at the first sentence with which the stranger, to whom they have just been introduced, attempts to open a conversation. They are generally without pity; their want of experience making them hard towards sorrows which they do not understand —let us charitably hope also making them ignorant of the pain they inflict. That famous article in the *Times* on the cruelty of young girls, *àpropos* of Constance Kent's confession, though absurdly exaggerated, had in it the core of truth which gives the sting to such papers, which makes them stick, and which is the real cause of the outcry they create.

Girls are cruel; there is no question about it. If passive rather than active, they are simply indifferent to the sufferings of others; if of a more active temperament, they find a positive pleasure in giving pain. A girl will say horribly cruel things to her dearest friend, then laugh at her because she cries. Even her own mother she will hurt and humiliate if she can; while, as for any unfortunate aspirant not approved of, were he as tough-skinned as a rhinoceros she would find means to make him wince. But all this acerbity is toned down in the mature woman. Experience has enlarged her sympathies, and knowledge of suffering has softened her heart to the sufferings of others. Her lessons of life too, have taught her tact; and tact is one of the most valuable lessons that a man or woman can learn. She sees at a glance the weak points and sore places in her companion, and she avoids them; or if she passes over them, it is with a hand so soft and tender, a touch so soothing, that she calms instead of irritating. A girl would have come down on those weak places heavily, and would have torn off the bandages from the sore ones, jesting at scars because she herself had never felt a wound, and deriding the sybaritism of diachylon because ignorant of the anguish it conceals.

Furthermore, the mature siren is thoughtful for others. Girls are self-asserting and aggressive. Life is so strong in them, and the instinct which prompts them to try their strength with all comers and to get the best of everything everywhere, is so irrepressible, that they are often disagreeable because of that instinctive selfishness, that craving, natural to the young, of taking all and giving back nothing. But the mature siren knows better than this. She knows that social success entirely depends on what each of us can throw into the common fund of society; that the surest way to win consideration for ourselves is to be considerate for others; that sympathy begets liking, and self-suppression leads to exaltation; and that if we want to gain love we must first show how well we can give it. Her tact then, and her sympathy, her moral flexibility and quick comprehension of character, her readiness to give herself to others, are some of the reasons, among others, why the society of a cultivated agreeable woman of a certain age is sought by those men to whom women are more than mere mistresses or toys. Besides, she is a good conversationalist. She has no pretensions to any special or deep learning —for, if pedantic, she is spoilt as a siren at any age —but she knows a little about most things; at all events, she knows enough to make her a pleasant companion in a *tête-à-tête* or at a dinner-table, and to enable her to keep up the ball when thrown. And men like to talk to intelligent women. They do not like to be taught nor corrected by them, but they like that quick sympathetic intellect which follows them readily, and that amount of knowledge which makes a comfortable cushion for their own. And a mature siren who knows what she is about would never do more than this, even if she could.

Though the mature siren rests her claims to admiration on more than mere personal charms, and appeals to something beyond the senses, yet she is personable and well preserved, and, in a favourable light, looks nearly as young as ever. So the men say who knew her when she was twenty; who loved her then, and have gone on loving her, with a difference, despite the twenty years which lie between this and then. Girls, indeed, despise her charms because she is no longer young; and yet she may be even more beautiful than youth. She knows all the little niceties of dress, and, without going into the vulgar trickery of paint and dyes—which would make her hideous—is up to the best arts of the toilet by which every point is made to tell and every minor beauty is given its fullest value. For part of the art and mystery of sirenhood is an accurate perception of times and conditions, and a careful avoidance of that suicidal mistake of which *la femme passée* is so often guilty—namely, setting herself in confessed rivalry with the young by trying to look like them, and so losing the good of what she has retained, and betraying the ravages of time by the contrast.

The mature siren is wiser than this. She knows exactly what she has and what she can do; and before all things avoids whatever seems too youthful for her years; and this is one reason why she is always beautiful, because always in harmony. Besides, she has very many good points, many positive charms still left. Her figure is still good—not slim and slender certainly, but round and soft, and with that slower, riper, lazier grace which, quite different from the antelope-like elasticity of youth, is in its own way as lovely. If her hair has lost its maiden luxuriance she makes up with crafty arrangements of lace, which are more picturesque than the fashionable wisp of hay-like ends tumbling half-way to the waist. She has still her white and shapely hands with their pink filbert-like nails; still her pleasant smile and square small teeth—those one or two new, matching so perfectly with the old as to be undiscoverable! Her eyes are bright yet, and if the upper muscles are a little shrunk, the consequent apparent enlargement of the orbit only makes them more expressive; her lips are not yet withered; her skin is not wrinkled. Undeniably, when well-dressed and in a favourable light, the mature siren is as beautiful in her own way as the girlish belle; and the world knows it and acknowledges it.

That mature sirens can be passionately loved,

even when very mature, history gives us more than one example; and the first name that naturally occurs to one's mind is that of the too famous Ninon de l'Enclos. And Ninon, if a trifle mythical, was yet a fact and an example. But not going quite to Ninon's age, we often see women of forty and upwards who are personally charming, and whom men love with as much warmth and tenderness as if they were in the heyday of life—women who count their admirers by dozens, and who end by making a superb marriage, and having quite an Indian summer of romance and happiness. The young laugh at this idea of the Indian summer for a bride of forty-five; but it is true; for neither romance nor happiness, neither love nor mental youth, is a matter of years; and after all we are only as old as we feel, and certainly no older than we look.

All women do not harden by time, nor wither, nor yet corrupt. Some merely ripen and mellow and get enriched by the passage of the years, retaining the most delicate womanliness—we had almost said girlishness—into quite old age, blushing as swiftly under their grey hairs, while shrinking from anything coarse or vulgar or impure as sensitively, as when they were girls. *La femme à quarante ans* is the French term for the opening of the great gulf beyond which love cannot pass; but human history disproves this date, and shows that the heart can remain fresh and the person lovely long after the age fixed for the final adieu to admiration—that the mature siren can be adored by her own contemporaries when the rising generation regard her as nothing better than a chimney-corner fixture. Mr. Trollope recognized the claims of the mature siren in his *Orley Farm* and *Miss Mackenzie*; and no one can deny the intense naturalness of the characters and the interest of the stories.

Another point which tells with the mature woman is, that she is not jealous nor exacting. She knows the world, and takes what comes with that philosophy which springs from knowledge. If she be of an enjoying nature—and she cannot be a siren else—she accepts such good as floats to the top, neither looking too deep into the cup nor speculating on the time when she shall have drained it to the dregs. Men feel safe with her. If they have entered on a tender friendship with her, they know that there will be no scene, no tears, no upbraidings, when an inexorable fate comes in to end their pleasant little drama, with the inevitable wife as the scene-shifter. The mature siren knows so well that fate and the wife must break in between her and her friend, that she is resigned from the first to what is foredoomed, and thus accepts her bitter portion, when it comes, with dignity and in silence. Where younger women would fall into hysterics and make a scene, perhaps go about the world taking their revenge in slander, the middle-aged woman holds out a friendly hand and takes the back seat gallantly, never showing by word nor look that she has felt her deposition. She becomes the best friend of the new household; and if any one is jealous, ten to one it is the husband who is jealous of her love for his wife. Of course it may be the wife herself, who cannot see what her husband can find to admire so much in Mrs. A , and who pouts at his extraordinary predilection for her, though of course she would scorn to be jealous—as, indeed, she has no cause. For even a mature siren, however delightful she may be, is not likely to come before a young wife in the heart of a young husband. Though the French paint the love of a woman of forty as pathetic, because slightly ridiculous and certainly hopeless, yet they arrange their theory of social life so that a youth is generally supposed to make his first love of a married woman many years his elder, while a mature siren finds her last love in a youth.

We have not come to this yet in England, either in theory or practice ; and it is to be hoped that we never shall come to it. Mature sirens are all very well for men of their own age, and it is pleasant to see them still loved and admired, and to recognize in them the claims of women to something higher than mere personal passion ; but the case would be very different if they became ghoulish seducers of the young, and kept up the habit of love by entangling boyish hearts and blighting youthful lives. As they are now, they form a charming element in society, and are of infinite use to the world. They are the ripe fruit in the garden where else everything would be green and immature—the last days of the golden summer set against the disappointing backwardness of spring and before the chills of autumn have come. They contain in themselves the advantages of two distinct epochs, and while possessing as much personal charm as youth, possess also the gains which come by experience and maturity. They keep things together as the young could not do ; and no gathering of friends is perfect which has not one or two mature sirens to give the tone, and prevent excesses. They soften the asperities of high-handed boys and girls, which else would be too biting ; and they set people at ease, and make them in good humour with themselves, by the courtesy with which they listen to them and the patience with which they bear with them. Even the very girls who hate them fiercely as rivals love them passing well as half maternal, half sisterly, companions ; and the first person to whom they would carry their sorrows would be a mature siren, quite capable for her own part of having caused them.

It would be hard indeed if the loss of youth did not bring with it some compensations ; but the mature siren suffers less from that loss than any other kind of woman. Indeed, she seems to have a private elixir of her own which is not quite drained dry when she dies, beloved and regretted, at threescore years and ten ; leaving behind her one or two old friends who were once her ardent lovers, and who still cherish her memory as that of the finest and most fascinating woman they ever knew—something which the present generation is utterly incapable of repeating.

PUMPKINS.

PUMPKINS are among the most imposing of all groundling growths. They have fine showy flowers, handsome leaves, roving stems, and they bear solid-looking fruit of a goodly size and gorgeous colour. To see them spreading over their domain with such rapid luxuriance, one would imagine them among the best things growing; but a critical examination proves their flesh to be about three parts water, while as for their stalks, they are of so pithless a nature that they can only creep along the earth, unable to stand upright without support;—which tells something against the pumpkin's claim for extra consideration. Still, their showy largeness attracts the eye, and not a few of us believe in pumpkins, and admire both their mode of growth and the fruit resulting. In like manner the human pumpkins—those beings of imposing presence and loud self-assertion—get themselves believed in by the simple; and, as occasions by which their watery and fibreless nature is revealed do not arise every day, they are for the most part accepted for the substantialities they assume to be, and the world is deceived by appearances as it ever has been.

These human pumpkins abound everywhere. In all states and professions, and in both sexes, we find them flourishing magnificently on the face of the earth, taking the lead in their society and setting themselves out as the finest fellows to be found in their respective gardens. Among them are the men of the Bombastes type, so dear to the older playwrights; braggadocios of the kill 'em and eat 'em school, who were such terrible fellows to look at and listen to, though only pumpkins of a singularly innocuous nature when stoutly squeezed and analyzed; fire-eaters of the juggling kind, with special care taken that the fire shall be harmless and that the danger shall lie only in the fear of the spectators. Now that duelling has gone out of fashion, and discharged captains who have signalized themselves in war are rare, our old swashbuckler type of pumpkins has gone out both in fact and fiction, on the stage and off it. To be sure we have a few travellers of slightly apocryphal courage, and more than doubtful accuracy, whose books of perilous adventure and breathless dangers are to us what Bombastes and Bobadil were to our fathers; and we have Major Wellington de Boots with his military swagger and his hare's heart. But he is a very weak imitation of the old fire-eater; and, on the whole, this special family of the pumpkins has dwindled into insignificance, and their place knows them no more.

Then there is the pumpkin after the cut of the Prince Regent—the man of deportment, big, handsome, showy, and specially noticeable for a loud voice, a broad chest, and an indescribable air of superiority and command; the man who has studied bowing as one of the fine arts, who walks with a swagger, and even now tips his curly-brimmed hat slightly to the side. This is the kind of man who influences women. Bombastes frightens the nervous and inexperienced of his own sex, but the man of deportment partly fascinates and partly overawes the other. They take him at his own valuation, and have not skill enough to find out the flaw in the summing up until perhaps it is too late, when they have come so near to him that they are able to appraise him for themselves, and have learnt by bitter experience of what unsound materials he is made. And then let him look out. There is nothing women resent so much as pumpkin manhood—nothing which humiliates them more in their own esteem than to discover that they have been taken in by appearances, and that what they had believed in as solid wood turns out to be only squash.

Women like to rely on men, and dread nothing so much as weakness and vacillation in their male protectors; save indeed those grim and bulky females in whom Hood so much delighted, who take small men *vi et armis*, and subjugate them body and soul, like two-legged poodles trained to fetch and carry at the word of command. But these are exceptions; the average woman prizing strength rather than poodle-like docility. The pumpkin of the Prince

Regent cut is generally notorious for laying down the law on all points. His voice is so loud and his manner of speech so dictatorial, that no one dreams of doubting still less of contradicting him, but everybody takes him as he represents himself to be—a man of prompt decision, of boundless resources, a granitic tower of strength to be leant against in all emergencies without the slightest fear of failure ; a man who is not only sufficient for himself but strong enough to bear the weaknesses of others. He is famous for giving advice—advice of a vague, rapid, sprawling kind, never quite exact to the circumstances, never quite practical nor to the point—large advice, general in scope but wonderfully positive in tone, and, until you analyze, grandly imposing in effect. Nail him to the point ; ask his advice seriously on any question where the responsibility of counsel will rest with him ; place yourself in his hands where the consequences of failure will touch him as well as you ; and then see to what meagre dimensions your goodly gourd will shrink. The confident assertion drops into a weak hesitation ; the arrogant dictum melts into a timid refusal to take such a serious responsibility on himself ; you have pricked your windbag, bisected your pumpkin, and henceforth you know the precise weight of substance remaining. Yet mankind sees him exactly where he was before, and he will go about the world in his large, loud way, saying to every one that if you had followed his advice you would have succeeded—supposing you have failed ;

or, if you have succeeded, he will take all the credit to himself, and say it was he who guided you and showed you how to go in and win. For himself, and his own affairs, he has no more moral stamina than he had leadership for you and yours. The least reverse knocks him over. Care or sorrow, when it touches him, shrivels him up as completely as frost shrivels up the pumpkin. In every circumstance requiring promptitude, coolness, keen perception, just decision, our swaggering man of froth fails ignominiously; and one hour of real pressure proves incontestably that he was only a pumpkin of imposing presence, good neither as meat nor staff when the time of trial came.

Very often the pumpkin has a wife whose fibre is as close as his is loose, and whose nature is as tough as his is soft; a hard-eyed, thin-lipped, tenacious woman, who speaks little and boasts not at all, but who does all she wishes to do, and whose iron will pins her pumpkin to the wall as the spear of the Bushman pins the elephant or the rhinoceros. It is very curious to see how a blatant blustering man who is so loud and confident abroad, knocks under at home; and how the high-crested deportment which carries things with such a lofty bearing out of doors droops into the meek submission of the hen-pecked husband so soon as the house-door closes on him, and he is subjected to the pitiless analysis of home. There is no question of flourish then; and if by chance the ambitious crest should make an effort to display itself, the wife knows how to lower it by a few decisive words of a keen-edged kind, and her pumpkin is made to feel sharply enough the difference existing between fibre and pulp. It is almost melancholy to see one of these fine flourishing fellows so subdued. Pumpkin as he may be, it is not pleasant to see him so cut down in his pride; and involuntarily one's sympathies go with him rather than with that tenacious, hard-mouthed wife of his, who would be none the worse perhaps for a little of her husband's essential softness and with less than her own hardness.

How often too, these big fellows have no physical stamina as well as but very shaky moral fibre! A small, wiry light-weight will do twice as much as they; not, of course, where muscle only is wanted, but where the question is of endurance. Large heavy men knock up far sooner than the light-weights; and though size and weight count for something at certain times and on occasions, fibre and tenacity go for more in the long run. In the Crimea, the men who first dropped off from exposure and privation were the magnificently-built Guardsmen—men apparently bred and fed to the highest point of physical perfection; while the undersized little liners, who had nothing to be admired in them, stood the strain gamely, and were brisk and serviceable when the others were either dead or in hospital. So far as we have gone yet, we have not solved the problem of how to combine toughness and bigness, solidity and size, but for the most part fail in the one in proportion as we succeed in the other.

Many of the dark-skinned races are what we may call emotional pumpkins. Their flashing black eyes and swarthy skins seem to be instinct with passion; they look like living furnaces filled with flames and molten metal, terrible fellows, dangerous to meddle with and almost impossible to subdue. But nine times out of ten we find them to be marvellously meek persons, timid, amenable to law, unable to give offence and incapable of taking it—lambs masquerading in tiger-skins. A fair-faced Anglo-Saxon, with his sensitive blush, good-humoured smile and light blue eyes, has more pluck and pith in him than a whole brigade of certain of these dark-skinned men. He has less ferocity perhaps than they when they are thoroughly roused, though our good-humoured Anglo-Saxon is by no means destitute of ferocity on occasions when his blood is up; but his is ferocity of the quarter-staff and bludgeon stand-up fight kind—the ferocity of strength fairly put out against an adversary, not the tigerish cruelty which is almost always found when moral weakness and physical submission have a momentary triumph and reaction. Cowardly men are like women in their revenge when once they get the upper hand; and their revenge is more cruel than that of the habitually brave man who, after a fair fight, overthrows his opponent. Some of the dark-skinned races look the very ideal of the melodramatic ruffian—operatic brigands painted with broad black lines, and up to any amount of deeds of daring and of crime ; but they are only pumpkins at the core. We need not go so far as Calcutta to find them ; we get examples nearer home, both in Houndsditch and in Rome ; for both Jews and Italians are soft-cored men in spite of their passionate outsides, and both would be better for an extra twist and toughness in their fibres.

Intellectual pumpkins are as common as those of the more specially physical kind. You meet with philosophers and 'thinkers'—perhaps they are poets, perhaps politicians—who flourish out a vague big declamation which, when you reduce it to its essence, you find to be a platitude worth nothing ; whipped cream, without any foundation of solid pudding. If they are of the philosophic sort, they quote you Fichte and Hegel, to the bewilderment of your brains unless you have gone into the metaphysical maze on your own account ; but they might have put all they have said into half a dozen words of three letters, like a child's first reading lesson. The flourish imposes, and people who cannot analyze take the whipped cream for solid pudding, and think that platitudes dressed in the garb of Fichte and Hegel are utterances worthy of deep respect and admiring wonder.

All the professions which talk, either by word of mouth or in print, are specially given to this manifestation of pumpkinhood. Preachers and authors sprawl and flourish over their small inheritance with a tremendous assumption of vital force and vigorous growth; and weak hands, with weaker heads, find support and shelter in their foliage. Poets too, with a knack for turning out large moulds in which they have run very small ideas, are pumpkins dear to the feminine mind. Have we not our Tupper? had we not our 'Satan' Montgomery? and a few others whom we might catalogue if we cared for the task, each with his multifarious female following and his spiritual harem of ardent admirers? All artists—that is, the men who create, or rather who assume to create—are liable to be proved pumpkins when called on to show themselves solid wood. They talk grandly enough, but when they have to translate their words into deeds, too often the noble aims and immortal efforts they have been advocating tail off into pulp and water, and we have botches and pot-boilers instead of masterpieces and high art. Perhaps we may take it as a rule that all doers who talk much and boast grandly are of the pumpkin order, and that art, like nature, elaborates best in silence.

Strong-visaged women are often pure pumpkins with a very rough and corrugated outside. It is astonishing how soon they break down, and for all their stern and powerful looks sink under burdens under which a frail little creature, as light as thistledown, will glide along quite easily. Women with black brows and harsh voices—brigandesses by appearance, or like the typical Herodias of unimaginative artists —are often the gentlest and most pithless of their sex, and may be seen acting quite compassionately towards their infants, or vindicating their womanhood by meekly sewing on their husbands' buttons and weeping at their rebukes; while a fair, silver-tongued, languid lady, as soft as if she were made of nothing harder than the traditional cream and rose-leaves, will give up her babies as a prey to unfeeling nurses and let her husband go buttonless and in rags, while she lounges before the fire indifferent to his wrath and callous to his wrongs. There is many a house mistress who looks as if she could use her fists when annoyed, who is absolutely afraid of her servants; and the maid is always the mistress when the one is fibre and the other pulp.

Heaven be praised that the strong-visaged women are not 'clear grit' all through. If they were as hard as they look, the world would go but queerly, and society would have to make new laws for the protection of its weaker male members. But nature is merciful as well as sportive, and while she amuses herself by creating pumpkins of formidable aspect, takes care that the core shall not always correspond to the rind. Like the Athenian images of the satyr which enclosed a god, the black-browed brigandesses and the men of magnificent deportment are sometimes impostors of a quite amiable kind; and when you have once learnt by heart the false analogies of form, you will cease to fear your typical Herodias, to be impressed by your copy of the Prince Regent, or to be influenced by your wordy Hegelian talking platitudes in the philosophic dialect.

WIDOWS.

THERE are widows and widows; there are those who are bereaved and those who are released; those who lose their support and those whose chains are broken; those who are sunk in desolation and those who wake up into freedom. Of the first we will not speak. Theirs is a sorrow too sacred to be publicly handled even with sympathy; but the second demand no such respectful reticence. The widow who is no sooner released from one husband than she plots for another, and the widow who leaps into liberty over the grave of a gaoler, not a lover, are fair game enough. They have always been favourite subjects whereon authors may exercise their wits; and while men are what they are—laughing animals apt to see the humour lying in incongruity, and with a spice of the devil to sharpen that same laughter into satire—they will remain favourite subjects, tragic as the state is when widowhood is deeper than mere outward condition.

There are many varieties of the widow and all are not beautiful. For one, there is the widow who is bent on re-marrying whether men like it or not;

that thing of prey who goes about the world seeking whom she may devour; that awful creature who bears down on her victims with a vigour in her assaults which puts to flight the popular fancy about the weaker sex and the natural distribution of power. No hawk poised over a brood of hedge birds, no shark cruising steadily towards a shoal of small fry, no piratical craft sailing under a free flag and accountable to no law save success, was ever more formidable to the weaker things pursued than is the hawk widow to men when she is bent on re-marrying. She knows so much!—there is not a manœuvre by which a victory can be stolen that she has not mastered and she is not afraid of even the most desperate measures. When she has once struck, he would be a clever man and a strong one who should escape her. Generally left but meagrely provided for in worldly goods—else her game would not be difficult—she makes up for her financial poverty by her wealth of bold resources, and by the courage with which she takes her own fortunes in hand and, with her own, those of her more eligible masculine associates. She is a woman of purpose and lives for an end; and that end is re-marriage, with the most favourable settlement that can be obtained by her lawyer from his. If fate has dealt hardly by her—though, may be, compassionately by her successive spouses—and has landed her in the widowed state twice or thrice, she is in nowise daunted and as little abashed. She merely refits after a certain time of anchorage, and goes out into the open again for a repetition of her chance. She has no notion of a perpetuity of weeds, and, though she may have cleared her half century with a margin besides, thinks the suggestive orange-blossoms of the bride infinitely more desirable than the fruitless heliotrope of the widow. If one husband is taken, she remembers the old proverb, and reflects on the many, quite as good, who are left potentially subject to her choice. And somehow she manages. It has been said that any woman can marry any man if she determines to do so, and follows on the line of her determination with tenacity and common-sense.

The hawk widow exemplifies the truth of this saying. She determines upon marriage; and she usually succeeds; the question being one of victim only, not of sacrifice. One has to fall to her share; there is no help for it; and the whole contest is, which shall it be? which is strongest to break her bonds? which craftiest to slip out of them? which most resolute not to bear them from the beginning? This the straggling covey must settle among themselves the best way they can. When the hawk pounces down upon its quarry, it is *sauve qui peut*! But all cannot be saved. One has to be caught; and the choice is determined partly by chance and partly by relative strength. When the widow of experience and resolve bears down on *her* prey, the result is equally certain. Floundering avails nothing; struggling and splashing are just as futile; one among the crowd has to come to the slaughter, like Mrs. Bond's ducks, and to assist at his own immolation. The best thing he can do is to make a handsome surrender, and to let the world of men and brothers believe he rather likes his position than not.

But there are pleasanter types of the re-marrying widow than this. There is the widow of the Wadman kind, who has outlived her grief and is not disinclined to a repetition of the matrimonial experiment, if asked humbly by an experimenter after her own heart. But she must be asked humbly that she may grant in a pretty, tender, womanly way—if not quite so timidly as a girl, yet as becomingly in her degree, and with that peculiar fascination which nothing but the combination of experience and modesty can give. The widow of the Wadman kind is no creature of prey, neither shark nor hawk; at the worst she is but a cooing dove, making just the sweetest little noise in the world, the tenderest little call to indicate her whereabouts, and to show that she is lonely and feels a-cold. She sits close, waiting to be found, and does not ramp and dash about like the hawk sisterhood; neither does she pretend that she is unwilling to be found, still less deny that a soft warm nest, well lined and snugly sheltered, is better than a lonely branch stretching out comfortless and bare into the bleak wide world. She, too, is almost sure to get what she wants, with the advantage of being voluntarily chosen and not unwillingly submitted to.

This is the kind of woman who is always mildly

but thoroughly happy in her married life ; unless indeed her husband should be a brute, which heaven forefend. She lives in peace and bland contentment while the fates permit, and when he dies she buries him decently and laments him decorously ; but she thinks it folly to spend her life in weeping by the side of his cold grave, when her tears can do no good to either of them. Rather she thinks it a proof of her love for him, and the evidence of how true was her happiness, that she should elect to give him a successor. Her blessed experience in the past has made her trustful of the future ; and because she has found one man faithful she thinks that all are Abdiels. As a rule, this type of woman does find men pleasant; and by her own nature she ensures domestic happiness. She is always tenderly, and never passionately, in love, even with the husband she has loved the best. She gives in to no excesses to the right nor to the left. Her temperament is of that serene moonlight kind which does not fatigue others nor wear out its possessor. Without ambition or the power to fling herself into any absorbing occupation, she lives only to please and be pleased at home ; and if she be not a wife, wearing her light fetters lovingly and proud that she is fettered, she is nothing. As some women are born mothers and others are born nuns, so is the Wadman woman a born wife, and shines in no other character nor capacity. But in this she excels ; and knowing this, she sticks to her *rôle*, how frequently so ever the protagonist may be changed.

There are widows, however, who have no thought nor desire for remaining anything but widows—who have gained the worth of the world in their condition. 'Jeune, riche, et veuve—quel bonheur!' says the French wife, eyeing 'mon mari' askance. Can the most exacting woman ask for more? And truly such a one is in the most enviable position possible to a woman, supposing always that she has not lost in her husband the man she loved. If she has lost only the man who sat by right at the same hearth with herself—perhaps the man who quarrelled with her across the ashes—she has lost her burden and gained her release.

The cross of matrimony lies heavy on many a woman who never takes the world into her confidence, and who bears in absolute silence what she has not the power to cast from her. Perhaps her husband has been a man of note, a man of learning, of elevated station, a political or a philanthropic power. She alone knew the fretfulness, the petty tyranny, the miserable smallness at home of the man of large repute whom his generation conspired to honour, and whose public life was a mark for the future to date by. When he died the press wrote his eulogy and his elegy; but his widow, when she put on her weeds, sang softly in her own heart a pæan to the great King of Freedom, and whispered to herself Laudamus with a sigh of unutterable relief. To such a woman widowhood has no sentimental regrets. She has come into possession of the goods for which perhaps she sold herself; she is young enough to enjoy the present and to project a future ; she has the free choice of a maid and the free action of a matron, as no other woman has. She may be courted and she need not be chaperoned, nor yet forced to accept. Experience has mellowed and enriched her ; for though the asperities of her former condition were sharp while they lasted, they have not permanently roughened nor embittered her. Then the sense of relief gladdens, while the sense of propriety subdues, her ; and the delicate mixture of outside melancholy, tempered with internal warmth, is wonderfully enticing. Few men know how to resist that gentle sadness which does not preclude the sweetest sympathy with pleasures in which she may not join—with happiness which is, alas ! denied her. It gives an air of such profound unselfishness; it asks so mutely, so bewitchingly, for consolation!

Even a hard man is moved at the sight of a pretty young widow in the funereal black of her first grief, sitting apart with a patient smile and eyes cast meekly down, as one not of the world though in it. Her loss is too recent to admit of any thought of reparation ; and yet what man does not think of that time of reparation ? and if she be more than usually charming in person and well dowered in purse, what man does not think of himself as the best repairer she could take ? Then, as time goes on and she glides gracefully into the era of mitigated grief, how beautiful is her whole manner, how tasteful her attire! The most exquisite colours of the prismatic scale look garish beside her dainty tints, and the untempered mirth of happy girls is coarse beside her subdued admission of moral sunshine. Greys as tender as a dove's breast; regal purples which have a glow behind their gloom; stately silks of sombre black softly veiled by clouds of gauzy white or brightened with the 'dark light' of sparkling jet—all speak of passing time and the gradual blooming of the spring after the sadness of the winter; all symbolize the flowers which are growing on the sod that covers the dear departed; all hint at a melting of the funereal gloom into the starlight of a possible bridal. She begins too to take pleasure in the old familiar things of life. She steals into a quiet back seat at the Opera; she just walks through a quadrille; she sees no harm in a fête or flower-show, if properly companioned. Winter does not last for ever; and a life-long mourning is a wearisome prospect. So she goes through her degrees in accurate order, and comes out at the end radiant.

For when the faint shadows cast by the era of mitigated grief fade away, she is the widow *par excellence*—the blooming widow, young, rich, gay, free; with the world on her side, her fortune in her hand, the ball at her foot. She is the freest woman alive; freer even than any old maid to be found. Freedom, indeed, comes to the old maid when too late to enjoy it; at least in certain directions; for while she is young she is necessarily in bondage, and when parents and guardians leave her at liberty, the world and Mrs. Grundy take up the reins and hold them pretty tight. But the widow is as thoroughly emancipated from the conventional bonds which confine the free action of a maid as she is from those which fetter the wife; and only she herself knows what she has lost and gained. She bore her yoke well while it pressed on her. It galled her but she did not wince; only when it was removed, did she become fully conscious of how great had been the burden, from her sense of infinite relief through her freedom. The world never knew that she had passed under the harrow; probably therefore it wonders at her cheerfulness, with the dear departed scarce two years dead; and some say how sweetly resigned she is, and others how unfeeling. She is neither. She is simply free after having lived in bondage; and she is glad in consequence. But she is dangerous. In fact, she is the most dangerous of all women to men's peace of mind. She does not want to marry again —does not mean to marry again for many years to come, if ever; granted; but this does not say that she is indifferent to admiration or careless of men's society. And being without serious intentions herself, she does not reflect that she may possibly mislead and deceive others who have no such cause as she has to beware of the pleasant folly of love and its results.

In the exercise of her prerogative as a free woman, able to cultivate the dearest friendships with men and fearlessly using her power, she entangles many a poor fellow's heart which she never wished to engage more than platonically, and crushes hopes which she had not the slightest intention to raise. Why cannot men be her friends? she asks, with a pretty, pleading look—a tender kind of despair at the wrongheadedness of the stronger sex. But, tender as she is, she does not easily yield even when she loves. The freedom she has gone through so much to gain she does not rashly throw away; and if ever the day comes when she gives it up into the keeping of another—and for all her protestations it comes sometimes—the man to whom she succumbs may congratulate himself on a victory more flattering to his vanity, and more complete in its surrender of advantages, than he could have gained over any other woman. Belle or heiress, of higher rank or of greater fame than himself, no unmarried woman could have made such a sacrifice in her marriage as did this widow of means and good looks, when she laid her freedom, her joyous present and potential future, in his hand. He will be lucky if he manages so well that he is never reproached for that sacrifice—if his wife never looks back regretfully to the time when she was a widow—if there are no longing glances forward to possibilities ahead, mingled with sighs at the difficulty of retracing a step when made. On the whole, if a woman can live without love, or with nothing stronger than a tender sentimental friendship, widowhood is the most blissful state she can attain. But if she be of a loving nature and fond of home, finding her own happiness in the happiness of others and indifferent to freedom—thinking, indeed, that feminine freedom is only another word for desolation—she will be miserable until she has doubled her experience and carried on the old into the new.

DOLLS.

THE love of dolls is instinctive with girl children; and a nursery without some of these silent simulacra for the amusement of the little maids is a very lifeless affair. But outside the nursery door dolls are stupid things enough; and, whether improvised of wisped-up bundles of rags or made of the costliest kind of composition, they are at the best mere pretences for the pastime of babies, not living creatures to be loved nor artistic creations to be admired. Certainly they are pretty in their own way, and some are made to simulate human actions quite cleverly; and one of their charms with children is that they can be treated like sentient beings without a chance of retaliation. They can be scolded for being naughty; put to bed in broad daylight for a punishment; seated in the corner with their impassive faces turned to the wall, just as the little ones themselves are dealt with; the doll all the time smiling exactly as it smiled before, its round blue beads staring just as they stared before; neither scolding nor cornering making more impression on its sawdust soul than do little missy's sobs and tears when nurse is cross and dolly is her only friend. But the child has had its hour of play and make-believe sentiment of companionship and authority; and so, if the doll can do no good of itself, it can at least be the occasion of pleasantness to others.

Now there are women who are dolls in all but the mere accident of material. The doll proper is a simple structure of wax or wood, 'its knees and elbows glued together;' and the human doll is a complex machine of flesh and blood. But, saving such structural differences, these women are as essentially dolls as those in the bazaar which open and shut their eyes at the word of command enforced by a wire, and squeak when you pinch them in the middle. There are women who seem born into the world only as the playthings and make-believes of human life. As impassive as the waxen creatures in the nursery, no remonstrance touches them and no experience teaches them. Their final cause seems to be to look pretty, to be always in perfect drawing-room order, and to be the occasions by which their friends and companions are taught patience and self-denial. And they perfectly fulfil their destiny ; which may be so much carried to their credit. A doll woman is hopelessly useless and can do nothing with her brains or her hands. In distress or sickness she can only sit by you and look as sorrowful as her round smooth face will permit; but she has not a helping suggestion to make, not a fraction of practical power to put forth.

When a man has married a doll wife he has assigned himself to absolute loneliness or a double burden. He cannot live with his pretty toy in any more reality of sympathy than does a child with her puppet. He can tell her nothing of his affairs, nothing of his troubles nor of his thoughts, because she can impart no new idea, even from the woman's point of view, not from want of heart but from want of brains to understand another's life. Is she not a doll? and does not the very essence of her dollhood lie in this want of perceptive faculty both for things and feelings? What are the hot flushes of passion, the bitter tears of grief, the frenzy of despair, to her? She sees them; and she wonders that people can be so silly as to make themselves and her so uncomfortable; but of the depth of the anguish they express she knows no more than does her waxen prototype when little missy sobs over it in her arms and confides her sorrows to its deaf ears. Whatever anxieties oppress her husband, he must keep them to himself, he cannot share them with her; and the last shred of his credit, like the last effort of his strength, must be employed in maintaining his toy wife in the fool's paradise where alone she can make her habitation. Many a man's back has broken under the strain of such a burden; and many a ruined fortune might have been held together and repaired when damaged, had it not been for the exigencies and necessities of the living doll, who had to be spared all want or inconvenience at the cost of everything else. How many men are groaning in spirit at this moment over the infatuation that made them sacrifice the whole worth of life for the sake of a pretty face and a plastic manner!

The doll woman is as helpless practically as she is useless morally. If she is in personal danger, she either faints or becomes dazed, according to her physiological conditions. Sometimes she is hysterical and frantic, and then she is actively troublesome. In general, however, she is just so much dead weight on hand, to be thought for as well as protected; a living corpse to be carried on the shoulders of those who are struggling for their own lives. She can foresee no possibilities, measure no distances, think of no means of escape. Never quick nor ready, pressure paralyzes such wits as she possesses; and it is not from selfishness so much as from pure incapacity to help herself or to serve others that the poor doll falls down in a helpless heap of self-surrender, and lets her very children perish before her eyes without making an effort to protect them.

As a mother indeed, the doll woman is perhaps more unsatisfactory than in any other character. She gives up her nursery into the absolute keeping of her nurse, and does not attempt to control nor to interfere. This again, is not from want of affection, but from want of capacity. In her tepid way she has a heart, if only half-vitalized like the rest of her being; and she is by no means cruel. Indeed, she has not force enough to be cruel nor wicked anyhow; her worst offence being a passive kind of selfishness, not from greed but from inactivity, by which she is made simply useless for the general good. As for her children, she understands neither their moral nature nor their physical wants; and beyond a universal 'Oh, naughty!' if the little ones express their lives in the rampant manner proper to young things, or as a universal 'Oh, let them have it!' if there is a howl over what is forbidden or unwise, she has no idea of discipline or management. If they teaze her, they are sent away; if they are naughty, they are whipped by papa or nurse; if they are ill, the doctor is summoned and they have medicine as he directs; but none of the finer and more intimate relations usual between mother and child exist in the home of the doll mother. The children are the property of the nurse only; unless indeed the father happens to be a specially affectionate and a specially domestic man, and then he does the work of the mother—at the best clumsily, but at the worst better than the doll could have done it.

Very shocking and revolting are all the more tragic facts of human life to the smooth-skinned easy-going doll. When it comes to her own turn to bear pain, she wonders how a good God can permit her to suffer. Had she brains enough to think, the great mystery of pain would make her atheistical in her angry surprise that she should be so hardly dealt with. As dolls have a constitutional immunity from suffering, her first initiation into even a minor amount of anguish is generally a tremendous affair; and though it may be pain of a quite natural and universal character, she is none the less indignant and astonished at her portion. She invariably thinks herself worse treated than her sisters, and cannot be made to understand that others suffer as much as, and more than, herself. As she has always shrunk from witnessing trouble of any kind, and as what she may have seen has passed over her mind without leaving any impression, she comes to her own sorrows totally inexperienced; and one of the most pitiable sights in the world is that of a poor doll woman writhing in the grasp of physical agony, and broken down or rendered insanely impatient by what other women can bear without a murmur.

When she is in the presence of the moral tragedies of life, she is as lost and bewildered as she is with the physical. All sin and crime are to her odd and inexplicable. She cannot pity the sinner, because she cannot understand the temptation; and she cannot condemn from any lofty standpoint, because she has not mind enough to see the full meaning of iniquity. It is simply something out of the ordinary run of her life, and the doll naturally dislikes disturbance, whether of habit or of thought. Yet if a noted criminal came and sat down by her, she would probably whisper to her next friend, 'How shocking!' but she would simper when he spoke, and perhaps in her heart feel flattered by the attention of even so doubtful a notoriety. If she be a doll with a bias towards naughtiness, the utmost limit to which she can go is a mild kind of curiosity about the outsides of things—the mere husk and rind of the forbidden fruit—such as wondering how such and such people look who have done such dreadful things; and what they felt the next morning; and how could they ever come to think of such horrors! She would be more interested in hearing about the dress and hair and eyes of the female plaintiff or defendant in a famous cause than many other women would be; but she would not give herself the trouble to read the evidence, and she would take all her opinions secondhand. But whether the colour of the lady's gown was brown or blue, and whether she wore her hair wisped or plaited, would be matters in which she would take as intense an interest as is possible to her.

The utmost limit to which enthusiasm can be carried with her is in the matter of dress and fashion; and the only subject that thoroughly arouses her is the last new colour, or the latest eccentricity of costume. Talk to her of books, and she will go to sleep; even novels, her sole reading, she forgets half an hour after she has turned the last page; while of any other kind of literature she is as profoundly ignorant as she is of mathematics; but she can discuss the mysteries of fashion with something like animation, these being to her what the wire is to the eyes of the dolls in the bazaar. Else she has no power of conversation. At the head of her own table she sits like a pretty waxen dummy, and can only simper out a few commonplaces, or simper without the commonplaces, satisfied if she is well appointed and looks lovely, and if her husband seems tolerably contented with the dinner. She is more in her element at a ball, where she is only asked to dance and not wanted to talk; but her ball-room days do not last for ever, and when they are over she has no available retreat.

If a rich doll woman is a mistake, a poor one who has been rich is about the greatest infliction that can be laid on a suffering household. Not all the teaching of experience can make wax and glue into flesh and blood, and nothing can train the human doll into a dignified or a capable womanhood. She still dresses in faded finery—which she calls keeping up appearances; and still has pretensions which no 'inexorable logic of facts' can destroy. She spends her money on sweets and ribbons and ignores the family need for meat and calico; and she sits by the fireside dozing over a trashy novel, while her children are in rags and her house is given over to disorder. But then she has a craze for the word 'lady-like,' and thinks it synonymous with ignorance and helplessness. She abhors the masculine-minded woman who helps her —sister, cousin, daughter—so far as she can abhor anything; but she is glad to lean on her strength, despite this abhorrence, and, while grumbling at her masculinity, does not disdain to take advantage of her power. The doll is only passively disagreeable though; and for all that she carps under her breath, will remain in any position in which she is placed. She will not act, but she will let you act unhindered; which is something gained when you have to deal with fools.

This quiescence of hers passes with the world for plasticity and amiability; it is neither; it is simply indolence and want of originating force. While she is young, she is nice enough to those who care only for a pretty face and a character founded on negatives; but when a man's pride of life has gone, and he has come into the phase of weakness, or under the harrow of affliction, or into the valley of the shadow of death, then she becomes in sorrowful truth the chain and bullet which make him a galley-slave for the remainder of his days, and which sign him to drudgery and despair.

As an old woman the doll has not one charm. She has learned none of that handiness, come to none of that grand maternal power of helping others, which should accompany maturity and age and has still to be thought for and protected, to the exclusion of the younger and naturally more helpless, as when she was young herself, and beautiful and fascinating, and men thought it a privilege to suffer for her sake. Nine times out of ten she has lost her temper as well as her complexion, and has become peevish and unreasonable. She gets fat and rouges; but she will not consent to get old. She takes to false hair, dyes, padded stays, arsenic or 'anti-fat,' and to artful contrivances of every description; but alas! there is no 'dolly's hospital' for her as there used to be for her battered old prototype in the nursery lumber-closet; and, whether she likes it or not, she has to succumb to the inevitable decree, and to become faded, worn out, unlovely, till the final *coup de grâce* is given and the poor doll is no more. Poor, weak, frivolous doll! it requires some faith to believe that she is of any good whatsoever in this overladen life of ours; but doubtless she has her final uses, though it would puzzle a Sanhedrim of wise men to discover them. Perhaps in the great readjustment of the future she may have her place and her work assigned to her in some inter-stellar Phalansterie ; when the meaning of her helpless earthly existence shall be made manifest and its absurd uselessness atoned for by some kind of celestial 'charing.'

CHARMING WOMEN.

THERE are certain women who are invariably spoken of as charming. We never hear any other epithet applied to them. They are not said to be pretty, nor amiable, nor clever, though they may be all three, but simply charming; which we may take as a kind of verbal amalgam—the concentration and concretion of all praise. The main feature about these charming women is their intense feminality. There is no blurring of the outlines here; no confusion of qualities admirable enough in themselves but slightly out of place considering the sex; no Amazonian virtues which leave one in doubt as to whether we have not before us Achilles in petticoats rather than a true Pyrrha or a more tender Deidamia.

A charming woman is woman all over—one who places her glory in being a woman and has no desire to be anything else. She is a woman rather than a human being, and a lady rather than a woman. One of her characteristics is the exquisite grace of her manner which so sweetly represents the tender nature within. She has not an angle anywhere. If she were to be expressed geometrically, Hogarth's Line of

Beauty is the sole figure that could be used for her. She is flowing, graceful, bending in mind as in body; she is neither self-asserting nor aggressive, neither rigid nor narrow; she is a creature who glides gracefully through life, and adjusts herself to her company and her circumstances in a manner little less than marvellous; working her own way without tumult or sharpness; creeping round the obstacles she cannot overthrow, and quietly wearing down more friable opposition with that gentle persistency which does so much more than turmoil and disturbance.

Even if enthusiastic—which she is for art, either as music, as painting, or yet as poetry—she is enthusiastic in such a sweet and graceful way that no one can be offended by a fire which shines and does not burn. There is no touch of scorn about her and no assumption of superior knowledge. She speaks to you, poor ignorant Philistine, with the most flattering conviction that you follow her in all her flights; and when she comes out, quite naturally, with her pretty little bits of recondite lore or professional technicalities, you cannot be so boorish as to ask for an explanation of these trite matters which she makes so sure you must understand. Are you not an educated person with a soul to be saved? can you then be ignorant of things with which every one of culture is familiar? She discourses confidentially of musicians and painters unknown to fame, and speaks as if she knew the secret doings of the Conservatoire and the R.A. council-chamber alike. The models and the methods, the loves and the hates, of the artistic world are to her things of everyday life, and you cannot tell her that she is shooting her delicate shafts wide of the mark, and that you know no more of what she means than if she were talking in the choicest Arabic.

If she has been abroad—and she generally has been more or less—she will pour out her tender little rhapsodies about palazzi and musei of which you have never heard, but every room of which she assumes you know by heart; and she will speak of out-of-the-way churches, and grim old castles perched upon vine-clad mounts, as if you were as well acquainted with them as with your native hamlet. She will bring into her discourse all manner of Italian technicalities, as if you understood the subject as well as she herself understands it; though your learning is limited to a knowledge of how much has been done in jute and tallow this last half year, or how many pockets of hops went off in the market last week. If she has a liking for high life and titles —and what charming woman has not?—she will mention the names of all manner of counts and dukes and monsignori unknown to English society, as though they were her brothers; but if you were to interrupt the gentle ripple of her speech with such rude breakwaters as 'who?' and 'what?' the charming woman would think you a horrid bore—and no man would willingly face that humiliation. One may be a rhinoceros in one's own haunts, but, as the fable tells us, even rhinoceroses are ashamed of their parentage when among gazelles.

Never self-asserting, never contradictory, only sweetly and tenderly putting you right when you blunder, the charming woman nevertheless always makes you feel her superiority. True, she lays herself as it were at your feet and gives you a thousand delicate flatteries—indeed among her specialities is that of being able to set you on good terms with yourself by her art of subtle flattery ; but despite her own self-abasement and your exaltation you cannot but feel her superiority; and, although she is too charming to acknowledge what would wound your pride, you know that she feels it too, and tries to hide it. All of which has the effect of making you admire her still more for her grace and tact.

The charming woman is generally notoriously in love with her husband, who is almost always inferior to her in birth, acquirements, manner, appearance. This Titania-like affection of hers only shows her feminine qualities of sacrifice and wifely devotion to greater advantage, and makes other men envy more ferociously the lucky fellow who has drawn such a prize. The husband of a charming woman is indeed lucky in the world's esteem ; no man more so. Though he may be one of the most ordinary, perhaps unpleasant, fellows you know, with a sour face, an underbred air, and by no means famous in his special sphere, his wife speaks of him enthusiastically as so good, so clever, so delightful ! No one knows how good he is, she says; though of course he has his little peculiarities of temper and the rest of it, and perhaps every one would not bear with them as she does. But then she knows him, and knows his wonderful worth and value! If they are not seen much together, that comes from causes over which they have no control, not from anything like disinclination to each other's society. Certainly, for so happy a marriage, it is a little surprising how very seldom they are together; and how all her friends are hers only and not his, and how much she goes into society without him. On the whole, counting hours, they live very much more apart than united; but that is the misfortune of his career, of his health, or of hers—a misfortune due to any cause but that of diversity of tastes, inharmoniousness of pursuits, or lack of love.

Full of home affection and the tenderest sentiment as she is, the charming woman does sometimes the oddest-looking things, which a rough little domestic creature without graceful pretensions would not dream of doing. Her child is lying dangerously ill, perhaps dying, and she appears at the grand ball of the season, subdued certainly—how well that sweet melancholy becomes her!—but always graceful, always thoughtful for others, and attentive to the minutest detail of her social duties. And though indeed, she will tell you, she does not know how she got dressed at all, because of the state of cruel anxiety in which she is, yet she is undeniably the best dressed woman in the room and the most carefully appointed. It is against her own will that she is there, you may be sure; but she has been forced to sacrifice herself, and tear herself away for an hour. The exigencies of society are so merciless!—the world is such a terrible Juggernaut! she says, raising her eyes with plaintive earnestness to yours in the breathing-times of the waltz.

She has another trial if her husband is ordered out to Canada or the West Indies. Dearly as she loves him, and though she is heart-broken at the idea of the separation, yet her health cannot stand the climate; and she must obey her doctor's orders. She is so delicate, you know—all charming women are delicate—and the doctor tells her she could not live six months either in Toronto or Port Royal. If her lord and master had to go on diplomatic service to St. Petersburg or Madrid, she might be able to stand the climate then; but that is different. A dull station, without any of her favourite pleasures, would be more than she could bear; so she remains behind, goes out into society, and writes her husband tender and amusing letters once a month.

The charming woman is the gentlest of her sex. She would not do a cruel thing nor say an unkind word for the world. When she tells you the unpleasant things which ill-natured people have said of your friends or hers, she tells them in the sweetest and dearest way imaginable. She is so sure there is not a syllable of truth in it all; and what a shame it is that people should be so ill-natured! In the gentle tone of sympathy and deprecation peculiar to her, she gives you all the ugly and uncomfortable reports which have come to her, and of which you have never heard a breath until this moment. Yet it is you who are stupid, not she who is initiative, for she tells them to you as if they were of patent notoriety to the whole world; only she does not believe them, remember! She takes the most scrupulous care to deny and defend as she retails, and you cannot class her with the tribe of the ill-natured whom she censures, setting, as she does, the whole strength of her gentle words and generous disbelief in opposition to these ugly rumours. Yet you wish she had not told you. Her disclaimers spring so evidently from the affectionate amiability of her own mind, which cannot bear to think evil, that they have not much effect upon you. The excuse dies away from your memory, but the ill-savoured report roots; and you feel that you have lost your respect for your former friends for ever; or, if they were only hers, then, that nothing should tempt you to know them. There is no smoke without some fire, you think; and the charming woman cannot possibly have kindled the flame herself out of sticks and leaves and rubbish of her own collecting. But how sweet and charitable she was when she told you! how much you love her for her tenderness of nature! what a guileless and delightful creature she is!

The charming woman is kind and graceful, but she does not command the stronger virtues. She flatters sweetly, but, it must be confessed, she fibs as sweetly. She sometimes owns to this, but only to fibs that do more good than harm—fibs into the utterance of which she is forced for the sake of peace and to avoid mischief. It is a feminine privilege, she says; and men agree with her. Truth at all times— bold, uncompromising, stern-faced truth—is coarse and indelicate she says; a masculine quality as little fitted for women as courage or great bodily strength. Her husband knows that she fibs; her friends at times find her out too; but though the women throw it at her as an accusation, the men accept it as a quality without which she would be less the charming woman that she is; and not only forgive it, but like her the better for the grace and tact and suppleness she displays in the process of manufacture. Hers are not the severer virtues, but the gentler, the more insinuating; and absolute truth—truth at any price and on all occasions—does not come into the list.

Charming women, with their plastic manners and non-aggressive force, always have their own way in the end. They are the women who influence by unseen methods and who shrink from any open display of power. They know that their *métier* is to soothe men, to put them on good terms with themselves, and so to get the benefit of the good humour they induce; and they dread nothing so much as a contest of wills. They coax and flatter for their rights, and consequently they are given privileges in excess of their rights; whereas the women who take their rights, as things to which they are entitled without favour, lose them and their privileges together. This art of self-abasement for future exaltation is one which it is given only to few to carry to perfection, but no woman is really charming without it. In fact it is part of her power; and she knows it. Though charming women are decidedly the favourites with men, they are careful to keep on good terms with their own sex; and in society you may often see them almost ostentatiously surrounded by women only, whom they take pains to please or exert themselves to amuse, but whom they throw into the shade in the most astonishing way.

Whatever these really charming women are, or do, or wear, is exactly the right thing; and every other woman fails in proportion to the distance she is removed from this model. When a charming woman is dressed richly, the simpler costumes of her friends look poor and mean; when she is *à la bergère*, the Court dresses about her are vulgar; when she is gay, quietness is dullness; when she is quiet, laughter is coarse. And there is no use in trying to imitate her. She is the very Will-o'-the-wisp of her circle, and no sooner shows her light here than she flits away there; she has no sooner set one fashion, which her admiring friends have adopted with infinite pains and trouble, than she has struck out a new one which renders all the previous labour in vain. This is part of her very essence; and the originality which is simply perfection that cannot be repeated, and not eccentricity that no one will imitate, comes in as one of the finest and most potent of her charms. When she lends her patterns to her friends, or tells them this or that little secret, she laughs in her heart, knowing that she has shown them a path they cannot possibly follow and raised up a standard to which they cannot attain. And even should they do either, then she knows that, by the time they have begun to get up to her, she will be miles away, and that no art whatever can approximate them to her as she is. What she was she tosses among them as a worn-out garment; what she is they cannot be. She remains still the unapproachable, the inimitable, the charming woman *par excellence* of her set, whom none can rival.

APRON-STRINGS.

AMONG other classifications, the world of men and women may be divided into those who wear aprons and those who are tied to the strings thereof—those who determine the length of the tether and those who are bound to browse within its circuit—those who hold the reins and those who go bitted. All men and women are fond of power, but there is a wide difference in the ways in which they use it. To men belong the grave political tyrannies at which nations revolt and history is outraged, to women the small conventional laws framed against individual liberty by Mrs. Grundy and society; men rule with rods of iron and drive with whips of steel, women shorten the tether and tie up close to apron-strings; men coerce, women forbid. In fact, the difference is just that which lies between action and negation, compulsion and restraint; between the masculine jealousy of equality and the feminine fear of excess. If men debar women from all entrance into their larger sphere, women try to dwarf men's lives to their own measure, and not a few hold themselves aggrieved when they fail. They think that everything which is impossible to them should be forbidden to others, and they maintain that to be a lamentable extreme which is simply in excess of their own powers. Not content with supremacy in the home which is their own undisputed domain, nor satisfied with binding on men the various rules distinguishing life in the drawing-room, the dining-room and the breakfast-parlour, they would, if they could, carry their code outside, and sweep into its narrow net the club-house and the mess-table, the billiard-room and the race-course, and wherever else men congregate together—delivered from the bondage of feminine conventionalities.

For almost all women have an uneasy feeling when their men are out of sight, enjoying themselves in their own way. They fear on all sides—both bodily harm and moral evil; and regard men's rougher sports and freer thoughts as a hen regards her wilful ducklings when they take to the water in which she would be drowned, and leave her high and dry lamenting their danger and self-destruction. The man they love best for his manliness they would, in their loving cowardice, do their utmost to make effeminate; and, while adoring him for all that makes him bold and strong in thought as well as in frame, they would tie him up to their apron-strings, and keep him there till he became as soft and narrow as themselves. Not that they would wish to do so; if you asked them they would tell you quite the contrary. But this would be the result if they had their own way, their love being at all times more timid than confident.

To home-staying women, a brilliant husband courted by the world and loving what courts him, is a painful cross to bear, however much he may be beloved—the pain, in fact, being proportionate to the love. Perhaps no life exemplifies this so much as Moore's. Poor "Bessy" suffered many things because of the looseness of the apron-string by which her roving husband was tied, and the length of the tether which he allowed himself. *Farfallone amoroso* as he was, his incessant flutterings out of range and reach caused her many a sad hour; and in after years she was often heard to say that the happiest time of her life was when his mind had begun to fail, for then she had him all to herself and no one came in between them—no great world swept him away to be the idol of a *salon*, and left her alone at home casting up her accounts with life and love, and quaking at the result that came out. When the brilliancy and the idolatry came to an end, then her turn began; and she tied up her dulled and faltering idol close to her side for ever after, and was happier to have him there helpless, affectionate, dependent and imbecile than when he was at his brightest—and a rover.

Many a wife has felt the same when sickness has broken down the strong man's power to a weakness below her own, and made her, so long the inferior, now the more powerful of the two, and the supreme. She gathers up the reins with that firm, tight hand peculiar to women, and ties her master to her apron-string so that he cannot escape. It is quite a matter of pride with her that she has got him into such good order. He obeys her so implicitly about his medicines, and going to bed early, and wrapping himself up, and avoidance of draughts and night-air, that she feels all the reflected glory of one who has conquered a hero. The Samson who used to defy the elements and break her careful strings like bands of tow, has at last laid his head in her lap and suffered himself to be covered by her apron. It is worth while to have had the anxiety and loss of his illness for the sake of the submission resulting; and she generally ends by gaining a hold over him which he can never shake off again.

It is pitiful though, to see the stronger life thus dwarfed and bound. But women like it; and while the need for it lasts men must submit. The danger is lest the habit of the apron-string should become permanent; for it is so perilously pleasant to be petted and made much of by women, that few men can resist the temptation when it offers; and many have been ruined for the remainder of their days by an illness which gave them up into the keeping of wife and sisters—those fireside Armidas who will coddle all the real manliness out of their finest heroes, if they are let. If this kind of thing occurs at the break of life, the *mezzo cammino* between maturity and age, it is doubly difficult to throw off; and many a man who had good years of vigour and strength before him if he had been kept up to the mark, sinks all at once into senility because his womankind got frightened at that last small attack of his, and thought the best way to preserve him from another was to weaken him by over-care out of all wish for dangerous exposure.

Perhaps the greatest misfortune that can befall a man is to have been an only son brought up by a timid widow mother. It is easy to see at a glance, among a crowd of boys, who has been educated under exclusively feminine influence. The long curled shining hair, the fantastic tunic—generally a kind of hybrid between a tunic and a frock—the lavish use of embroidery, the soft pretty-behaved manner, the clean unroughened hands, all mark the boy of whom his mother has so often wished that he had been a girl, and whom she has made as much like a girl as possible. His intellectual education has been as unboylike as his daily breeding. Mothers' boys are taught to play the piano, to amuse themselves with painting, or netting, or perhaps a little woolwork in the evenings—anything to keep them quietly seated by the family table, without an outbreak of boyish restlessness or inconvenient energy; but they are never taught to ride, to hunt, to shoot, to swim, to play at cricket, football, nor billiards, unless a stalwart uncle happens to be about who takes the reins in his own hand at times, and insists on having a word to say to his nephew's education.

There is danger in all, and evil in some, of

these things; and women cannot bear that those they love should run the risk of either. Wherefore their boys are modest and virtuous truly, but they are not manly; and when they go out into the world, as they must sooner or later, they are either laughed at for their priggishness, or they go to the bad by the very force of reaction. The mother has allowed them to learn nothing that will be of solid use to them, and they enter the great arena wholly unprepared either to fight or to resist, to push their own way or to take their own part. They have been kept tied up to the apron-string to the last moment, and only when absolutely forced by the necessity of events will she cut the knot and let them go free. But she holds on to the last moment. Even when the time comes for college-life and learning, she often goes with her darling, and takes lodgings in the town, that she may be near at hand to watch over his health and morals, and continue her careful labours for his destruction.

The chances are that a youth so brought up never becomes a real man, nor worth his salt anyhow. He is a prig if he is good, a debauchee of the worst kind if he kicks over the traces at all. He is more likely the first, carrying the mark of the apron-string round his wrist for life. Like a tame falcon used to the hood and the perch and the lure home, no matter what the temptation of the quarry afield, he is essentially a domestic man, at ease only in the society of women; a fussy man; a small-minded man; delicate in health; with a dread of strong measures, physical, political, or intellectual; a crotchety man given to passing quackeries; but not a man fit for man's society nor for man's work. When there are many boys, instead of only one, in a widow's family, the opposite of all this is the case. So soon as they have escaped from the nursery, they have escaped from all control whatsoever; and if one wants to realize a puerile pandemonium of dirt, discomfort, noise and general disorganization, the best place in the world is the household of a feeble-spirited mother of many sons where there is no controlling masculine influence.

Daughters, who are naturally and necessarily tied up to the mother's apron-string, suffer occasionally from too tight a strain; though certainly it is not the fault of the present day that girls are too closely fettered, too home-staying or subdued. Still, every now and then one comes across a matron who has crushed all individuality out of her family, and whose grown-up daughters are still children to her in moral go-carts and intellectual leading-strings. They may be the least attractive of their sex, but a mother of this kind has one fixed delusion respecting them—namely, that the world is full of wolves eager to devour her lambs, and that they are only safe when close to the maternal apron and browsing within an inch of the tether stake. These are the girls who become hopeless old maids. Men have an instinctive dread of the maternal apron-string. They do not want to marry a mother as well as a wife, and to live under a double dominion and a reduplicated opposition.

It is all very well to say that a girl so brought up is broken in already, and therefore more likely to make a good wife than many others, seeing that it is only a transfer of obedience. That may do for slaves who cannot be other than slaves whoever is the master; but it does not do for women who, seeing their friends freer than themselves, reflect with grief and longing that, had fate so ordered it, they might have been free too. The chances here, as with the mothers' boys, are, that the girl kept too close to the apron-string during her spinsterhood goes all abroad so soon as she gets on the free ground of matrimony, and lets her liberty run into license. Or she keeps her old allegiance to her mother intact, and her husband is never more than the younger branch at best. Most likely he is a usurper, whom it is her duty to disobey in favour of the rightful ruler when they chance to come into collision.

If women had their will, all national enterprise would be at an end. There would be no Arctic Expeditions, no Alpine Clubs, no dangerous experiments in science, no firearms at home, no volunteering—in their own family at least. All the danger would be done by the husbands and brothers and sons of other women, but each would guard her own. For women cannot go beyond the individual; and the loss of one of their own, by misadventure, weighs more with them than the necessity of keeping up the courage and hardihood of the nation. Nor do they see the difference between care and coddling, refinement and effeminacy; consequently, men are obliged to resist their influence, and many cut the apron-string altogether, because delicate fingers will tie the knots too tight. They do not remember that the influence to which men yield as a voluntary act of their own grace is a very different thing from obedience to the open denial, the undisguised interference and restraint, which some women like to show. Men respect the higher standard of morality kept up by women; they obey the major and the minor laws of refinement which are framed for home life and for society; and they confess that, without woman's influence, they would soon degenerate into mere savages and be no better than so many Choctaws before a generation was over; but they do not like being pulled up short, especially in public, and hounded into the safe sheepfold for all the world to see them run. And they resent the endeavour. And the world resents it too, and feels that something is wrong when a woman shows that she has the whip hand, and that she can treat her husband like a petted child or bully him like a refractory one; that she has him tied to her apron-strings and tethered to the stake of her will. But there is more of this kind of thing in families than the world at large always knows of; and many a fine, stalwart fellow who holds his own among men, who is looked up to at his club and respected in his office for his courage, decision and self-reliance, sinks into mere poodledom at home, where his wife has somehow managed to get hold of the leading-strings, and has taught him that the only way to peace is by submission and obedience.

FINE FEELINGS.

THERE are people who pride themselves on the possession of what it pleases them to call fine feelings. Perhaps, if we were all diligent to call spades spades, these same fine feelings would come under a less euphemistic heading; but, as things are, we may as well adopt the softening gloze that is spread over the whole of our language, and call them by a pretty name with the rest. People who possess fine feelings are chiefly remarkable for the ease with which they take offence; it being indeed impossible, even for the most wary of their associates, to avoid giving umbrage in some shape, and generally when least intended and most innocently minded. Nothing satisfies them. No amount of attention, short of absolute devotion and giving them the place of honour everywhere, sets them at ease with themselves or keeps them in good-humour. If you ask them to your house, you must not dream of mixing them up with the rest. Though you have done them an honour in asking them at all, you must give them a marked position and bear them on your hands for the evening. They must be singled out from the herd and specially attended to ; introduced to the nicest people ; made a fuss with and taken care of ; else they are offended, and feel they have been slighted—their sensitiveness or fine feelings being a kind of Chat Moss which will swallow up any quantity of *petits soins* that may be thrown in, and yet never be filled. If they are your intimate friends, you have to ask them on every occasion on which you receive. They make it a grievance if they hear that you have had even a dinner party without inviting them, though your space is limited and you had them at your last gathering. Still, if it comes to their ears that you have had friends and did not include them, they will come down on you to a dead certainty if they are of the franker kind, and ask you seriously, perhaps pathetically, how they have offended you ? If they are of the sullen sort they will meet you coldly, or pass you by without seeing you ; and will either drift into a permanent estrangement or come round after a time, according to the degree of acidity in their blood and the amount of tenacity in their character. They have lost their friends many times for no worse offence than this.

They are as punctilious too, as they are exacting. They demand visit for visit, invitation for invitation, letter for letter. Though you may be overwhelmed with serious work, while they have no weightier burden strapped to their shoulders than their social duties and social fineries, yet you must render point for point with them, keeping an exact tally with not a notch too many on their side, if you want to retain their acquaintance at all. And they must be always invited specially and individually, even to your open days ; else they will not come at all ; and their fine feelings will be hurt. They suffer no liberties to be taken with them and they take none with others ; counting all frock-coat friendliness as taking liberties, and holding themselves refined and you coarse if you think that manners *sans façon* are pleasanter than those which put themselves eternally into stays and stiff buckram, and are never in more undress than a Court suit. They will not go into your house to wait for you, however intimate they may be ; and they would resent it as an intrusion, perhaps an impertinence, if you went into theirs in their absence. If you are at luncheon when they call, they stiffly leave their cards and turn away ; though you have the heartiest, jolliest manner of housekeeping going, and keep a kind of open house for luncheon casuals. They do not understand heartiness or a jolly manner of housekeeping ; open houses are not in their line and they will not be luncheon casuals ; so they turn away grimly, and if you want to see them you have to send your servant panting down the street after them, when, their dignity being satisfied, their sensitiveness smoothed down and their fine feelings reassured, they will graciously turn back and do what they might have done at first without all this fuss and fume.

When people who possess fine feelings are poor,

their sensitiveness is indeed a cross both for themselves and their friends to bear. If you try to show them a kindness or do them a service, they fly out at you for patronizing them, and say you humiliate them by treating them as paupers. You may do to your rich acquaintances a hundred things which you dare not attempt with your poor friends cursed with fine feelings; and little offices of kindness, which pass as current coin through society, are construed into insults with them. Difficult to handle in every phase, they are in none more dangerous to meddle with than when poor, though they are as bad if they have become successful after a period of struggle. Then your attention to them is time-serving, bowing to the rising sun, worshipping the golden calf, &c. Else why did you not seek them out when they were poor? Why were you not cap in hand when they went bare-headed? Why have you waited until they were successful before you recognized their value?

It is funny to hear how bitter these sensitive folks are when they have come out into the sunlight of success after the dark passage of poverty; as if it had been possible to dig them out of their obscurity when their name was still to make—as if the world could recognize its prophets before they had spoken. But this admission into the penetralia after success is a very delicate point with people of fine feelings, supposing always the previous struggle to have been hard; and even if there has been no struggle to speak of, then there are doubts and misgivings as to whether they are liked for themselves or not, and morbid speculations on the stability and absolute value of the position they hold and the attentions they receive, and endless surmises of what would be the result if they lost their fame or wealth or political power or social standing— or whatever may be the hook whereon their success hangs, and their fine feelings are impaled. The act of wisdom most impossible to be performed by these self-torturers is the philosophic acceptance of life as it is and of things as they fall naturally to their share.

Women remarkable for fine feelings are also remarkable for that uneasy distrust, that insatiable craving which continually requires reassuring and allaying. As wives or lovers they never take a man's love, once expressed and loyally acted on, as a certainty, unless constantly repeated; hence they are always pouting or bemoaning their loveless condition, getting up pathetic scenes of tender accusation or sorrowful acceptance of coolness and desertion, which at the first may have a certain charm to a man because flattering to his vanity, but which pall on him after a short time, and end by annoying and alienating him; thus bringing about the very catastrophe which was deprecated before it existed.

Another characteristic with women of fine feelings is their inability to bear the gentlest remonstrance, the most shadowy fault-finding. A rebuke of any gravity throws them into hysterics on the spot; but even a request to do what they have not been in the habit of doing, or to abstain from doing that which they have used themselves to do, is more than they can endure with dry-eyed equanimity. You have to live with them in the fool's paradise of perfectness, or you are made to feel yourself an unmitigated brute. You have before you the two alternatives of suffering many things which are disagreeable and which might easily be remedied, or of having your wife sobbing in her own room and going about the house with red eyes and an expression of exasperating patience under ill-treatment, far worse to bear than the most passionate retaliation. Indeed women may be divided broadly into those who cry and those who retort when they are found fault with; which, with a side section of those wooden women who 'don't care,' leaves a very small percentage indeed of those who can accept a rebuke good-temperedly, and simply try to amend a failing or break off an unpleasant habit, without parade of submission and sweet Griseldadom unjustly chastised, but kissing the rod with aggravating meekness.

For there are women who can make their meekness a more potent weapon of offence than any passion or violence could give. They do not cry, neither do they complain, but they exaggerate their submission till you are driven half mad under the slow torture they inflict. They look at you so humbly; they speak to you in so subdued a voice, when they speak to you at all, which is rarely and never unless first addressed; they avoid you so pointedly, hurrying away if you are going to meet them about the house, on the pretext of being hateful to your sight and doing you a service by ridding you of their presence; they are so ostentatiously careful that the thing of which you mildly complained under some circumstances shall never happen again under any circumstances, that you are forced at last out of your entrenchments, and obliged to come to an explanation. You ask them what is amiss? or, what do they mean by their absurd conduct? and they answer you 'Nothing,' with an injured air or affected surprise at your query. What have they done that you should speak to them so harshly? They are sure they have done all they could to please you, and they do not know what right you have to be vexed with them again. They have kept out of your way and not said a word to annoy you; they have only tried to obey you and to do as you ordered, and yet you are not satisfied! What can they do to please you? and why is it that they never can please you whatever they do? You get no nearer your end by this kind of thing; and the only way to bring your Griselda to reason is by having a row; when she will cry bittery, but finally end by kissing and making up. You have to go through the process. Nothing else, save a sudden disaster or an unexpected pleasure of large dimensions, will save you from it; but as we cannot always command earthquakes nor godsends, and as the first are dangerous and the last costly, the short and easy method remaining is to have a decisive 'understanding,' which means a scene and a domestic tempest with smooth sailing till the next time.

Sometimes fine feelings are hurt by no greater barbarity than that which is contained in a joke. People with fine feelings are seldom able to take a joke; and you will hear them relating, with an injured accent and as a serious accusation, the merest bit of nonsense you flung off at random, with no more intention of wounding them than had the merchant the intention of putting out the Efreet's eye when he flung his date-stones in the desert. As you cannot deny what you have said, they have the whip-hand of you for the moment; and all you can hope for is that the friend to whom they detail their grievance will see through them and it, and understand the joke if they cannot. Then there are fine feelings which express themselves in exceeding irritation at moral and intellectual differences of opinion—fine feelings bound up in questions of faith and soundness of doctrine, having taken certain moral and theological views under their especial patronage and holding all diversity of judgment therefrom a personal offence. The people thus afflicted are exceedingly uncomfortable folks to deal with, and manage to make every one else uncomfortable too. You hurt their feelings so continually and so unconsciously, that you might as well be living in a region of steel-traps and spring-guns, and set to walk blindfold among pitfalls and water-holes. You fling your date-stone here too, quite carelessly and thinking no evil, and up starts the Efreet who swears you have injured him intentionally. You express an opinion without attaching any particular importance to it, but you hurt the fine feelings which oppose it, and unless you wish to have a quarrel you must retract or apologize. As the worst temper always carries the day, and as fine feelings are only bad tempers under another name, you very probably do apologize; and so the matter ends.

Other people show their fineness of feeling by their impatience of pain and the tremendous grievance they think it that they should suffer as others —they say, so much more than others. These are the people who are great on the theory of nervous differences, and who maintain that their cowardice and impatience of suffering means an organization like an Æolian harp for sensibility. The oddest part of the business is the sublime contempt which these sensitives have for other persons' patience and endurance, and how much more refined and touching they think their own puerile sensibility. But this is a characteristic of humanity all through; the masquerading of evil under the name of good being one of the saddest facts of an imperfect nature and a confused system of morals. If all things showed their faces without disguise, we should have fine feelings placed in a different category from that in which they stand at this moment, and the world would be the richer by just so much addition of truth.

SPHINXES.

THERE are people to whom mystery is the very breath of life and the main element of their existence. Without it they are insignificant nobodies; by its aid they are magnified into vague and perhaps awful potentialities. They are the people who take the Sphinx for their model, and like her, speak darkly and in parables; making secrets of every-day matters which would be patent to the whole world in their simplicity, but which, by the magic of enigmatic handling, become riddles that the curious would give their lives to unravel.

Nothing with these people is confessed and above board, and nothing is shown openly so that you may look at it all round and judge for yourself what it is like and what it is worth. The utmost they do is to uncover just a corner of something they keep back in the bulk, tantalizing you with glimpses that bewilder and mislead; or they will dangle before you the end of a clue which they want you to take up and follow, making you believe that you will be guided thereby into the very heart of a mystery, and that you will find a treasure hidden in the centre of the maze which will abundantly repay you for the trouble of hunting it out. Nine times out of ten you will find nothing but a scarecrow of no more value than the rags of which it is composed—if even you find that. They are the people who repeat to you the most trivial things you may have said, and who remind you of the most unimportant things you may have done, years ago, all of which you have totally forgotten; but they will speak of them in a mysterious manner, as if they had been matters of vital meaning at the time —things which would open, if followed up, a page in your private history that it were better should be forgotten. As it is a question of memory, you cannot deny point-blank what they affirm; and as we all have pages of private history which we would rather not hear read aloud at the market-cross, you are obliged to accept their highly suggestive recollections with a queer feeling of helplessness and being somehow in their power—not knowing how much they are really acquainted with your secret affairs, nor whether the signal they have flashed before your eyes is a feint or a revelation.

Of the same sort, with a difference, are those who are always going to tell you something some day— people burdened with a perennial mystery which never sees the light. You are for ever tormented with these folks' possibilities of knowledge. You turn over in your own mind every circumstance that you think they could have got hold of; you cunningly subject all your common friends to crafty cross-examination; you go, link by link, through the whole chain connecting you with them; but you can find nothing that leads to the mere outskirts of the mystery. You can make nothing of it; and your sphinx goes on to the end promising some day to tell you something which dies with him untold. Your only consolation is the inner conviction that there was nothing to tell after all.

Then there are sphinxes of a more personal kind— people who keep their affairs a profound secret from every one, who wash all their dirty linen scrupulously at home and double-lock the door of the cupboard where the family skeleton lives. They are dungeons of silence, unfathomable abysses of reserve. You never know more of them, mind nor estate, than what you can learn from the merest outside of things. Look back, and you cannot recollect that you have ever heard them speak of their family or of their early days; and you are not acquainted with a living soul with whom they are connected. You may visit them for years without knowing that such and such a friend is their cousin, or maybe their sister. If they are unmarried men, they have no address save at their club; and neither you nor their most intimate friends have an idea where they sleep. For all you know to the contrary they may be married, with a fine flourishing family snugly stowed away in some suburban villa, where perhaps they live under another name, or with the omission or addition of a title that effectually masks their real individuality.

If this is their special manifestation of sphinxhood, they take as many precautions against being identified as a savage when out on a scouting expedition. They obliterate all traces of themselves so soon as they leave their office in the City, and take it as a terrible misfortune if the truth is ever discovered; though there is nothing disgraceful in their circumstances, and their wives and children are healthy and presentable.

Most of us have been startled by the sudden discovery, in our own circle of friends, of the wife and children of some member of our society hitherto supposed to be a bachelor and unshackled. All the time that we have been joking him on his celibacy and introducing him to various young ladies likely to make good wives if properly taught, he has been living in the holy estate a little way out of town, where he is at last stumbled on by some Œdipus who tells the secret to all the world and blows the mystery to the winds. We may be very sure that the officious Œdipus in question gets no thanks for his pains, and that the sphinx he has unmasked would rather have gone on living in congenial secrecy with his unacknowledged family in that remote suburban villa, than be forced into publicity and recognition. Leading two lives and personating two men—the one as imagined by his friends, the other as known to his belongings—was a kind of existence he liked infinitely better than the commonplace respectability of being *en évidence* throughout.

With certain sphinxes, no one but the officials

concerned ever knows what they have done, where they have served, what laurels they have gained. It comes out quite by accident that they were in the Crimea, where, like Jack Poyntz in *School*, they were heroes in their own way, though they don't talk about it; or that they performed prodigies of valour in the Indian Mutiny and obtained the Victoria Cross, which they never wear. This kind has at least the merit of being unboastful; keeping their virtues hidden like the temple which the real sphinx held between her paws, and to which only those had access who knew the secret of the way. But though it is hateful to hear a man blowing his own trumpet in season and out of season, yet it is pleasant to know the good deeds of one's neighbours, and to have the power of admiring what is worthy of admiration. Besides, modesty and mystery are not the same things; and there is a mean to be found between the secrecy of a sphinx making riddles of commonplace matters, and the cackle of a hen when she has laid an egg for the family breakfast.

The monetary or financial sphinx is one of the oddest of the whole tribe and one of the most mysterious. There are people who live on notoriously small incomes—such as the widows, say, of naval or military men, whose pensions are printed in blue-books and of whose yearly receipts the world can take exact cognizance—yet who dress in velvet and satin, perpetually go about in cabs and hired carriages, and are never without money to spend, though always complaining of poverty. How these financial sphinxes manage surpasses the understanding of every one; and by what royal road they arrive at the power of making two do the work of four is hidden from the ordinary believers in Cocker. You know their ostensible income; indeed, they themselves put it at so much; but they keep up a magnificent appearance on a less sum than that on which you would go shabby and dilapidated. When you ask them how it is done, they answer, 'by management.' Anything can be done by management, they say, by those who have the gift; which you feel to be an utterance of the sphinx—a dark saying the key to which has not yet been forged.

You calculate to the best of your ability, and you know that you are sound in your arithmetic; but, do what you will, you can never come to the rule by which five hundred a year can be made to compass the expenditure of a thousand. If you whisper secret supplies, concealed resources, your sphinx will not so much as wink her eyelid. How she contrives to make her ostensible five hundred do the work of a thousand—how she gets velvet and satin for the value of cotton and stuff, and how, though always complaining of poverty, she keeps unfailingly flush of cash—how all this is done is her secret, and she holds it sacred. And you may be quite sure of one thing—it is a secret she will never share with you nor any one else.

The rapidly-working *littérateur* is another sphinx

worth studying as a curiosity—we might say, indeed, a living miracle. There he stands, a jovial, self-indulgent, enjoying man, out in society every night in the week; by no means abstinent from champagne, and as little given to early rising as he is to consumption of the midnight oil. But he gets through a mass of work which would be respectable in a mere copyist, and which is little less than miraculous in an original producer. How he thinks, when he finds time to make up his plots, to work out his characters, even to correct his proofs, are riddles unanswerable by all his friends. Taking the mere mechanical act alone, he must write faster than any living man has ever been known to write, to get through all that goes under his name. And when is it done? Literary sphinxes of this kind go about unchallenged; indeed, they are very much about, and to be beheld everywhere; and one looks at them with respect, not knowing of what material they are made, nor of what mysterious gifts they are the possessors. Novels, plays, essays, poems, come pouring forth in never slackening supply. The railway stations and all hoardings are made gorgeous by the announcement of their feats set out in red and blue and yellow. No sooner has one blaze of triumph burnt itself out than another blaze of triumph flares up; and nothing but death or a rich inheritance seems likely to stop their mysterious fecundity. How is it done? That is the secret of the literary sphinx, to which the admiring and amazed brotherhood is anxiously seeking some clue; but up to the present hour it has been kept jealously guarded and no solution has been arrived at.

There is another form of the literary sphinx in the Nobodies and Anons who speak from out the darkness and let no man see whence the voice proceeds. They are generally tracked to their lair sooner or later, and the sphinx's head turns out to be only a pasteboard mask behind which some well-known Apuleian hid himself for a while, working much amazement among the wondering crowd while the clasps held good, but losing something of that fervid worship when the reality became known. Others, again, of these Anons have, like Junius, kept their true abode hidden and their name a mystery still, though there be some who swear they have traced the footsteps and know exactly where the sphinx lives, and what is the name upon his frontlet, and of what race and complexion he is without his mask. It may be so. But as every discoverer has a track of his own, and as each swears that his sphinx is the real one and no other, the choice among so many becomes a service of difficulty; and perhaps the wisest thing to do is to suspend judgment until the literary sphinx of the day chooses to reveal himself by the prosaic means of a title-page, with his name as author printed thereon and his place of abode jotted down at the foot of the preface.

FLIRTING.

THERE are certain things which can never be accurately described—things so shadowy, so fitful, so dependent on the mood of the moment, both in the audience and the actor, that analysis and representation are equally at fault. And flirting is one of them. What is flirting? Who can define or determine? It is more serious than talking nonsense and not so serious as making love; it is not chaff and it is not feeling; it means something more than indifference and yet something less than affection; it binds no one; it commits no one though it raises expectations in the individual and sets society on the look-out for results; it is a plaything in the hands of the experienced but a deadly weapon against the breast of the unwary; and it is a thing so vague, so protean, that the most accurate measurer of moral values would be puzzled to say where it exactly ends and where serious intentions begin.

But again we ask: What is flirting? What constitutes its essence? What makes the difference between it and chaff on the one hand, and it and love-making on the other? Has it a cumulative power, and, according to the old saying of many a pickle making a mickle, does a long series of small flirtings make up a concrete whole of love ? or is it like an unmortared heap of bricks, potential utilities if conditions were changed, but valueless as things are ? The man who would be able to reduce flirting to a definite science, who could analyze its elements and codify its laws, would be doing infinite service to his generation; but we fear that this is about as difficult as finding the pot of gold under the end of a rainbow, or catching small birds with a pinch of salt.

Every one has his or her ideas of what constitutes flirting; consequently every one judges of that pleasant exercise according to individual temperament and experience. Faded flowers, who see impropriety in everything they are no longer able to enjoy, say with more or less severity that Henry and Angelina are flirting if they are laughing while whispering together in an alcove, probably the most innocent nonsense in the world; but the fact that they are enjoying themselves in their own way, albeit a silly one, is enough for the faded flower to think they are after mischief, flirting being to her mind about the worst bit of mischief that a fallen humanity can perpetrate. The watchful mother, intent on chances, says that dancing together oftener than is necessary for good breeding and just the amount of attention demanded by circumstances, is flirting; timid girls newly out, and not yet used to the odd ways of men, think they are being flirted with outrageously if their partner fires off the meekest little compliment at them, or looks at them more tenderly than he would look at a cabbage ; but bolder spirits of both sexes think nothing worthy of the name which does not include a few questionable familiarities, and an equivoke or two, more or less risky. With some, flirting is nothing but the passing fun of the moment ; with others, it is the first lesson of the great unopened book and means the beginning of the end ; with some, it is not even angling with intent ; with others, it is deep-sea fishing with a broad, boldly-made net, and taking all fish that come in as good for sport if not for food.

Flirts are of many kinds as well as of all degrees. There are quiet flirts and demonstrative flirts ; flirts of the subtle sort whose practice is made by the eyes alone, by the manner, by the tender little sigh, by the bend of the head and the wave of the hand, to give pathos and point to the otherwise harmless word ; and flirts of the open and rampant kind, who go up quite boldly towards the point, but who never reach it, taking care to draw back in time before they fairly cross the border. This is the kind which, as the flirt male, does incalculable damage to the poor little fluttering dove to whom it is as a bird of prey, handsome, bold, cruel ; but this is the kind which has unlimited success, using as it does that immense moral leverage we call 'tantalizing'—for ever rousing hopes and exciting expectations, and luring a woman on as an *ignis fatuus* lures us on across the marsh, in the vain belief that it will bring us to our haven at last.

Akin to this kind are those male flirts who are great in the way in which they manage to insinuate things without committing themselves to positive statements. They generally contrive to give the impression of some mysterious hindrance by which they are held back from full and frank confession. They hint at fatal bonds, at unfortunate attachments, at a past that has burnt them up or withered them up, at any rate that has prevented their future from blossoming in the direction in which they would fain have had it blossom and bear fruit. They sketch out vaguely the outlines of some thrilling romance ; a few, of the Byronic breed, add the suspicion of some dark and melancholy crime as a further romantic charm and personal obstacle ; and when they have got the girl's pity, and the love that is akin to pity, then they cool down scientifically, never creating any scandal, never making any rupture, never coming to a moment when awkward explanations can be asked, but cooling nevertheless, till the thing drops of its own accord and dies out from inanition ; when they are free to carry their sorrows and their mysteries elsewhere. Some men spend their lives in this kind of thing, and find their pleasure in making all the women they know madly or sentimentally in love with them ; and if by chance any poor moth who has burned her wings makes too loud an outcry, the tables are turned against her dexterously, and she is held up to public pity—contempt would be a better word—as one who has suffered herself to love too well and by no means wisely, and who has run after a Lothario by no means inclined to let himself be caught.

Then there are certain men who flirt only with married women, and others who flirt only with girls; and the two pastimes are as different as tropical sunlight and northern moonshine. And there are some who are 'brothers,' and some who are 'fathers' to their young friends — suspicious fathers on the whole, not unlike Little Red Ridinghood's grandmother the wolf, with perilously bright eyes, and not a little danger to Red Ridinghood in the relationship, how delightful soever it may be to the wolf. Some are content with cousinship only —which however breaks down quite sufficient fences; and some are 'dearest friends,' no more, and find that an exceedingly useful centre from which to work onward and outward. For, if any peg will do on which to hang a discourse, so will any relationship or adoption serve the ends of flirting, if it be so willed.

But what is flirting? Is sitting away in corners, talking in low voices and looking personally affronted if any unlucky outsider comes within earshot, flirting? Not necessarily. It is just possible that Henry may be telling Angelina all about his admiration for her sister Grace; or Angelina may be confessing to Henry what Charley said to her last night;—which makes her lower her eyes as she is doing now, and play with the fringe of her fan so nervously. May be, if not likely. So that sitting away in corners and whispering together is not necessarily flirting, though it may look like it. Is dancing all the 'round' dances together? This goes for decided flirting in the code of the ball-room. But if the two keep well together? If they are really fond of dancing, as one of the fine arts combining science and enjoyment, they would dance with each other all night, though outside the 'marble halls' they might be deadly enemies—Montagues and Capulets, with no echo of Romeo and Juliet to soften their mutual dislike. So that not even dancing together oftener than is absolutely necessary is unmistakeable evidence, any more than is sitting away in corners, seeing that equal skill and keeping well in step are reasons enough for perpetual partnership, making all idea of flirtation unnecessary. In fact, there is no outward sign nor symbol of flirting which may not be mistaken and turned round, because flirting is so entirely in the intention and not in the mere formula, that it becomes a kind of phantasm, a Proteus, impossible to seize or to depict with accuracy.

One thing however, we can say—taking gifts and attentions, offered with evident design and accepted with tacit understanding, may be certainly held as constituting an important element of flirting. But this is flirting on the woman's side. And here you are being continually taken in. Your flirt of the cunningly simple kind, who smiles so sweetly and seems so flatteringly glad to see you when you come, who takes all your presents and acted expressions of love with the most bewitching gratitude and effusion, even she, so simple as she seems to be, slips the thread and will not be caught if she does not wish to be caught. At the decisive moment when you think you have secured her, she makes a bound and is away ; then turns round, looks you in the face, and with many a tear and pretty asseveration declares that she never understood you to mean what you say you have meant all along ; and that you are cruel to dispel her dream of a pleasant and harmless friendship, and very wicked indeed because you press her for a decision. Yes ; you are cruel, because you have believed her honest ; cruel, because you did not see through the veil of flattery and insincerity in which she clothed her selfishness ; cruel, because she was false. This is the flirt's logic when brought to book, and forced to confess that her pretended love was only flirting, and that she led you on to your destruction simply because it pleased her vanity to make you her victim.

Then there are flirts of the open and rollicking kind, who let you go far, very far indeed, when suddenly they pull up and assume an offended air as if you had wilfully transgressed known and absolute boundaries—girls and women who lead you on, all in the way of good fellowship, to knock you over when you have got just far enough to lose your balance.

That is their form of the art. They like to see how far they can make a man forget himself, and how much stronger their own delusive enticements are than prudence, experience and common-sense. And there are flirts of the artful and ' still waters ' kind, something like the male flirts spoken of just now ; sentimental little pusses—perhaps pretty young wives with uncomfortable husbands, whose griefs have by no means soured nor scorched, but just mellowed and refined, them. Or they may be of the sisterly class ; creatures so very frank, so very sisterly and confiding and unsuspicious of evil, that really you scarcely know how to deal with them at all. And there are flirts of the scientific kind ; women who have studied the art thoroughly ; and who are adepts in the use of every weapon known—using each according to circumstances and the nature of the victim, and using each with deadly precision. From such may a kind Providence deliver us ! As the tender mercies of the wicked, so are the scientific flirts—the women and the men who play at bowls with human hearts, for the stakes of a whole life's happiness on the one side and a few weeks of gratified vanity on the other.

It used to be an old schoolboy maxim that no real gentleman could be refused by a lady, because no real gentleman could presume beyond his line of encouragement. *À fortiori*, no lady would or could give more encouragement than she meant. What are we to say then of our flirts if this maxim be true ? Are they really 'no gentlemen' and 'no ladies,' according to the famous formula of the kitchen? Perhaps it would be said so if gentlehood meant now, as it meant centuries ago, the real worth and virtue of humanity. For flirting with intent is a cruel, false, heartless amusement; and time was when cruelty and falsehood were essentially sins which vitiated all claims to gentlehood. And yet the world would be very dull without that innocent kind of nonsense which often goes by the name of flirting —that pleasant something which is more than mere acquaintanceship and less than formal loverhood— that bright and animated intercourse which makes the hours pass so easily, yet which leaves no bitter pang of self-reproach—that indefinite and undefinable interest by which the one man or the one woman becomes a kind of microcosm for the time, the epitome of all that is pleasant and of all that is lovely. The only caution to be observed is :—Do not go too far.

SCRAMBLERS.

There are people who are never what Northern housewives call 'straight'—people who seem to have been born in a scramble, who live in a scramble, and who, when their time comes, will die in a scramble, just able to scrawl their signature to a will that ought to have been made years ago, and that does not embody their real intentions now. Emphatically the Unready, they are never prepared for anything, whether expected or unexpected; they make no plans more stable than good intentions; and they neither calculate nor foresee. Everything with them is hurry and confusion; not because they have more to do than other people, but because they do it more loosely and less methodically—because they have not learnt the art of dovetailing nor the mystery of packing. Consequently half their pleasures and more than half their duties slip through their fingers for want of the knack of compact holding; and their lives are passed in trying to pick up what they have let drop and in frantic endeavours to remedy their mistakes. For scramblers are always making mistakes and going through an endless round of forgetting. They never remember their engagements, but accept in the blandest and frankest way imaginable two or more invitations for the same day and hour, and assure you quite seriously when, taught by experience, you push them hard and probe them deep, that they have no engagement whatever on hand and are certain not to fail you. In an evil hour you trust to them. When the day comes they suddenly wake to the fact that they had accepted Mrs. So-and-So's invitation before yours; and all you get for your empty place and your careful arrangements ruthlessly upset, is a hurried note of apology which comes perhaps in the middle of dinner, perhaps sometime next day, when too late to be of use.

If they forget their own engagements they also ignore yours, no matter how distinctly you may have tabulated them; and are sure to come rattling to your house on the day when you said emphatically you were engaged and could not see them. If you keep to your programme and refuse to admit them, more likely than not you affront them. Engagements being in their eyes moveable feasts, which it does not in the least degree signify whether they keep on the date set down or not, they cannot understand your rigidity of purpose; and were it not that as a tribe they are good-natured, and too fluid to hold even annoyance for any length of time, you would in all probability have a quarrel fastened on you because your scrambling friends chose to make a calendar for themselves and to insist on your setting your diary by it.

As they ignore your appointed hours, so do they

forget your street and number. They always stick to your first card, though you may have moved many times since it was printed, duly apprizing them of each change as it occurred. That does not help you, for they never note the changes of their friends' addresses, but keep loyally to the first. It all comes to the same in the end, they say, and the postman is cleverer than they. But they do not often trouble their friends with letters on their own account, for they have a speciality for not answering such as are written to them. When they do by chance answer them, they never reply to the questions asked nor give the news demanded. They do not even reply to invitations like other people, but leave you to infer from their silence the acceptance or rejection they are meditating. When they in their turn invite you, they generally puzzle you by mismatching the day of the week with the date of the month, leaving you tormented with doubt which you are to go by ; and they forget to give you the hour. Besides this, they write an illegible hand ; and they are famous for the blots they make and the Queen's heads they omit.

A scrambling wife is no light cross to a man who values order and regularity as part of his home life. She may be, and probably is, the best-tempered creature in the world—a peevish scrambler would be too unendurable—but a fresh face, bright eyes and a merry laugh do not atone for never-ending disorder and discomfort. This kind of thing does not depend on income and is not to be remedied by riches. The households where my lady has nothing to do but let her maid keep her to the hours she herself has appointed are just as uncomfortable in their way as poorer establishments, if my lady is a scrambler, and cannot be taught method and the value of holding on by the forelock. Sometimes my lady gets herself into such an inextricable coil of promises and engagements, all crossing each other, that in despair she takes to her bed and gives herself out as ill, and so cuts what she cannot untie. People wonder at her sudden indisposition, looking as she did only yesterday in the bloom of health; and they wonder at her radiant reappearance in a day or two without a trace of even languor upon her. They do not know that her retirement was simply a version of the famous rope trick, and that, like the Brothers Davenport, she went into the dark to shake herself free of the cords with which she had suffered herself to be bound. It is a short and easy method certainly, but it has rather too much of the echo of 'Wolf' in it to bear frequent repetition.

In houses of a lower grade, where the lady is her own housekeeper, the habit of scrambling of course leads to far greater and more manifest confusion. The servants catch from the mistress the trick of overstaying time; and punctuality at last comes to mean an elastic margin, where fixed duties and their appointed times appear cometically at irregular intervals. The cook is late with dinner; the coachman begins to put-to a little after the hour he was ordered to be at the door; but they know that, however late they are, the chances are ten to one their mistress will not be ready for them, and that in her heart she will be grateful to them for the shelter their own unpunctuality affords her. This being so, they take their time and dawdle at their pleasure; thus adding to the pressure which always comes at the end of the scrambler's day, when everything is thrown into a chaotic mass and nothing comes out straight or complete.

Did any one ever know a scrambling woman ready at the moment in her own house? That she should be punctual to any appointment out of her house is, of course, not to be thought of; but she makes an awkward thing of it sometimes at home. Her guests are often all assembled, and the dinner hour has struck, before she has torn off one gown and dragged on another. What she cannot tie she pins; and her pins are many and demonstrative. She wisps up her hair, not having left herself time to braid it; and the consequence is that before she has been half an hour in the room ends and tails are sure to stray playfully from their fastenings and come tumbling about her ears. Her jewels are mismatched, her colours ill-assorted, her belt is awry, her bouquet falling to pieces. She rushes into the drawing-room in her morning slippers, smiling and good-tempered, with a patch-work look about her—something forgotten in her attire that makes her whole appearance shaky and unfinished—fastening her last button or clasping on her first bracelet. She is full of regrets and excuses delivered in her joyous, buoyant manner, or in a voice so winning, an accent so coaxing, that you cannot be annoyed. Besides, you leave the annoyance to her husband, who is sure to have in reserve a pickle quite sufficiently strong for the inevitable rod, as the poor scrambler knows too well. All you can do is to accept her apologies with a good grace, and to carry away with you a vivid recollection of an awkward half-hour, a spoilt dinner, and a scrambling hostess all abroad and out of time, sweeping through the room very heated, very good-tempered, only half-dressed and chronically out of breath.

Scramblers can never learn the value of money, neither for themselves nor for others. They are famous for borrowing small sums which they forget to return ; but, to do them justice, they are just as willing to lend what they never dream of asking for again. Long ago they caught hold of the fact that money is only a circulating medium, and they have added an extra speed to the circulation at which slower folk stand aghast. To be sure, the practical results of their theory are not very satisfactory, and the confusion between the possessive pronouns which distinguishes their financial catechism is apt to lead to unpleasant issues.

Scrambling women are especially notorious for the way in which they set themselves afloat without sufficient means to carry them on; finding themselves stranded in mid-career because they have made no calculations and have forgotten the rule of subtraction. They find themselves at a small Italian town, say, where the virtues of the British banking system are unknown, and where their letters of credit and circular notes are not worth more than the value of the paper they are written on. More than one British matron of respectable condition and weak arithmetic has found herself in such a plight as this, with her black-eyed landlord perfectly civil and well-bred, but as firm as a rock in his resolution that the Signora shall not depart out of his custody till his little account is paid—a plight out of which she has to scramble the best way she can, with the loss perhaps of a little dignity and of more repute—at least in the locality where her solid scudi gave out and her precious paper could not be cashed. This is the same woman who offers an omnibus conductor a sovereign for a threepenny fare; who gives the village grocer a ten-pound note for a shilling's-worth of sugar; and who, when she comes up to London for a day's shopping, and has got her last parcel made up and ready to be put into her cab, finds she has not left herself half enough money to pay for it—with a shopman whose faith in human nature is by no means lively, and who only last week was bitten by a lady swindler of undeniable manners and appearance, and not very unlike herself. She has been known too, to go into a confectioner's and, after having made an excellent luncheon, to find to her dismay that she has left her purse in the pocket of her other dress at home, and that she has not sixpence about her. In fact there is not an equivocal position in which forgetfulness, want of method, want of foresight, and all the other characteristics which make up scrambling in the concrete, can place her, in which she has not been at some time or other. But no experience teaches her; the scrambler she was born, the scrambler she will die, and to the last will tumble through her life, all her ends flying and deprecating excuses on her lips.

Scramblers are notoriously great for making promises, and as notorious for not performing what they promise. Kindhearted as they are in general, and willing to do their friends a service—going out of their way indeed to proffer kindnesses quite beyond your expectations and the range of their duties towards you, and always undertaking works of supererogation; which works in fact lead to more than half their normal scramble—they forget the next hour the promise on which you have based your dearest hopes. Or, if they do not forget it, they find it is crowded out of time by a multitude of engagements and prior promises, of all of which they were innocently oblivious when they offered to do your business so frankly, and swore so confidently they would set about it now at once and get it out of hand without delay. The oath and the offer which you took to be as sure as the best chain-cable, you will find on trial to be only a rope of sand that could not bind so much as a bunch of tow together, still less hold the anchor of a life; and many a heart, sick with hope deferred and wrung with the disappointment which might have been so easily prevented, has been half broken before now from the anguish that has followed on the failure of the kindhearted scrambler to perform the promise voluntarily made, and the service earnestly pressed on a reluctant acceptor.

This is the tragic side of the scrambler's career, the shadow thrown by almost every one of the class. For all the minor delinquencies of hurry and unpunctuality in social affairs it is not difficult to find full and ample forgiveness; but when it comes to untrustworthiness in graver matters, then the scrambler becomes a scourge instead of only an inconvenience. The only safe way of dealing with the class is to take them when we can get hold of them, and to accept them for what they are worth; but not to rely on them, and not to attempt any mortising of our own affairs with their promises. They are the froth and foam of society, pretty and pleasant enough in the sunlight as they splash and splutter about the rocks; but they are not the deep waters which bear the burden of our ships and by which the life of the world is maintained.

FLATTERY.

NOTHING is so delightful as flattery. To hear and believe pleasant fictions about oneself is a temptation too seductive for weak mortals to resist, as the typical legends of all mythologies and the private histories of most individuals show; in consequence of which, home truths, to one used to ideal portraiture, come like draughts of 'bitter cup' to the dram-drinker. And flattery is dram-drinking; and yet not quite without good uses to balance its undeniable evil, if it be only exaggeration and not wholly falsehood; that is, if it assumes as a matter of course the presence of virtues potential to your character but not always active, and praises you for what you might be if you chose to live up to your best. Many a weak brother and weaker sister, and all children, can be heartened into goodness by a little dash of judicious praise or flattery where ponderous exhortation and grave reproof would fail; just as a heavily-laden horse can be coaxed up-hill when the whip and spur would lead to untimely jibbing. If, on the contrary, the flattery is of a kind that makes you believe yourself an exceptionally fine fellow when you are only 'mean trash'—a king of men when you are nothing better nor nobler than a moral nigger—making you satisfied with yourself when at your worst—then it is an unmitigated evil; for it then becomes dram-drinking of a very poisonous kind, which sooner or later does for your soul what unlimited blue ruin does for your body. But this is what we generally mean when we speak of flattery; and this is the kind which has such a deservedly bad name from moralists of all ages.

The flatteries of men to women, and those of women to men, are very different in kind and direction. Men flatter women for what they are—for their beauty, their grace, their sweetness, their charmingness in general; while a woman will flatter a man for what he does—for his speech in the House last night, of which she understands little; for his book, of which she understands less; or for his pleading, of which she understands nothing at all. Not that this signifies much on either side. The most unintellectual little woman in the world has brains enough to look up in your face sweetly, and breathe out something that sounds like 'beautiful—charming—so clever,' vaguely sketching the outline of a hymn of praise to which your own vanity supplies the versicles. For you must have an exceptionally strong head if you can rate the sketch at its real value and see for yourself how utterly meaningless it is.

You may be the most mystical poet of the day, suggesting to your acutest readers grave doubts as to your own power of comprehending yourself; or you may be the most subtle metaphysician, to follow whom in your labyrinth of reasoning requires perhaps the rarest order of brains to be met with; but you will nevertheless believe any narrow-browed, small-headed woman who tells you in a low sweet voice, with a gentle uplifting of her eyes and a suggestive curve of her lip, that she has found you both intelligible and charming, and that she quite agrees with you and shares your every sentiment. If she further tells you that all her life long she has thought in exactly the same way but was wholly unable to express herself, and that you have now supplied her want and translated into words her vague ideas, and if she says this with a reverential kind of effusiveness, you are done for, so far as your critical power goes; and should some candid friend, whom she has not flattered, tell you with brutal frankness that your bewitching little flatterer has neither the brains nor the education to understand you, you will set him down as a slanderer, spiteful and malignant, and call his candour envy because he has not been so lucky as yourself.

The most subtle form of flattery is that which asks your advice with the pretence of needing it—your advice, particularly—yours above that of all other persons, as the wisest, best, most useful to be obtained. This too is a form that belongs rather to women in their relations with men than the converse; though sometimes men will pretend to want a woman's advice about their love affairs, and will perhaps make-believe to be guided by it. Not unfrequently, however, asking one woman's opinion and advice about another is a masked manner of love-making on its own account; though sometimes it may be done for flattery only, when there are reasons. Of course not all advice-asking is flattery; but when intended only to please and not meant to be genuine, it is perhaps one of the most potent instruments of the art to be met with.

But if seeking advice be the most subtle form of flattery, the most intoxicating is that which pretends to moral elevation or reform by your influence. The reformation of a rake is a work which no woman alive could be found to resist if the rake offered it to her as his last chance of salvation; and to lead a pretty sinner back to the ways of picturesque virtue by his own influence only is a temptation to self-reliance which no man could refuse—a flattery which not Diogenes nor Zeno himself could see through. The pretensions of any one else would be laughed at cruelly enough; but this is one of the things where personal experience and critical judgment never go in harness together—one of the manifestations of flattery which would overcome the calmest and bewilder the wisest.

Priests of all denominations are especially open to this kind of flattery; not only from pretty sinners who have gone openly out of the right line, but from quite comely and respectable maids and matrons who have lived blamelessly so far as the broad moral distinctions go, yet who have not lived the Awakened Life until roused thereunto by this peculiarly favoured minister. It is a tremendous trial of a man's discernment when such flattery is offered to him. How much of this pretended awakening is real? How much of this sudden spiritual insight is true, and not a mere phrasing, artfully adopted for pleasantness only? These are the cases where we most want that famous spear of Ithuriel to help us to a right estimate, for they are beyond the power of any ordinary man to determine.

But if priests are subject to these delusions of flattery on the one hand, they know how to practise them on the other. Take away the flattery which, mingled with occasional rebuke, forms the great ministerial spur, and both Revivalism and Ritualism would flag like flowers without 'the gentle dews.' Scolded for their faults in dress, for their vanity, extravagance and other feminine vices, are not women also flattered as the favourites of heaven and of the Church? Are they not told that they are the lilies of the ecclesiastical garden? the divinely appointed missionaries for the preservation of virtue and godly truth in the world? without whom the coarser race of men would be given over to inconceivable spiritual evil, to infidelity and all immorality. We may be very sure of this, that if humanity, and especially feminine humanity, were not flattered as well as chastened, clerical influence would not last for a day.

There is one kind of flattery which is common to both men and women, and that is the expressed preference of sex. Thus, when men want to flatter women, they say how infinitely they prefer their society to that of their own sex; and women will say the same to men. Or, if they do not say it, they will act it. See a set of women congregated together without the light of a manly countenance among them. They may talk to each other certainly; and one or two will sit away together and discuss their private affairs with animation; but the great mass of them are only half vitalized while waiting the advent of the men to rouse them into life and the desire to please. No man who goes up first from the dinner-table, and earlier than he was expected, can fail to see the change which comes over those wearied, limp, indifferent-looking faces and figures so soon as he enters the room. He is like the prince whose kiss woke up the Sleeping Beauty and all her court; and can any one say that this is not flattery of the most delightful kind? To be the Pygmalion even for a moment, and for the weakest order of soul-giving, is about the greatest pleasure that a man can know, if he be susceptible to the finer kinds of flattery.

Some women indeed, not only show their preference for men, but openly confess it, and confess at the same time to a lofty contempt or abhorrence for the society of women. These are generally women who are, or have been, beauties; or who have literary and intellectual pretensions; or who despise babies and contemn housekeeping, and profess themselves unable to talk to other women because of their narrowness and stupidity. But for the most part they are women who, by their beauty or their position, have been used to receive extra attention from men; and thus their preference is not flattery so much as *exigence*. Women who have been in India, or wherever else they are in the minority in society, are of this kind; and nothing is more amazing to them when they first come home than the attentions which a certain style of Englishwoman pays to men, instead of demanding and receiving attentions from them.

There are also those sweet, humble, caressing women who flatter you with every word and look, but whose flattery is nothing but a pretty dress put on for show and taken off when the show is done with. Anything serves for an occasion with these people. Why, the way in which certain unmarried women will caress a child before you is an implied flattery; and they know it. If only they would be careful to carry these pretty ante-nuptial ways into the home where nothing is to be gained by them but a humdrum husband's happiness! But too often the woman whose whole attitude was one of flattering devotion before her end was gained, gives up every shred of that which she had in such profusion, when she has attained her object, and lets the home go bare of that which was so beautiful and seductive in the ball-room and the flirting corner.

Some men however, want more home flattery to keep them tolerably happy and up to the mark than any woman with a soul to be saved by truth can give. Poets and artists are of this kind—men who literally live on praise, without which they droop and can do nothing. With them it is absolutely necessary that the people with whom they are associated should be of appreciative and sympathetic natures; but the burden comes heavy when they want, as they generally do, so much more than this. For, in truth, they want flattery in excess of sympathy; and if they do not get it they hold themselves as the victims of an unkind fate, and fill the world with the echo of their woes. This is nine-tenths of the cause why great geniuses are so often unhappy in married life. They demand more incessant flattery than can be kept up by one woman, unless she has not only an exceptional power of love but also an exceptional power of self-suppression. They think that by virtue of their genius they are entitled to a Benjamin's mess of devotion double that given to other men; and when they get only Judah's share, they cry out that they are ill-used, and make the world think them ill-used as well.

But though a little home flattery helps the home life immeasurably, and greases the creaking domestic wheels more than anything else can, a great deal is just the most pernicious thing that can be offered. The belief prevalent in some families that all the very small and commonplace members thereof are the world's wonders and greater than any one else—that no one is so clever as Harry, no one so pretty as Julia, that Amy's red hair is of a more brilliant gold than can be found elsewhere, and Edward's mathematical abilities about equal to Newton's—this belief, nourished and acted on, is sure to turn out an insufferable collection of prigs and self-conceited damsels who have to be brought down innumerable pegs before they find their own level. But we often see this; especially in country places where there is not much society to give a standard for comparative measurement; and we know that those fond parents and doting relations are blindly and diligently sowing seeds of bitterness for a future harvest of sorrow for their darlings. These young people must be made to suffer if they are to be of any good whatever in the world; and finding their level, after the exalted position which they have been supposed to fill so long, and being pelted with the unsavoury missiles of truth in exchange for all the incense of flattery to which they have been used, will be suffering enough. But it has to be gone through; this being one of the penalties to which the unwisdom of love so often subjects its objects.

The flattery met with in society is not often very harmful save to coarse or specially simple natures. You must be either one or the other to be able to believe it. Lady Morgan was perhaps the most unblushing and excessive of the tribe of social flatterers; but that was her engine, the ladder by which she did a good part of her climbing. We must not confound with this kind of flattery the impulsive expression of praise or love which certain outspoken people indulge in to the last. You may as well try to dam up Niagara as to make some folks reticent of their thoughts and feelings. And when one of this kind sees anything that he or she likes, the praise has to come out, with superlatives if the creature be prone to exaggeration. But this is not flattery; it is merely a certain childlike expansiveness which lasts with some into quite old age. Unfortunately, very few understand this childlike expansiveness when they see it. Hence it subjects its possessor to misrepresentation and unfriendly jibes, so soon as his or her back is turned, and the explosion of exaggerated but perfectly sincere praise is discussed critically by the uninterested part of the audience.

LA FEMME PASSÉE.

WITHOUT doubt it is a time of trial to all women, more or less painful according to individual disposition, when they first begin to grow old and lose their good looks. Youth and beauty make up so much of their personal value, so much of their natural final cause, that when these are gone many feel as if their whole career were at an end, and as if nothing were left to them now that they are no longer young enough to be loved as girls are loved, or pretty enough to be admired as mature sirens are admired. For women of a certain position have so little wholesome occupation, and so little ambition for anything save indeed that miserable thing called 'getting on in society,' that they cannot change their way of life with advancing years. Hence they do not attempt to find interest in things outside themselves, and independent of the personal attractiveness which in youth constituted their whole pleasure of existence.

This is essentially the case with fashionable women, who have staked their all on appearance, and to whom good looks are of more account than noble deeds ; and, accordingly, the struggle to remain young is a frantic one with them, and as degrading as it is frantic.

With the ideal woman of middle age—that pleasant She with her calm face and soft manner, who unites the charms of both epochs, retaining the ready responsiveness of youth while adding the wider sympathies of experience—with her there has been no such struggle to make herself an anachronism. Consequently she remains beautiful to the last—far more beautiful than all the pastes and washes in Madame Rachel's shop could make her. Sometimes, if rarely in these latter days, we meet her in society, where she carries with her an atmosphere of her own—an atmosphere of honest, wholesome truth and love, which makes every one who enters it better and purer for the time. All children and all young persons love her, because she understands and loves them. For she is essentially a mother—that is, a woman who can forget herself; who can give without asking to receive ; and who, without losing any of the individualism which belongs to self-respect, can yet live for and in the lives of others, and find her best joy in the well-being of those about her. There is no exaggerated sacrifice in this ; it is simply the fulfilment of woman's highest duty—the expression of that grand maternal instinct which need not necessarily include the fact of personal maternity, but which, with all women worthy of the name, must find utterance in some line of unselfish action.

The ideal woman of middle age understands the young because she has lived with them. If a mother, she has performed her maternal duties with cheerfulness and love. There has been no giving up her nursery to the care of a hired servant who is expected to do for so many pounds a year things which the tremendous instinct of a mother's love could not find strength to do. When she had children, she attended to them in great part herself, and learnt all about their tempers, their maladies, and the best methods of management. As they grew up she was still the best friend they had—the Providence of their young lives who gave them both care and justice, both love and guidance. Such a manner of life has forced her to forget herself. When her child lay ill, perhaps dying, she had no heart and no time to think of her own appearance, and whether this dressing-gown was more becoming than that; and what did the doctor think of her with her hair pushed back from her face?—and what a fright she must have looked in the morning light after her sleepless night of watching! The world and all its petty pleasures and paltry pains faded away in the presence of the stern tragedy of the hour; and not the finest ball of the season seemed to be worth a thought compared to the all-absorbing question of whether her child slept after his draught and whether he ate his food with better appetite. And such a life, in spite of all its cares, has kept her young as well as unselfish; we should rather say, young because unselfish. As she comes into the room with her daughters, her kindly face unpolluted by paint, her dress picturesque or fashionable according to her taste, but decent in form and consistent in tone with her age, it is often remarked that she looks more like the sister than the mother of her girls. This is because she is in harmony with her age, and has not therefore put herself in rivalry with them; and harmony is the very keystone of beauty. Her hair is thickly streaked with white; the girlish firmness and transparency of her skin have gone; the pearly clearness of her eye is clouded; the slender grace of line is lost—but for all that she is beautiful, and she is intrinsically young. What she has lost in outside material charm—in that mere *beauté du diable* of youth—she has gained in character and expression; and by not attempting to simulate the attractiveness of a girl, she keeps what nature gave her—the attractiveness of middle age. And as every epoch has its own beauty—if women would but learn that truth—she is as beautiful now as a matron of fifty, because in harmony with her years, as she was when a maiden of sixteen.

This is the ideal woman of middle age, met with even yet at times in society—the woman whom all men respect; whom all women envy, and wonder how she does it; and whom all the young adore, and wish they had for an elder sister or an aunt. And the secret of it all lies in truth, in love, in purity, and in unselfishness.

LA FEMME PASSÉE.

Standing far apart from this sweet and wholesome idealization is *la femme passée* of to-day—the reality as we meet with it at balls and fêtes and afternoon At Homes, ever foremost in the mad chase after pleasure, for which alone she seems to think she has been sent into the world. Dressed in the extreme of youthful fashion; her thinning hair dyed and crimped and fired till it is more like red-brown tow than hair; her flaccid cheeks ruddled; her throat whitened; her bust displayed with unflinching generosity—as if beauty is to be measured by cubic inches; her lustreless eyes blackened round the lids, to give the semblance of limpidity to the tarnished whites; perhaps the pupils dilated by belladonna; perhaps a false and fatal brilliancy for the moment given by opium, or by eau de cologne, of which she has a store in her carriage, and drinks as she passes from ball to ball; no kindly drapery of lace nor of gauze to conceal the breadth of her robust maturity, to soften the dreadful shadows of her leanness—there she stands, the wretched creature who will not consent to grow old, and who still affects to be a fresh coquettish girl when she is nothing but *la femme passée—la femme passée et ridicule* into the bargain.

There is not a folly for which even the thoughtlessness of youth is but a poor excuse into which she, in all the plenitude of her abundant experience, does not plunge. Wife and mother as she may be, she flirts and makes love as if an honourable issue were as open to her as to her young daughter;

or as if she did not know to what end flirting and making love lead in all ages. If we watch the career of such a woman, we see how, by slow but very sure degrees, she is obliged to lower the standard of her adorers, and to take up at last with men of inferior social position, who are content to buy her patronage by their devotion. To the best men of her own class she can give nothing that they value; so she barters with snobs, who go into the transaction with their eyes open, and take the whole affair as a matter of exchange, and *quid pro quo* rigidly exacted. Or she does really dazzle some very young and low-born man who is weak as well as ambitious, and who thinks the fugitive regard of a middle-aged woman of high rank something to be proud of and boasted about. That she is as old as his own mother—at this moment selling tapes behind a village counter, or gathering up the eggs in a country farm—tells nothing against the association with him; and the woman who began her career of flirtation with the son of a duke ends it with the son of a shopkeeper, having between these two terms spanned all the several degrees of degradation which lie between giving and buying. She cannot help herself; for it is part of the insignia of her artificial youth to have the reputation of a love-affair, or the pretence of one, even if the reality be a mere delusion. When such a woman as this is one of the matrons, and consequently one of the leaders of society, what can we expect from the girls? What worse example could be given to the young? When we see her with her own daughters we feel instinctively that she is the most disastrous adviser they could have; and when in the company of girls or young married women not belonging to her, we doubt whether we ought not to warn their natural guardians against allowing such association, for all that her standing in society is undeniable, and not a door is shut against her.

What good in life does this kind of woman do? All her time is taken up, first in trying to make herself look twenty or thirty years younger than she is, and then in trying to make others believe the same. She has neither thought nor energy to spare from this, to her, far more important work than is feeding the hungry or nursing the sick, rescuing the fallen or soothing the sorrowful. The final cause of her existence seems to be the impetus she has given to a certain branch of trade manufacture—unless we add to this, the corruption of society. For whom, but for her, are the 'little secrets' which are continually being advertised as woman's social salvation—regardless of grammar? The 'eaux noire, brun, et châtain, which dyes the hair any shade in one minute;' the 'kohhl for the eyelids;' the 'blanc de perle,' and 'rouge de Lubin'—which does not wash off; the 'bleu pour les veines;' the 'rouge of eight shades,' and 'the sympathetic blush,' which are cynically offered for the use and adoption of our mothers and daughters, find their chief patroness in the *femme passée* who makes herself up—the middle-aged matron engaged in her frantic struggle against time, and obstinately refusing to grow old in spite of all that nature may say or do. Bad as the Girl of the Period is, this horrible travesty of her vices in the modern matron is even worse. Indeed, were it not for her, the girls would never have gone to such lengths as those to which they have gone; for elder women naturally have immense influence over younger ones, and if mothers were resolutely to set their faces against the follies of the day, daughters would and must give in. As it is, some go even ahead of the young, and, by example on the one hand and rivalry on the other, sow the curse of corruption broadcast where they were meant to have only a pure influence and to set a wise example. Were it not for those who still remain faithful—women who regard themselves as the trustees for humanity and virtue—the world would go to ruin forthwith; but so long as the five righteous are left we have hope and a certain amount of security for the future, when the present disgraceful madness of society shall have passed away.

SPOILT WOMEN.

LIKE children and all soft things, women are soon spoilt if subjected to unwholesome conditions. Sometimes the spoiling comes from over-harshness, sometimes from over-indulgence; what we are speaking of to-day is the latter condition—the spoiling which comes from being petted and given way to and indulged, till they think themselves better than everybody else, and living under laws made specially for them. Men get spoilt too in the same manner; but for the most part there is a tougher fibre in them which resists the flabby influences of flattery and exaggerated attention better than can the morale of the weaker sex; besides, even arbitrary men meet with opposition in certain directions, and the most self-contented social autocrat knows that his adherents criticize though they dare not oppose.

A man who has been spoilt by success and a gratified ambition, so that he thinks himself a small Alexander in his own way and able to conquer any obstacles which may present themselves, has a certain high-handed activity of will about him that does not interfere with his duties in life; he is not made fretful and impatient and exigeant as a woman is—as if he alone of all mankind ought to be exempt from misfortunes and annoyances; as if his friends must never die, his youth never fade, his circumstances run always smooth, protected by the care of others from all untoward hitch; as if time and tide, which wait for no one else, are bound to him as humble servants dutifully observant of his wishes. The useful art of finding his level, which he learnt at school and in his youth generally, keeps him from any very weak manifestation of being spoilt; save indeed, when he has been spoilt by women at home, nursed up by an adoring wife and a large circle of wife's sisters almost as adoring, to all of whom his smallest wishes are religious obligations and his faintest virtues godly graces, and who vie with each other which of them shall wait upon him most servilely, flatter him most outrageously, coax and coddle him most entirely, and so do him the largest amount of spiritual damage, and unfit him most thoroughly for the worth and work of masculine life. A man subjected to this insidious injury is simply ruined so far as any real manliness of nature goes. He is made into that sickening creature, 'a sweet being,' as the women call him—a woman's man with æsthetic tastes and a turn for poetry; full of highflown sentiment and morbid sympathies; a man almost as much woman as man, who has no backbone of useful ambition in him, but who puts his whole life into love, and who becomes at last emphatically not worth his salt.

Bad as it is for men of the world to be kowtowed to by men, it is not so bad, because not so weakening, as the domestic idolatry which sometimes goes on when one man is the centre of a large family of women, and the only object upon which the natural feminine instinct can expend itself. No greater damage can be done to a man than is done by this kind of domestic idolatry. But, in truth, the evil is too pleasant to be resisted; and there is scarcely a man so far master of himself as to withstand the subtle intoxication, the sweet and penetrating poison, of woman's tender flattery and loving submission. To a certain extent he holds it so entirely the right thing, because it is natural and instinctive, that it is difficult to draw the line and map out exactly the division between right and wrong, pleasantness and harmfulness, and where loving submission ends and debasing slavishness begins.

Spoilt women are spoilt mainly from a like cause: over-attention from men. A few certainly are to be found, as pampered daughters, with indulgent mammas and subservient aunts given up to ruining their young charges with the utmost despatch possible; but this is comparatively a rare form of the disease, and one which a little wholesome matrimonial discipline would soon cure. For it is seldom that a petted daughter becomes a spoilt wife—human affairs having that marvellous power of equation, that inevitable tendency to readjust the balance, which prevents the continuance of a like excess under different forms. Besides, a spoilt daughter generally makes such a supremely unpleasant wife that the husband has no inducement to continue the mistake, and therefore either lowers her tone by a judicious exhibition of snubbing, or, if she be aggressive as well as unpleasant, leaves her to fight with her shadows in the best way she can, glad for his own part to escape the strife she will not forego.

The spoilt woman is impatient of anything like rivalry. She never has a female friend—certainly not one of her own degree, and not one at all in the true sense of the word. Friendship presupposes equality; and a spoilt woman knows no equality. She has been so long accustomed to consider herself as lady-paramount that she cannot understand it if any one steps in to share her honours and divide her throne. To praise the beauty of any other woman, to find her charming, and to pay her the attention due to a charming woman, is to insult our spoilt darling, and to slight her past forgiveness. If there is only one good thing, it must be given to her—the first seat, the softest cushion, the most protected situation; and she looks for the best of all things as if naturally consecrated from her birth to the sunshine of life, and as if the 'cold shade' which may do for others were by no means the portion allotted to her.

It is almost impossible to make the spoilt woman understand the grace or the glory of sacrifice. By rare good fortune she may sometimes be found to possess an indestructible germ of conscience which sorrow and necessity can develope into active good; but only sometimes. The spoilt woman *par excellence* understands only her own value, only her own merits and the absolutism of her own requirements; and sacrifice, self-abnegation, and the whole class of virtues belonging to unselfishness, are as much unknown to her as is the Decalogue in the original, or the squaring of the circle. The spoilt woman, as the wife of an unsuccessful husband or the mother of sickly children, is a pitiable spectacle. If obliged to sacrifice her usual luxuries, to make an old gown serve when a new one is desired, to sit up all night watching by the sick-bed, to witness the painful details of illness, perhaps of death, to meet hardship face to face and to bend her back to the burden of sorrow, she is at the first absolutely lost. Not the thing to be done, but her own discomfort in doing it, is the one master idea—not others' needs, but her own pain in supplying them, is the great grief of the moment. Many are the hard lessons set us by life and fate, but the hardest of all is that given to the spoilt woman when she is made to think for others rather than for herself, and is forced by the exigencies of circumstances to sacrifice her own ease for the greater necessities of her kind.

All that large part of the true woman's nature which expresses itself in serving is an unknown function to the spoilt woman. She must be waited on, but she cannot in her turn serve even the one she loves. She is the woman who calls her husband from one end of the room to the other to put down her cup, rather than reach out her arm and put it down for herself; who, however weary he may be, will bid him get up and ring the bell, though it is close to her own hand, and her longest walk during the day has been from the dining-room to the drawing-room. It is not that she cannot do these small offices for herself, but that she likes the feeling of being waited on; and it is not for love, and the amiable if weak pleasure of attracting the notice of the beloved, but it is for the vanity of being a little somebody for the moment, and of playing off the small regality involved in the procedure, that she claims his attention. She would not return that attention. Unlike the Eastern women, who wait on their lords hand and foot, and who place their highest honour in their lowliest service, the spoilt woman of Western life knows nothing of the natural grace of womanly serving for love, for grace, or for gratitude.

This kind of thing is peculiarly strong among the *demi-monde* of the higher class, and among women who are of the *demi-monde* by nature. The respect they cannot command by their virtues they demand in the simulation of manner; and perhaps no women are more tenacious of the outward forms of deference than those who have lost their claim to the vital reality. It is very striking to see the difference between the women of this type, the *petites maîtresses* who require the utmost attention and almost servility from man, and the noble dignity of service which the pure woman can afford to give—which she finds indeed, that it belongs to the very purity and nobleness of her womanhood to give. It is the old story of the ill-assured position which is afraid of its own weakness, and the security which can afford to descend—the rule holding good for other things besides mere social place.

Another characteristic of the spoilt woman is the changeableness and excitability of her temper. All suavity and gentleness and delightful gaiety and perfect manners when everything goes right, she startles you by her outburst of petulance when the first cross comes. If no man is a hero to his valet, neither is a spoilt woman a heroine to her maid; and the lady who has just been the charm of the drawing-room, upstairs in her boudoir makes her maid go through spiritual exercises to which walking among burning ploughshares is easy-going. A length of lace unstarched, a ribbon unsewed, a flower set awry, anything that crumples one of the myriad rose-leaves on which she lies, and the spoilt woman raves as much as if each particular leaf had become suddenly a bunch of thorns. If a dove were to be transformed to a hawk the change would not be more complete, more startling, than that which occurs when the spoilt woman of well-bred company manners puts off her mask to her maid, and shows her temper over trifles. Whoever else may suffer the grievances of life, she cannot understand that she also must be at times one of the sufferers with the rest; and if by chance the bad moment comes, the person accompanying it has a hard time of it.

There are spoilt women also who have their peculiar exercises in thought and opinion, and who cannot suffer that any one should think differently from themselves, or find those things sacred which to them are accursed. They will hear nothing but what is in harmony with themselves; and they take it as a personal insult when men or women attempt to reason with them, or even hold their own without flinching. This kind is to be found specially among the more intellectual of a family or a circle—women who are pronounced clever by their friends, and who have been so long accustomed to think themselves clever that they have become spoilt mentally as others are personally, and fancy that minds and thoughts must follow in their direction, just as eyes and hands must follow and attend their sisters. The spoilt woman of the mental kind is a horrid nuisance generally. She is greatly given to large discourse. But discourse of a kind that leans all to one side, and that denies the right of any one to criticize, doubt, or contradict, is an intellectual Tower of Pisa under the shadow of which it is not pleasant to live.

DOVECOTS.

TIMES must be very bad indeed if a faithful few are not still left to keep the sources of society sweet and wholesome. When corruption has gone through the whole mass and all classes are bad alike, everything comes to an end, and there is a general overthrow of national life; but while some are left pure and unspotted, we are not quite undone, and we may reasonably hope for better days in the future. In the midst of the reign of the Girl of the Period, with her slang and her boldness—of the fashionable woman, with her denial of duty and her madness for pleasure—we come every now and then upon a group of good girls of the real old English type; the faithful few growing up silently among us, but none the less valuable because they are silent and make no public display; doves who are content with life as they have it in the dovecot, and have no desire to be either eagles dwelling on romantic heights, or peacocks displaying their pride in sunny courts. We find these faithful few in town and country alike; but they are rifest in the country, where there is less temptation to go wrong than there is in the large towns, and where life is simpler and the moral tone undeniably higher. The leading feature of these girls is their love of home and of their own family, and their power of making occupation and happiness out of apparently meagre materials. If they are the elders, they find amusement and interest in their little brothers and sisters, whom they consider immensely funny and to whom they are as much girl-mothers as sisters; if they are the youngers, they idolize their baby nephews and nieces. For there is always a baby going on somewhere about these houses—babies being the great excitement of home-life, and the antiseptic element among women which keeps everything else pure. They are passionately attached to papa and mamma, whom they think the very king and queen of humanity, yet whom they do not call by even endearing slang names. It has never occurred to them to criticize them as ordinary mortals; and as they have not been in the way of learning the prevailing accent of disrespect, they have not shaken off that almost religious veneration for their parents which all young people naturally feel, if they have been well brought up and are not corrupted.

The yoke in most middle-class country-houses is one fitting very loosely round all necks; and as they have all the freedom they desire or could use, the girls are not fretted by undue pressure, and are content to live in peace under such restraints as they have. They adore their elder brothers who are from home just beginning the great battle of life for themselves, and confidently believe them to be the finest fellows going, and the future great men of the day if only they care to put out those splendid talents of theirs, and take the trouble of plucking the prizes within their reach. They may have a slight reservation perhaps, in favour of the brother's friend, whom they place on a pedestal of almost equal height. But they keep their mental architecture a profound secret from every one, and do not suffer it to grow into too solid a structure unless it has some surer foundation than their own fancy. For, though doves are loving, they are by no means lovesick, and are too healthy and natural and quietly busy for unwholesome dreams. If one of them marries, they all unite in loving the man who comes in among them. He is adopted as one of themselves, and leaps into a family of idolizing sisters who pet him as their brother—with just that subtle little difference in their petting, in so much as it comes from sisters unaccustomed, and so has the charm of novelty without the prurient excitement of naughtiness. But this kind of thing is about the most dangerous to a man's moral nature that can befall him. Though pretty to see and undeniably pleasant to experience, and though perfectly innocent in every way, still, nothing enervates him so much as this idolatrous submission of a large family of women. In a widow's house, where there are many daughters and no sons, and where the man who marries one marries the whole family and is worshipped accordingly, the danger is of course increased tenfold ; but if there are brothers and a father, the sister's husband, though affectionately cooed over, is not made quite such a fuss with, and the association is all the less hurtful in consequence.

These girls lead a by no means stupid life, though it is a quiet one, and without any spasmodic events or tremendous cataclysms. They go a great deal among the village poor, and they teach at the Sunday-school, and attend the mothers' meetings and clothing-clubs and the like, and learn to get interested in their humbler friends, who after all are Christian sisters. They read their romances in real life instead of in three-volume novels, and study human nature as it is—in the rough certainly, but perhaps in more genuine form than if they learnt it only in what is called society. Then they have their pleasures, though they are of an unexciting kind and what fast girls would call awfully slow. They have their horses and their croquet parties, their lawn tennis and their archery meetings; they have batches of new music, and a monthly box from Mudie's—and they know the value of both; they go out to tea, and sometimes to dinner, in the neighbourhood; and they enjoy the rare county balls with a zest unknown to London girls who are out every night in the week. They have their village flower-shows, which the great families patronize in a free-and-easy kind of way, and which give occupation for weeks before and subject for talk for weeks after; their school feasts, where the pet parson of the district comes out with his best anecdotes, and makes mild jokes at a long distance from Sydney Smith; their periodical missionary meetings, where they have great guns from London, and where they hear unctuous stories about the saintliness of converted cannibals, and are required to believe in the power of change of creed to produce an ethnological miracle; they have their friends to stay with them—schoolgirl friends—with whom they exchange deep confidences, and go back over the old days—so old to their youth!—their brothers come down in the summer, and their brothers' friends come with them, and do a little spooning in the shrubbery. But there is more spooning done at picnics than anywhere else; and more offers are made there under the shadow of the old ruin, or in the quiet leafy nook by the river side, than at any other gathering time of the country. And as we are all to a certain extent what we are made by our environment, the doves take to these pleasures quite kindly and gratefully, as being the only ones known to them, and enjoy themselves in a simplicity of circumstances which would give no pleasure at all to girls accustomed to more highly-spiced entertainments.

Doves know very little of evil. They are not in the way of learning it; and they do not care to learn it. The few villagers who are supposed to lead ill lives are spoken of below the breath, and carefully avoided without being critically studied. When the railway is to be carried past their quiet nest, there is an immense excitement as the report goes that a knot of strange men have been seen scattering themselves over the fields with their little white flags and theodolites, their measuring lines and levels. But when the army of navvies follows after, the excitement is changed to consternation, and a general sense of evil to come advancing ruthlessly towards them. The clergy of the district organize special services, and the scared doves keep religiously away from the place where the navvies are hutted. They think them little better than the savages about whom the Deputation tell them once or twice a year; and they create almost as much terror as an encampment of gipsies. They represent the lawless forces of the world and the unknown sins of strong men; and the wildest story about them is not too wild to be believed. The railway altogether is a great offence to the neighbourhood, and the line is assumed to destroy the whole scenic beauty of the place. There are lamentations over the cockneys it will bring down; over the high prices it will create, the immorality it will cause. Only the sons who are out in the world and have learnt how life goes on outside the dovecot, advocate keeping pace with the times; and a few of the stronger minded of the sisters listen to them with a timid admiration of their breadth and boldness, and think there may be two sides to the question after all. When the dashing captain and his fast wife suddenly appear in the village—as often happens in these remote districts—the doves are in a state of great moral tribulation. They are scandalized by Mrs. Highflyer's costume and complexion, and think her manners odd and doubtful ; her slang shocks them ; and when they meet her in the lanes, talking so loudly and laughing so shrilly with that horrid-looking man in a green cutaway, they feel as fluttered as their namesakes when a hawk is hovering over the farmyard. The dashing captain, who does not use a prayer-book at church, who stares at all the girls so rudely, and who has even been seen to wink at some of the prettier cottage girls, and his handsome wife with her equivocal complexion and pronounced fashions, who makes eyes at the curate, are never heartily adopted by the local magnates, though vouched for by some far-away backer; and the doves always feel them to be strange bodies among them, and out of their rightful element somehow. If things go quietly without an explosion, well and good ; but if the truth bursts to the surface in the shape of a London detective, and the Highflyers are found to be no better than they should be, the consternation and half-awed wonderment at the existence of so much effrontery and villany in their atmosphere create an impression which no time effaces. The first clash of innocence with evil is an event in the life of the innocent the effect of which nothing ever destroys.

The dovecot is rather dull in the winter, and the doves are somewhat moped ; but even then they have the church to decorate, and the sentiment of Christmas to enliven them. The absent ones of the family too, return to the old hearth while they can; and as the great joy of the dovecot lies in the family union that is kept up, and in the family love which is so strong, the visits of those who no longer live at home bring a moral summer as warm and cheering as the physical sunshine. But they do not all assemble. For many of the doves marry men whose work lies abroad; these quiet country-houses being the favourite matrimonial hunting-grounds for colonists and Anglo-Indians. So that some are always absent whose healths are drunk in the traditional punch, while eyes grow moist as the names are given. Doves are not disinclined to marry men who have to go abroad, for all the passionate family love common to them. Travel is a golden dream to them in their still homes; but travel properly companioned. For even the most adventurous among them are not independent, as we mean when we speak of independence in women. They are essentially home-girls, family-girls, doves who cannot exist without a dovecot, however humble. The family is everything to them; and they are utterly unfit for the solitude which so many of our self-supporting women can accept quite resignedly. Not that they are necessarily useless even as breadwinners. They could work, if pushed to it; but it must be in a quiet womanly way, with the mother, the sister, the husband as the helper—with the home as the place of rest and the refuge. Their whole lines are laid in love and quietness; not by any means in inaction, but all centred within the home circle. If they marry, they find the love of their husband enough for them, and have no desire for other men's admiration. Their babies are all the world to them, and they do not think maternity an infliction, as so many of the miserably fashionable think it. They like the occupation of housekeeping, and feel pride in their fine linen and clean service, in their well-ordered table and neatly-balanced accounts. They are kind to their servants, who generally come from the old home, and whose families they therefore know; but they keep up a certain dignity and tone of superiority towards them in the midst of all their kindness, which very few town-bred mistresses can keep to town-bred maids. They have always been the aristocracy in their native place; and they carry through life the ineffaceable stamp which being 'the best' gives.

Doves are essentially mild and gentle women; not queens of society even when they are pretty, because not caring for social success and therefore not laying themselves out for it; for if they please at home that is all they care for, holding love before admiration, and the esteem of one higher than the praise of many. If a fault is to be found with them it is that they have not perhaps quite enough salt for the general taste, used as it is to such highly-seasoned social food; but do we really want our women to have so very much character? Do not our splendid passionate creatures lead madly wretched lives and make miserably uncomfortable homes ? and are not our glorious heroines better in pictures and in fiction than seated by the domestic fire, or checking the baker's bill ? No doubt the quiet home-staying doves seem tame enough when we think of the gorgeous beings made familiar to us by romance, and history, which is more romantic still; but as our daily lives run chiefly in prose, our doves are better fitted for things as they are ; and to men who want wives and not playthings, and who care for the peace of family life and the dignity of home, they are beyond price when they can be found and secured. So that, on the whole, we can dispense with the splendid creatures of character and the magnificent queens of society sooner than with the quiet and unobtrusive doves. And though they do spoil men most monstrously, they know where to draw the line, and while petting their own at home they keep strangers abroad at a distance, and make themselves respected as only modest and gentle women are respected by men.

BORED HUSBANDS.

THE curtain falls on joined hands when it does not descend on a tragedy; and novels for the most part end with a wreath of orange-blossoms and a pair of high-stepping greys, as the last act that claims to be recorded. For both novelists and playwrights assume that with marriage all the great events of life have ceased, and that, once wedded to the beloved object, there is sure to be smooth sailing and halcyon seas to the end of time. It sounds very cynical and shocking to question this pretty belief; but unfortunately for us who live in the world as it is and not as it is supposed to be, we find that even a union with the beloved object does not always ensure perfect contentment in the home, and that bored husbands are by no means rare.

The ideal honeymoon is of course an Elysian time, during which nothing works rusty nor gets out of joint; and the ideal marriage is only a life-long honeymoon, where the happiness is more secure and the love deeper, if more sober; but the prose reality of one and the other has often a terrible dash of weariness in it, even under the most favourable conditions. Boredom begins in the very honeymoon itself. At first starting in married life there are many dangers to be encountered, not a shadow of which was seen in the wooing. There are odd freaks of temper turning up quite unexpectedly; there is the sense, so painful to some men, of being tied for life, of never being able to be alone again, never free and without responsibilities; there are misunderstandings to-day and the struggle for mastery to-morrow—the cloud, no bigger than a man's hand, which may prove to be the tempest that will destroy all; there is the unrest of travelling, and the awkwardness of unusual association, to help in the general discomfort; or, if the happy pair have settled down in a vale and a cottage for their month, there is the 'sad satiety' which all men feel after a time when they have had one companion only, with no outside diversion to cause a break. But the honeymoon at last draws to a close, and the relieved bridegroom gets back to his old haunts, to his work, his friends, and his club; and though he takes to all these things again with a difference, still they are helps and additions. This is the time of trial to a woman. If she gets over this pinch, and is sensible enough to understand that human nature cannot be kept up at high pressure, even in love, and that a man must sooner or later come down from romance to work-a-day prose, from the passionate lover to the cool and sober husband—if she can understand this, and settle into his pace, without fretting on the one hand or casting about for unhealthy distractions on the other—she will do well, and will probably make a pleasant home, and thereby diminish the boredom of life. But unfortunately, not every woman can do this; and it is just during this time of the man's transition from the lover to the friend that so many women begin to make shipwreck of their own happiness and his. They think to keep him a romantic wooer still, by their tears at his prosaic indifference to the little sentimentalities once so eagerly accepted and offered; they try to hold him close by their flattering but somewhat tiresome exactions; their jealousies—very pretty perhaps, and quite as flattering—are infinite, and as baseless as they are infinite; all of which is very nice up to a certain point and in the beginning of things, but all of which gets wearisome as time goes on, and a man wants both a little change and a little rest. But women do not see this; or seeing it, they cannot accept it as a necessary condition of things; wherefore they go on in their fatal way, and by the very unwisdom of their own love bore their husband out of his. Or they grow substantially cold because he is superficially cooler, and think themselves justified in ceasing to love him altogether because he takes their love for granted, and so has ceased to woo it.

If they are jealous, or shy, or unsocial, as so many women are, they make life very heavy by their exclusiveness, and the monastic character they give the home. A man married to a woman of this kind is, in fact, a house prisoner, whose only free spaces lie beyond the four walls of home. His bachelor friends are shut out. They smoke; or entice him to drink more than his wife thinks is good for him; or they induce him to bet on the Derby; or to play for half-crowns at whist or billiards; or they lead him in some other way of offence abhorrent to women. So the bachelor friends are shouldered out; and when the husband wants to entertain them, he must invite them to his club—if he has one— and pay the penalty when he gets home. In a few years' time his wife will be glad to encourage her sons' young friends to the house, for the sake of the daughters on hand; but husbands and sons are in a different category, and there are few fathers who do not learn, as time goes on, how much the mother will allow that the wife refused.

If bachelor friends are shouldered out of the house, all female friends are forbidden anything like an intimate footing, save those few whom the wife thinks specially devoted to herself and of whom she is not jealous. And these are very few. There are perhaps no women in the world so exclusive in their dealings with their husbands as are Englishwomen. A husband is bound to one woman only, no doubt; but the average wife thinks him also bound to have no affection whatever outside her and perhaps her family. If he meets an intelligent woman, pleasant to talk to, of agreeable manners and ready wit, and if he talks to her in consequence with anything like persistency or interest, he offends against the unwritten law ; and his wife, whose utmost power of conversation consists in putting in a yes or no with tolerable accuracy of aim, thinks herself slighted and ill-used. She may be young and pretty, and dearly loved for her own special qualities ; and her husband may not have a thought towards his new friend, or any other woman, in the remotest degree trenching on his allegiance to her ; but the fact that he finds pleasure, though only of an intellectual and æsthetic kind, in the society of any other woman, that he feels an interest in her life, chooses her for his friend, or finds community of pursuits or sympathy in ideas, makes his wife by just so much a victim and aggrieved.

And yet what a miserably monotonous home is that to which she would confine him ! He is at his office all day, badgered and worried with various business complications, and he comes home tired, perhaps cross—even well-conducted husbands have that way sometimes. He finds his wife tired and cross too ; so that they begin the evening together mutually at odds, she irritated by small cares and he disturbed by large anxieties. Or he finds her preoccupied and absorbed in her own pursuits, and quite disinclined to make any diversion for his sake. He asks her for some music ; she used to be ready enough to sing and play to him in the old love-making days ; but she refuses now. Either she has some needlework to do, which might have been done during the day when he was out, or baby is asleep in the nursery, and music in the drawing-room would disturb him—at all events she cannot sing or play to-night; and even if she does—he has heard all her pieces so often! If he is not a reading-man, those long, dull, silent evenings are very trying. She works, and drives him wild with the click of her needle; or she reads the last new novel, and he hates novels, and gets tired to death when she insists on telling him all about the story and the characters; or she chooses the evening for letter-writing, and if the noise of her pen scratching over the paper does not irritate him, perhaps it sends him to sleep, when at least he is not bored. But dull, objectless, and vacant as their evenings are, his wife would not hear of any help from without to give just that little fillip which would prevent boredom and not create ceremony. She would think her life had gone to pieces, and that only desolation was before her, if he hinted that his home was dull, and that though he loves her very dearly and wants no other wife but her, yet that her society only—*toujours perdrix*, without change or addition—is a little stupid, however nice the partridge may be, and that things would be bettered if Mrs. or Miss So-and-So came in sometimes, just to brighten up the hours. And if he were to make a practice of bringing home his men friends, she would probably let all parties concerned feel pretty distinctly that she considered the home her special sanctuary, and that guests whom she did not invite were intruders. She would perhaps go willingly enough to a ball or crowded *soirée*, or she might like to give one; but that intimate form of society, which is a mere enlargement of the home life, she dreads as the supplementing of deficiencies, and thinks her married happiness safer in boredom than in any diversion from herself as the sole centre of her husband's pleasure.

Home life stagnates in England; and in very few families is there any mean between dissipation and this stagnation. We can scarcely wonder that so many husbands think matrimony a mistake as we have it in our insular arrangements; that they look back regretfully to the time when they were unfettered and not bored; or that their free friends, who watch them as wild birds watch their caged companions, curiously and reflectively, share their opinion. Wife and home, after all, make up but part of a man's life; they are not his all, and do not satisfy the whole of his social instinct; nor is any one woman the concentration of all womanhood to a man, leaving nothing that is beautiful, nor in its own unconjugal way desirable, on the outside. Besides, when with his wife a man is often as much isolated as when alone, for any real companionship there is between them. Few women take a living interest in the lives of men, and fewer still understand them. They expect the husband to sympathize with them in the kitchen gossip and the nursery chatter, the neighbours' doings and all the small household politics; but they are utterly unable to comprehend his pleasures, his thoughts, his duties, the responsibilities of his profession, or the bearings of any public question in which he takes a part.

Even if this were not so, and granting that they could enter fully into his life and sympathize with him as intelligent equals, not only as compassionate saints or loving children, there would still be the need of novelty, and still the certainty of boredom without it. For human life, like all other forms of life, must have a due proportion of fresh elements continually added to keep it sweet and growing, else it becomes stagnant and stunted. And daily intercourse undeniably exhausts the moral ground. After the close companionship of years no one can remain mentally fresh to the other, unless indeed one or both be of the rarest order of mind and of a practically inexhaustible power of acquiring knowledge. Save these exceptional instances, we must all of necessity get worn out by constant intercourse. We know every thought, every opinion, and almost every square inch of information possessed; we have heard the old stories again and again, and know exactly what will lead up to them, and at what point they will begin; we have measured the whole sweep of mind, and have probed its depths; and though we may love and value what we have learnt, yet we want something new—fresh food for interest, though not necessarily a new love for the displacement of the old. But this is what very few Englishwomen can understand or will allow. They hold so intensely by the doctrine of unity that they are even jealous of a man's pursuits, if they think these take up any place in his mind which might also be theirs. They must be good for every part of his life; and the poorest of them all must be his only source of interest, suffering no other woman to share his admiration nor obtain his friendship, though this would neither touch his love nor interfere with their rights. Friendship is a hard saying to them, and one they cannot receive. Wherefore they keep a tight grasp on the marital collar, and suffer no relief of monotony by judicious loosening, nor by generous faith in integral fidelity. The practical result of which is that most men are horribly bored at home, and that the mass of them really suffer from the domestic stagnation to which national customs and the exclusiveness of women doom them so soon as they become family men. It must however, in fairness be added, that in general they obtain some kind of compensation; and that very few walk meekly in their bonds without at times slipping them off, with or without the concurrence of their wives.

END OF THE FIRST VOLUME.

Lightning Source UK Ltd.
Milton Keynes UK
UKHW011016210820
368606UK00002B/388